WITHDRAWN

THE ROYAL HISTORICAL SOCIETY
ANNUAL BIBLIOGRAPHY OF BRITISH
AND IRISH HISTORY
Publications of 1978

WITHDRAWN

ROYAL HISTORICAL SOCIETY

ANNUAL BIBLIOGRAPHY OF BRITISH AND IRISH HISTORY

Publications of 1978

General Editor: G. R. Elton

R. Barker	D.A.L. Morgan
A. Bennett	J.S. Morrill
N. Brooks	G. Mac Niocaill
R.A. Griffiths	T.I. Rae
M.W.C. Hassall	A.T.Q. Stewart
	J.A. Woods

HARVESTER PRESS LIMITED
HUMANITIES PRESS INC

For the Royal Historical Society

First published in 1979 for
The Royal Historical Society by
THE HARVESTER PRESS LIMITED
Publisher: John Spiers
16 Ship Street, Brighton,
Sussex England
and in the USA in 1979 by
HUMANITIES PRESS INC.,
Atlantic Highlands,
N.J. 07716

© 1979 Royal Historical Society

British Library Cataloguing in Publication Data
Annual bibliography of British and Irish history.
   Publications of 1978
   1. Great Britain — History — Bibliography
   I. Elton, Geoffrey Rudolph II. Royal
   Historical Society
   016.941   Z2016

ISBN 0-85527-536-7
ISSN 0308-4558

Humanities Press Inc.
ISBN 0-391-01054-9

Printed in Great Britain by
Redwood Burn Limited, Trowbridge and Esher

CONTENTS

PREFACE

The Bibliography is meant in the first place to serve the urgent needs of scholars, which has meant subordinating absolutely total coverage and refinements of arrangement to speed of production. Nevertheless, it is comprehensive and arranged for easy use. Because the sectional headings are those approved by section editors they are not uniform. Searchers are advised to use the subdivisions in conjunction with the Subject Index which, apart from covering all place and personal names, is designed to facilitate a thematic and conceptual analysis.

Pieces contained in collective works (under Bc and sometimes in a chronological section) are individually listed in the appropriate place and there referred to the number the volume bears in the Bibliography.

Items covering more than two sections are listed in B; any that extend over two sections appear as a rule in the first and are cross-referenced at the head of the second.

The editors wish to express their gratitude to the assistance received from the Institute of Historical Research (London), the International Medieval Bibliography (Leeds), especially Mr R.J. Walsh, and Mr S.J. Hills (Cambridge University Library).

Abbreviations

Arch. — Archaeological
B.   — Bulletin
HMSO — Her Majesty's Stationery Office
J.   — Journal
P.   — Proceedings
Q.   — Quarterly
R.   — Review
Soc.   — Society
T.   — Transactions
UP   — University Press

A. AUXILIARY

(a) *Bibliography and archives*

1. Public Record Office. *Metropolitan Police, Office of the Commissioner, correspondence and papers (MEPO 2): class list.* London; List and Index Soc. 138; 1977. Pp 297.
2. Public Record Office. *State Papers Domestic, George I (SP 35): calendar, part 1 (1714–1719).* London; List and Index Soc. 139; 1977. Pp 224.
3. Public Record Office. *Cabinet Office: class list, part 2.* London; List and Index Soc. 140; 1977. Pp 235.
4. Public Record Office. *Chancery Patent Rolls, 23–29 Elizabeth I, index to grantees.* London; List and Index Soc.; 1977. Pp 273.
5. Public Record Office. *British Transport Commission historical records: class list.* London; List and Index Soc.; 1977. Pp 380.
6. University College, London, Library. *The Gaster papers: a collection of letters, documents, etc., of the late Hahan Dr Moses Gaster (1856–1939).* London; The Library; 1976. Pp 52.
7. Baldwin, J., 'Glasgow University Library's manuscripts: the non-Hunterian collections,' *Bibliotheck* 8 (1977), 127–55.
8. Schweizer, K.W., 'A handlist to the additional Weston papers,' *Bulletin of the Institute for Historical Research* 51 (1978), 99–102.
9. *Kelvin Papers: index to the manuscript collection of William Thomson, baron Kelvin in Glasgow University Library.* Glasgow; The Library; 1977. Pp 93.
10. Walles, P.J. and R. *Newton and Newtonians, 1672–1975: a bibliography.* Folkestone; Dawson; 1977. Pp xxiv, 362.
11. Knight, R.J.B. (ed.). *Guide to the manuscripts in the National Maritime Museum; vol. 1: the personal collections.* London; Mansell; 1977. Pp xxiv, 234.
12. Hook, E. *A guide to the papers of John Swire and Sons Ltd.* London; School of Oriental and African Studies; 1977. Pp 176.
13. Friedman, J.E. *Castleton parish library, the Farran collection: a catalogue.* University of Sheffield; 1977. Pp v, 150.
14. Sawyer, P.J.; Walsh, R.J. *International Medieval Bibliography, January–June 1977.* Leeds; 1977. Pp i, 231; *July–December,* pp. lii, 236.
15. 'Bibliography 1977', *B. of the Soc. for the Study of Labour History* 36 (1978), 79–104.
16. Harrison, J.F.C.; Thompson, D. *Bibliography of the Chartist movement, 1837–1976.* Hassocks; Harvester; 1978. Pp xvi, 214.

1

17. Mullett, M., 'Historical documents at Friends' Meeting House, Lancaster,' *J. of the Friends' Historical Soc.* 54 (1976), 33—4.

18. Kavanagh, M.V. *A contribution towards a bibliography of the history of County Kildare in printed books.* Kildare County Council; 1976. Pp 328.

19. Wilkinson, B. *Bibliographical handbooks: the high middle ages in England (1154—1377).* Cambridge UP; 1978. Pp ix, 130.

20. Philpin, C.H.E.; Creaton, H.J. *Writings on British History 1960—1961.* London; Institute of Historical Research; 1978. Pp xxi, 279.

21. Todd, J.M. *Mary Woolstonecraft: an annotated bibliography.* New York/London; Garland Publishing; 1976. Pp 124.

22. Griffiths, D. *A catalogue of the printed music published before 1850 in York Minster Library.* York; [The Library] ; 1977. Pp xxi, 118.

23. *Handlist of the Denbigh Borough Records.* Hawarden; Clwyd Record Office; 1976. Pp 70.

24. Pargeter, S. *A catalogue of the library at Tatton Park, Knutsford, Cheshire.* Chester; Cheshire Libraries and Museums; 1977. Pp 409.

25. Smith, N.A. et al. *Catalogue of the Pepys Library at Magdalene College, Cambridge; Vol. 1: printed books.* Ipswich; Brewer; 1978. Pp 201.

26. Skempton, A.W. *Early printed reports and maps (1665—1850) in the library of the Institution of Civil Engineers.* London; The Institution; 1977. Pp xv, 84.

27. Holloway, M. *Steel engravings in nineteenth century British topographical books.* London; Holland Press; 1977. Pp vii, 205.

28. *Manuscript collections in the library of University College, London: a handlist.* (2nd ed.). London; The Library; 1978. Pp 21.

29. Percival, J. *The papers of Sir Edwin Chadwick (1800—1890): a handlist.* London; University College Library; 1978. Pp 186.

30. *Smyth of Nibley papers.* Gloucester; Gloucestershire County Library; 1978. Pp 108.

31. Mackworth-Young, R., 'The Royal Archives, Windsor Castle,' *Archives* 13 (1978), 115—30.

32. Richards, P.S., 'The London & Birmingham Railway Company: an annotated bibliography,' *Transport History* 8 (1977), 209—16; 9 (1978), 24—9.

33. *Register of admissions to the Honourable Society of the Middle Temple*; vol. 4: January 1945—October 17th, 1967. London; Middle Temple; [1978] . Pp 401.

34. Meekings, C.F.A., 'King's Bench files,' Bc5, 97—139.

35. Elton, G.R. (ed.). *Annual bibliography of British and Irish history: 1977.* Hassocks; Harvester Press; 1978. Pp ix, 174.

36. Franklin, L.C. *Antiques and collectibles: a bibliography of works*

in English, 16th century to 1976. Metuchen/London; Scarecrow Press; 1978. Pp xxiii, 1091.

37. 'Research in Irish history in Irish universities, 1976—7,' *Irish Historical Studies* 20 (1977), 334—44.

38. Tobias, R.C., 'Victorian bibliography for 1977,' *Victorian Studies* 21 (1978), 527—628.

39. Dyer, G., 'Classified list of archive deposits, 1976,' *Soc. for the Study of Labour History* 37 (1978), 81—4.

40. Field, C.D., 'Bibliography of Methodist historical literature, 1976—,' *P. of the Wesley Historical Soc.* 41 (1978), 143—51.

41. Sheppard, J., 'The Liddell Hart Centre for military archives at King's College, London,' *Archives* 13 (1978), 190—5.

42. Riley, 'Methodist archives: some recent additions,' *P. of the Wesley Historical Soc.* 41 (1978), 139—42.

43. Keary, M.Y.; Howard, B.M. *Civil Service Department: its organisation and history: a bibliography.* London; The Department; 1977., Pp 30.

44. 'Writings on Irish history,' *Irish Historical Studies* 20 (1977), 464—89.

(b) *Works of reference*

1. *A guide to genealogical sources in Guildhall Library.* London; Corporation of London; 1976. Pp 25.

2. Turley, R.V. (ed.). *A directory of Hampshire and Isle of Wight art: local subjects featured in principal London exhibitions during the late-18th and 19th centuries, arranged by artist and indexed topographically.* University of Southampton; 1977. Pp 110.

3. Royal Commission on Historical Monuments (England). *Archaeological sites in central Northamptonshire.* London; HMSO; 1977. Pp 6.

4. *Guide to census reports, Great Britain, 1801—1966.* London; HMSO; 1977. Pp vii, 279.

5. Somers Cocks, J.V. *Devon topographical prints, 1660—1870: a catalogue and guide.* Exeter; Devon Library Services; 1977. Pp viii, 324.

6. Stewart, J.C. *Pioneers of a profession: chartered accountants to 1879: being biographical notes on the members of the Scottish Chartered Societies, 1854 to 1879.* Edinburgh; Institute of Chartered Accountants of Scotland; 1977. Pp xii, 181.

7. Wolstenholme, G.; Kerslake, J.F.; Ekkart, R.E.O.; Piper, D. *The Royal College of Physicians of London: portraits: catalogue 2.* Amsterdam/Oxford; Elsevier; 1977. Pp ix, 239.

8. Currie, R.; Gilbert, A.; Horsley, L. *Churches and churchgoers: patterns of church growth in the British Isles since 1700.* Oxford; Clarendon; 1977. Pp xi, 244.

9. Armstrong, N.E.S. *Local collections in Scotland.* Glasgow; Scottish Library Association Publications; 1977. Pp ix, 174.

10. Ellis, M. *Maps of Colne and district: a classified catalogue of the collection held for reference at Colne Library.* Nelson; The Library; 1977. 33 leaves.

11. Donaldson, G.; Morpeth, R.S. *A dictionary of Scottish history.* Edinburgh; Donald; 1977. Pp 234.

12. McDonnell, M. *The Registers of St Paul's School, 1509–1748.* [London; The School] ; 1977. Pp xxvii, 479.

13. Wallis, P.J. *An eighteenth-century book trade index based on 'Newtonia' and book subscription lists.* Newcastle; School of Education; 1977. Pp iv, 54.

14. Greenway, D.E. *Fasti Ecclesiae Anglicanae, 1066–1300; 3: Lincoln* (new ed.). London; Institute of Historical Research; 1977. Pp xxviii, 195.

15. Lewis Jones, D., 'Theses on Welsh history, III,' *Welsh History R.* 9 (1978), 84–94.

16. Scanlon, P.A., 'A checklist of prose romances in English, 1474–1603,' *The Library* 5th ser. 33 (1978), 143–52.

17. Middleton, D.M., 'Guide to the publications of the Royal Geographical Society, 1830–1892,' *Geographical J.* 144 (1978), 99–116.

18. Stenton, M.; Lees, S. (ed.). *Who's who of British members of Parliament, vol. 2: 1886–1918; a biographical dictionary of the House of Commons.* Hassocks; Harvester; 1978. Pp xvi, 401.

19. Hine, M., 'Dissenting meeting places in the city of London [a note on an MS index] ,' *Baptist Q.* 27 (1978), 259–60.

20. *A directory for local historians in the County Palatine of Lancaster/Lancashire Library* (3rd ed.). Preston; The Library; 1977. Pp 40.

21. Pratt, D.; Veysey, A.G. *A handlist of the topographical prints of Clwyd.* Hawarden; Clwyd Record Office; 1977. Pp 90–94.

22. Turnbull, H. *Artists of Yorkshire: a short dictionary* [artists born before 1921] . Bedale; Thornton Gallery; 1976. Pp xiv, 68.

23. Grant, G.L. *The standard catalogue of provincial banks and banknotes.* London; Spink; 1977. Pp xxiv, 133.

24. Craik, L. *General index to the Transactions of the Thoroton Society of Nottinghamshire, volumes 1–130, 1897–1976, and the Thoroton Society Record Series, volumes 1–31.* Nottingham; The Society; 1977. Pp 34.

25. Colvin, H.M. *A biographical dictionary of British architects, 1600–1840* (new ed.). London; Murray; 1978. Pp 1080.

26. Allan, A.R.; Cook, M. (ed.). *Records management.* London; Society of Archivists; 1977. Pp 63.

27. Bergess, W.F.; Riddell, B.R.M. (ed.). *Kent directories located.* [Maidstone] ; Kent County Council; 1976. Pp 361.

28. Gooder, E.A. *Latin for local history: an introduction* (2nd ed.). London; Longman; 1978. Pp 171.
29. Bradley, H.W. *A handbook of coins of the British Isles*. London; Hale; 1978. Pp vii, 210.
30. Ward, K., 'Film section: British documentaries of the 1930s,' *History* 62 (1977), 426—30.
31. Morris, J. *Provincial printing and publishing in Great Britain: an annotated catalogue of a collection of books and related material (with a reprint of Power's checklist of first printings)*. York; K Books; 1978. Pp 83.
32. Colvin, H.M. *English architectural history: a guide to sources* (2nd ed.). London; Pinhorns; 1976. Pp 23.
33. Standing Conference for Local History. *Directory of national organisations*. London; The Conference; 1978. 10 leaves.
34. 'Baptist records: Oxfordshire and East Gloucestershire Baptist Association,' *Baptist Q*. 27 (1978), 343—5.
35. Addison, W. *Understanding English place-names*. London; Batsford; 1978. Pp 159.
36. *A calendar of Scottish railway documents held by Paisley College of Technology Library*. Paisley; The Library; 1978. Pp 131.
37. Collinge, J.M. *Navy Board officials, 1660—1832*. London; Institute of Historical Research; 1978. Pp xii, 153.
38. Gibson, R. *Catalogue of portraits in the collection of the earl of Clarendon*. London; Paul Mellon Centre; 1977. Pp xix, 146.
39. Garside, P.L., 'The development of London: a classified list of theses presented to the universities of Great Britain and Ireland and the CNAA, 1908—1977,' *Guildhall Studies in London History* 3 (1978), 175—94.
40. Tate, W E. (ed. M.E. Turner). *A domesday of English enclosure acts and awards*. Reading; University Library; 1978. Pp viii, 459.
41. Boylan, H. *A dictionary of Irish biography*. Dublin; Gill & Macmillan; 1978. Pp xi, 385.
42. Sayers, J.E., 'Collection of papal letters addressed to recipients in England and Wales (1216—1303),' *J. of the Soc. of Archivists* 6 (1978), 92—4.

(c) *Historiography*

1. Sutton, D.G. *Parish records: a brief introduction*. Kingston on Thames; Surrey Record Office; 1977. Pp 13.
2. Macfarlane, A.; Harrison, S.; Jardine, C. *Reconstructing historical communities*. Cambridge UP; 1977. Pp xii, 222.
3. McCord, N., 'Photographs as historical evidence,' *Local Historian* 13 (1978), 23—36.
4. Pugh, R.B., 'The Victoria County Histories,' ibid. 15—22.
5. Marshall, J.D., 'Local or regional history — or — both?,' ibid. 3—10.

6. Barker, N. *Bibliotheca Lindesiana: the lives and collections of Alexander William, 25th earl of Crawford and 8th earl of Balcarres, and James Ludovic, 26th earl of Crawford and 9th earl of Balcarres.* London; Quaritch (for Roxburgh Club); 1977. Pp xviii, 415.

7. Garside, P.L., 'Local history in undergraduate history courses: a survey of universities and polytechnics in the United Kingdom,' *Local Historian* 13 (1978), 67—74.

8. Rogers, A. (ed.). *Group projects in local history.* Folkestone; Dawson; 1977. Pp 246.

9. Thompson, P. *The voice of the past: oral history.* Oxford UP; 1978. Pp xii, 257.

10. Hull, F., 'Jenkinson and the "acquisitive" record office,' *J. of the Soc. of Archivists* 6 (1978), 1—9.

11. Iredale, D. *Discovering local history* (2nd ed.). Aylesbury; Shire Publications; 1977. Pp 64.

12. Taylor, C. *Looking at cows: field archaeology in the 1980s.* London; Council for British Archaeology; 1978. Pp xv.

13. Page, E. *Michael Hechter's internal colonial thesis: some theoretical and methodological problems.* Glasgow; University of Strathclyde; 1977. Pp 30.

14. Whyte, I.D., 'Scottish historical geography — a review,' *Scottish Geographical Magazine* 94 (1978), 4—23.

15. Levine, J.M., 'The autonomy of history: R.G. Collingwood and Agatha Christie,' *Clio* 7 (1978), 253—64.

16. Dray, W.H., 'Concepts of causation in A.J.P. Taylor's account of the origins of the Second World War,' *History and Theory* 17 (1978), 149—74.

17. Storey, R.A., 'The development of the modern records centre, University of Warwick Library,' *Archives* 13 (1978), 137—42.

18. Boyce, D.G., 'Public opinion and historians,' *History* 63 (1978), 214—28.

19. Hudson, G., 'Printed ephemera and the industrial historian,' *Industrial Archaeology* 12 (1977), 357—68.

20. Cook, M., 'The Cunard Archives at Liverpool,' *Business History* 20 (1978), 240—52.

21. Hillier, R., 'Auction catalogues and notices: their vàlue for the local historian,' *Local Historian* 13 (1978), 131—9.

22. Winter, J.M. (ed.). *History and society: essays by R.H. Tawney.* London; Routledge; 1978. Pp 260.

23. Ugawa, K., 'Diplomatic and palaeography in England,' *Komonjo Kenkyu (Japanese J. of Diplomatic)* 12 (1978), 42—54.

24. Shaw, G., 'The content and reliability of nineteenth-century trade directories,' *Local Historian* 13 (1978), 205—9.

25. Pugh, P.M., 'The Oxford Colonial Records Project and the Oxford Development Records Project,' *J. of the Soc. of Archivists* 6 (1978), 76—86.

26. Emmison, F.G., 'Archives and the local historian,' *Local Historian* 13 (1978), 217–22.
27. Dray, W.H., 'Concepts of causation in A.J.P. Taylor's account of the origins of the Second World War,' *History and Theory* 17 (1978), 149–74.
28. Forster, G.C.F., 'Record publishing in the north-west in retrospect and prospect,' *Northern History* 14 (1978), 243–51.
29. Gowing, M., 'Some general problems [concerning source materials for the history of science] and British experience,' *Human Implications of Scientific Advance: proceedings of the XVth International Congress of the History of Science* (ed. E.G. Forbes; Edinburgh UP; 1978), 409–13.
30. Simpson, E., 'Oral history — some thoughts and experiences,' *Baptist Q.* 27 (1978), 370–5.
31. Musty, J., 'The developing role of the natural sciences in archaeological interpretation,' Bc6, 71–84.
32. Miles, D. *An introduction to archaeology.* London; Ward Lock; 1978. Pp 112.
33. Hair, P.E.H.; Quinn, A.M., 'The writings of D.B. Quinn,' Bc14, 303–10.
34. Kearney, H., 'The problems of perspective in the history of colonial America,' Bc14, 290–302.
35. Bennett, J.A.W., 'Carlyle and the medieval past,' *Reading Medieval Studies* 4 (1978), 3–18.

B. GENERAL

(a) *Long periods: national*

1. Harvie, C. *Scotland and nationalism: Scottish society and politics, 1707–1977.* London; Allen & Unwin; 1977. Pp 318.
2. Gathorne-Hardy, J. *The public school phenomenon, 597–1977.* London; Hodder & Stoughton; 1977. Pp 478.
3. Wilson, M.I. *The English country house, and its furnishings.* London; Batsford; 1977. Pp 216.
4. Flinn, M. (ed.). *Scottish population history from the 17th century to the 1930s.* Cambridge UP; 1977. Pp xxv, 547.
5. *The Royal Bank of Scotland, 1727–1977.* Edinburgh; The Bank; 1977. Pp 56.
6. Thoms, L. (ed.). *The archaeology of industrial Scotland: Scottish archaeological forum 8.* Edinburgh UP; 1977. Pp vii, 105.
7. Cunnington, P.; Lucas, C. *Charity costumes of children, scholars, almsfolk, pensioners.* London; Black; 1978. Pp x, 331.
8. Hawksworth, D.L.; Seaward, M.R.D. *Lichenology in the British Isles, 1568–1975: an historical and bibliographical survey.*

Richmond, Surrey; Richmond Publishing Company; 1977. Pp ix, 231.

9. Sparkes, I.G. *The English country chair: an illustrated history of chairs and chairmaking* (2nd revd. ed.). Bourne End; Spurbooks; 1977. Pp 160.

10. Carson, E.A., 'The Customs Quarantine Service,' *Mariner's Mirror* 64 (1978), 63—9.

11. Bernasconi, J.R. *The English domestic chair*. Reading; College of Estate Management; 1977. Pp 32.

12. Kolbert, C.F.; Mackay, N.A.M. *History of Scots and English land law*. Berkhamsted; Geographical Publications; 1977. Pp xxi, 379.

13. Zupko, R.E. *British weights and measures: a history from antiquity to the seventeenth century*. Madison/London; University of Wisconsin Press; 1977. Pp xvi, 248.

14. Ward, J.R., 'The profitability of sugar planting in the British West Indies, 1650—1834,' *Economic History R.* 2nd ser. 31 (1978), 197—213.

15. Adams, I.H. *The making of urban Scotland*. London; Croom Helm; 1978. Pp 303.

16. Butler, D. (ed.). *Coalitions in British politics: essays by Robert Blake et al.* London; Macmillan; 1978. Pp 128.

17. Gelling, M. *Signposts to the past: place-names and the history of England*. London; Dent; 1978. Pp 256.

18. Squibb, G.D. *Doctors' Commons: a history of the College of Advocates and Doctors of Law*. Oxford; Clarendon; 1977. Pp xvi, 244.

19. Hassall, T.G., 'Urban archaeology in England, 1975,' *European towns: their archaeology and early history* (ed. M.W. Barley; London; Academic Press; 1977), 3—18.

20. Johnson, P. *The National Trust Book of British castles*. London; Weidenfeld & Nicolson; 1978. Pp 288.

21. Rolt, L.T.C. *Red for danger: a history of railway accidents and railway safety* (3rd rev. ed.). London; Pan Books; 1978. Pp 301.

22. Lovell-Knight, A.V. *The story of the Royal Military Police*. London; Cooper; 1977. Pp xxi, 360.

23. Critchley, T.A. *A history of police in England and Wales* (rev. ed.). London; Constable; 1978. Pp xxiv, 360.

24. Hallam, E.M.; Roper, M., 'The capital and the records of the nation: seven centuries of housing the public records in London,' *London J.* 4 (1978), 73—94.

25. Cameron, K. *English place-names* (3rd ed.). London; Batsford; 1977. Pp 258.

26. Lenman, B. *An economic history of modern Scotland, 1660—1976*. London; Batsford; 1977. Pp 288.

27. Sproule, A. *Port out, starboard home: the rise and fall of the ocean passage*. Poole; Blandford Press; 1978. Pp 128.

28. Barty-King, H. *A tradition of English wine: the story of two thou-

sand years of English wine made from English grapes. Oxford; Oxford Illustrated Press; 1977. Pp xiv, 250.

29. Williams, K. *The English newspaper: an illustrated history to 1900.* London; Springwood Books; 1977. Pp 128.

30. Bristow, E.J. *Vice and vigilance: purity movements in Britain since 1700.* Dublin; Gill & Macmillan; 1977. Pp xii, 274.

31. Brookes, C. *English cricket: the game and its players through the ages.* London; Weidenfeld & Nicolson; 1978. Pp xiii, 210.

32. Cawte, E.C. *Ritual animal disguise: a historical and geographical study of animal disguise in the British Isles.* Ipswich; Brewer; 1977. Pp xv, 293.

33. Mead, W.R.; Kain, R.J.P., 'Ridge-and-furrow in Kent,' *Archaeologia Cantiana* 92 (1977 for 1976), 165–71.

34. Sturdy, D. *Historic monuments of England and Wales.* London; Dent; 1977. Pp 218.

35. Wynn Jones, M. *A cartoon history of the monarchy.* London; Macmillan; 1978. Pp 207.

36. Garrett, A. *A history of British wood engraving.* Tunbridge Wells; Midas Books; 1978. Pp 407.

37. Hoskins, W.G. *One man's England.* London; British Broadcasting Corporation; 1978. Pp 144.

38. Cranfield, G.A. *The press and society: from Caxton to Northcliffe.* London; Longman; 1978. Pp vii, 242.

39. Beeson, C.F.C. *English church clocks, 1200–1850: their history and classification* (new ed.). Ashford; Brant Wright Associates; 1977. Pp xvi, 172.

40. Babington, A. *The rule of law in Britain from the Roman occupation to the present day: the only liberty – a short history of the rule of law in Britain 54 BC – AD 1975.* Chichester; Rose; 1978. Pp xxix, 313.

41. Gladwin, D.D. *British waterways: an illustrated history.* Bourne End; Spurbooks; 1977. Pp 159.

42. Weinberg, J.R. *Ockham, Descartes and Hume: self-knowledge, substance, and causality.* Madison/London; University of Madison Press; 1977. Pp x, 179.

43. Collins, E.J.T. *The economy of upland Britain, 1750–1950: an illustrated review.* Reading; Centre for Agricultural Strategy (of the University); 1978. Pp 116.

44. Hyndman, M. *Schools and schooling in England and Wales, a documentary history.* London; Harper & Row; 1978. Pp 269.

45. Lance, D., 'Meals on the mess deck,' *History Today* 28 (1978), 476–9.

46. Miles, D. *The Royal National Eisteddfford of Wales.* Swansea; C. Davies; 1977. Pp 172.

47. Dunbar, J.G. *The architecture of Scotland* (2nd revd. ed.). London; Batsford; 1978. Pp 209.

48. Austen, B., *English provincial posts, 1633–1840: a study based on Kent examples.* London; Phillimore; 1978. Pp viii, 192.

49. Underhill, N. *The lord chancellor.* Lavenham; T. Dalton; 1978. Pp xiv, 210,

50. Kynaston, D. *The secretary of state.* Lavenham; T. Dalton; 1978. Pp xiv, 177.

51. Nixon, H.M. *Five centuries of English bookbinding.* London; Scolar Press; 1978. Pp 241.

52. Summerson, J. *Architecture in Britain, 1530 to 1830* (5th revd. ed.). Harmondsworth; Penguin; 1978. Pp 611.

53. Anderson, W.; Hicks, C. *Cathedrals in Britain and Ireland: from early times to the reign of Henry VIII.* London; Macdonald & Jane's; 1978. Pp 184.

54. Hampshire, A.C. *The secret navies.* London; Kimber; 1978. Pp 272.

55. Quinton, A.M. *The politics of imperfection: the religious and secular traditions of conservative thought in England from Hooker to Oakeshott.* London; Faber; 1978. Pp 105.

56. Patten, J. *English towns 1500–1700.* Folkestone; Dawson; 1978. Pp 348.

57. Coombs, D. *Sport and the countryside in English paintings, water-colours and prints.* Oxford; Phaidon; 1978. Pp 192.

58. Girouard, M. *Life in an English country house: a social and archi-tectural history.* New Haven/London; Yale UP; 1978. Pp 344.

59. Boyce, G.; Curran, J.; Wingate, P. (ed.). *Newspaper history from the seventeenth century to the present day.* London; Constable; 1978. Pp 423.

60. Mitchison, R. *Life in Scotland.* London; Batsford; 1978. Pp 181.

61. Bowyer, J. *The evolution of church building.* London; Crosby Lockwood Staples; 1977. Pp viii, 139.

62. Pimlott, J.A.R. *The Englishman's Christmas: a social history.* Hassocks; Harvester Press; 1978. Pp xii, 230.

63. Kiernan, V.G., 'Britons old and new,' Bc1, 23–59.

64. Rolph, C.H. *The queen's pardon.* London; Cassell; 1978. Pp ix, 173.

65. Newby, H. (et al.). *Property, paternalism and power: class and control in rural England.* London; Hutchinson; 1978. Pp 432.

66. Porter, R.S., 'Gentlemen and geology: the emergence of a scien-tific career, 1660–1920,' *Historical J.* 21 (1978), 809–36.

67. Kellenbenz, H., 'German immigrants in England,' Bc1, 63–80.

68. Dodgshon, R.A.; Butlin, R.A. (ed.). *An historical geography of England and Wales.* London; Academic Press; 1978. Pp xx, 450.

69. Oman, C. *English engraved silver, 1150 to 1900.* London; Faber; 1978. Pp 158.

(b) *Long periods: local*

1. Roxburgh, R. *The records of the Honourable Society of Lincoln's*

Inn: the black books, vol. 5; two postscripts. London; Lincoln's Inn; 1977. Pp 31.

2. Thomas, D.B. *The Council of Brechin: a study in local government.* Brechin; Soc. of Friends of Brechin Cathedral; 1977. Pp 214.

3. Boyes, J.; Russell, R. *The canals of eastern England.* Newton Abbot; David & Charles; 1977. Pp 368.

4. Hume, J.R. *The industrial archaeology of Scotland, 2: The Highlands and Islands.* London; Batsford; 1977. Pp 335.

5. Bourne, J. *Place-names of Leicestershire and Rutland.* Leicester Libraries and Information Services; 1977. Pp 30.

6. Morgan, R.R., 'Chichester — documenting a city,' *Local Historian* 13 (1978), 11—14.

7. Hartley, D. *The St Aubyns of Cornwall, 1200—1977.* Chesham; Barracuda Books; 1977. Pp 116.

8. Greenwood, C. *Famous houses of the west country.* Bath; Kingsmead; 1977. Pp vii, 116.

9. Crawford, A. *A history of the Vintner's Company.* London; Constable; 1977. Pp 319.

10. Blaxland, G. *The Middlesex Regiment (Duke of Cambridge's Own) (The 57th and 77th of Foot).* London; Cooper; 1977. Pp xiv, 144.

11. Dickens, G. *The dress of the British sailor* (2nd ed.). London; HMSO; 1977. Pp 24.

12. Brett, C.E.B. *Buildings in the town and parish of Saint Helier.* Belfast; Ulster Architectural Heritage Soc.; 1977. Pp 84.

13. Jowett, E.M. *Morden Park, Morden.* London; Merton Historical Soc.; 1977. Pp 16.

14. Perkins, A. *The book of Sonning: the story of an English village.* Chesham; Barracuda Books; 1977. Pp 160.

15. Hall, B. *Burnley: a short history.* Burnley and District Historical Soc.; 1977. Pp 40.

16. Runcie, R. (ed.). *Cathedral and city: St Albans ancient and modern.* St Albans; Martyn Associates; 1977. Pp 149.

17. Whitehead, R.A. *Steam in the village* [agricultural machinery]. Newton Abbot; David & Charles; 1977. Pp 160.

18. Nockolds, H. (ed.). *The coachmakers: a history of the Worshipful Company of Coachmakers and Coach Harness Makers.* London; J.A. Allen; 1977. Pp 239.

19. Filmer, R.M. *Deep-rooted in Kent: an account of the Filmer family.* London; Research Publishing Co.; 1977. Pp 69.

20. Day, J.W. *King's Lynn and Sandringham through the ages.* Ipswich; East Anglian Magazine Ltd; 1977. Pp 140.

21. Firth, G., 'The Northbrook Chemical Works, Bradford, 1750—1920,' *Industrial Archaeology R.* 2 (1977—8), 52—68.

22. Burgess, H.F. *A history of the Reading Blue Coat School (Aldworth's Hospital), 1660—1960.* Reading; The School; 1977. 159 leaves.

23. Rhodes, P. *Doctor John Leake's Hospital: a history of the General Lying-in Hospital, York Road, Lambeth, 1765–1971: the birth, life and death of a maternity hospital.* London; Davis-Poynter; 1977. Pp 400.

24. Pond, C.C. *George Monoux's School, Walthamstow, 1527–1977.* London; Walthamstow Antiquarian Soc.; 1977. Pp 43.

25. Biggs, H. *The sound of maroons: the story of life-saving services on the Kent and Sussex coasts.* Lavenham; T. Dalton; 1977. Pp 176.

26. Brook, F. *The industrial archaeology of the British Isles, 1: the West Midlands.* London; Batsford; 1977. Pp 223.

27. Marshall, J.D.; Davies-Shiel, M. *The industrial archaeology of the Lake Counties* (2nd revd. ed.). Beckermet; Michael Moon; 1977. Pp 287.

28. Davies, K.; Williams, C.J. *The Greenfield valley: an introduction to the history and industrial archaeology of the Greenfield valley, Holywell, North Wales.* Holywell; The Council; 1977. Pp 40.

29. Neale, K.J. *Essex in history.* London; Phillimore; 1977. Pp xiv, 208.

30. Brandon, P. *A history of Surrey.* London; Phillimore; 1977. Pp 128.

31. Wright, A.P.M. (ed.). *A history of the county of Cambridge and the Isle of Ely, vol. 6* [Victoria County History]. Oxford UP; 1978. Pp xvi, 314.

32. Jones, I.G. (ed.). *Aberystwyth, 1277–1977: eight lectures to celebrate the seventh centenary of the foundation of the borough.* Llandysul; Gomer Press; 1977. Pp ix, 142.

33. Stevenson, G. *Oxfordshire.* Chesham; Barracuda Press; 1977. Pp 124.

34. Cusden, P.E. *Coley: portrait of an urban village.* Reading Branch of the W.E.A.; 1977. Pp 94.

35. Rennison, R.W., 'The supply of water to Newcastle upon Tyne and Gateshead, 1680–1837,' *Archaeologia Aeliana* 5th ser. 5 (1977), 179–96.

36. Durkan, J., 'The early history of Glasgow University Library, 1475–1710,' *Bibliothek* 8 (1977–8), 102–26.

37. Stubbings, F.II. *Emmanuel College Chapel, 1677–1977.* Cambridge; The College; 1977. Pp 32.

38. Kohler, M.K. (ed.). *Memories of old Dorking.* Dorking; Kohler & Coombes; 1977. Pp 252.

39. Waltham Abbey Historical Society. *The worthies of Waltham: a history of the town of Waltham Abbey; part 1: to the dissolution of the Abbey, 1500 A.D.* The Society; 1977. Pp 23.

40. Stevens, J. *Old Jersey houses and those who lived in them; vol. 2: from 1700 onwards.* London; Phillimore; 1977. Pp xvi, 246.

41. Beresford, H. de la P. *The book of the Beresfords.* Chichester; Phillimore; 1977. Pp viii, 353.

42. Andrews, C.T. *The dark awakening: a history of St Lawrence's Hospital, Bodmin.* [Truro; the Hospital] ; 1978. Pp xii, 276.

43. Perry, N.R. *Extracts from the poor law documents in the parish chest of Oldswinford Church, formerly in Worcestershire.* Birmingham and Midland Soc. for Genealogy and Heraldry; 1977. Pp v, 136.

44. Green, I. *The book of Dover: cinque port, port of the passage, gateway to England.* Chesham; Barracuda Books; 1978. Pp 144.

45. Scott-Giles, C.W.; Slater, B.V. *The history of Emanuel School, 1594–1964.* [London; The School] ; 1977. Pp x, 258.

46. Carter, I., 'Social differentiation in the Aberdeenshire peasantry, 1696–1870,' *J. of Peasant Studies* 5 (1977), 48–65.

47. Barker, N. *The Oxford University Press and the spread of learning, 1478–1978: an illustrated history.* Oxford; Clarendon; 1978. Pp xiv, 70, 332.

48. Sutcliffe, P.H. *The Oxford University Press: an informal history.* Oxford; Clarendon; 1978. Pp xxviii, 303.

49. Nicolson, J.R. *Traditional life in Shetland.* London; Hale; 1978. Pp 206.

50. Robinson, G. *Hertfordshire.* Chesham; Barracuda Books; 1978. Pp 138.

51. Weit, R.B. *The history of the Malt Distillers' Association of Scotland.* [Elgin; The Association; ?1975] . Pp 200 in various pagings.

52. *Charlton Parish Register, 1653–1753,* and *1754–1798,* (2 vols.). London; Local History Library; [1977] . Pp 36; 18.

53. Hammond, P. *Royal fortress: the Tower of London through nine centuries.* London; HMSO; 1978. Pp 62.

54. Burnett, D. *Longleat: the story of an English country house.* London; Collins; 1978. Pp 208.

55. Hopkins, S. *Planning in Oxford: an historical survey and bibliography.* Oxford Polytechnic; 1978. Pp 41.

56. Johnston, P. *A short history of Guernsey.* [?1978] . Pp 71.

57. Palgrave-Moore, P.; Page, R.A.F. *Census of Norwich, 1851, part 2.* Norfolk and Norwich Genealogical Society; 1977. Pp 204.

58. Brooke, L.E.J. *The book of Yeovil: a portrait of the town.* Chesham; Barracuda Books; 1978. Pp 148.

59. Godwin, H. *Fenland: its ancient past and uncertain future.* Cambridge UP; 1978. Pp vii, 196.

60. [Bodleian Library] . *Painting and publishing at Oxford: the growth of a learned press, 1478–1978.* Oxford; The Library; 1978. Pp xvi, 96.

61. *The parish registers of Bishopstoke.* 2 vols: 1657–1812; 1813–1837. Eastleigh, Hants; Chinchen; 1977. 120 and 36 leaves.

62. Palgrave, D.A. *The history and lineage of the Palgraves.* Doncaster; Palgrave Society; 1978. Pp 350.

63. McCallum, D.M., 'A demographic study of the parishes of Bruton

and Pitcombe,' *Somerset Archaeology and Natural History* 121 (1977), 77–87.

64. M-N B. *History of the Russian Orthodox Church in London, 1707–1977.* London; the author; 1978. Pp 46.

65. Carter, R.W. et al. *Parish surveys in Somerset: 1, Wambrook.* Taunton; Somerset Arch. Soc.; 1977. Pp 19.

66. *The making of Havant*, vol. 1. Havant Local History Group; 1977. Pp 42.

67. Wilson, D. *The Tower, 1078–1978.* London; Hamilton; 1978. Pp x, 257.

68. Arundell, D. *The story of Sadler's Wells, 1683–1977* (2nd ed.). Newton Abbot; David & Charles; 1978. Pp xvi, 352.

69. Gray, R. *A history of London.* London; Hutchinson; 1978. Pp 352.

70. Hall, C.C. *Sheffield transport.* Glossop; Transport Publishing Co.; 1977. Pp 330.

71. Rees, D. *Rings and rosettes: the history of the Pembrokeshire Agricultural Society, 1784–1977.* [Llandysul; Gomer Press] ; 1977. Pp xv, 234.

72. Stephenson, D. *The book of Colchester: a portrait of the town.* Chesham; Barracuda Books; 1978. Pp 144.

73. Stonebanks, J.A. *Mount Felix, Walton-on-Thames.* Walton & Weybridge Local History Soc.; 1978. Pp 20.

74. Stewart, F., 'Life and death in an Oxfordshire churchyard,' *Local Historian* 13 (1978), 149–59.

75. Smith, G.R. *In well beware: the story of Newburgh Priory and the Belasyse family, 1145–1977.* Kineton; Roundwood Press; 1978. Pp xi, 227.

76. Liversidge, M.J.H. *The Bristol high cross.* Bristol Branch of the Historical Association; 1978. Pp 21.

77. Richard, P.S., 'Brick manufacture in Flintshire,' *Industrial Archaeology* 12 (1978), 226–46.

78. Shornland-Ball, R., 'Worsbrough corn mill, South Yorkshire,' *Industrial Arch R.* 2 (1978), 240–64.

79. Trinick, G.M.A., 'The Tregurtha Downs mines, Marazion, 1700–1965,' ibid. 111–28.

80. Anon., 'The clay industries of Shropshire,' *Industrial Archaeology* 12 (1978), 221–5.

81. Warren, C.D. *History of St Peter's Church, Petersham, Surrey* (new ed.). Petersham; Manor House Press; 1978. Pp 190.

82. Underwood, E. *Brighton.* London; Batsford; 1978. Pp 176.

83. Bush, R. *The book of Exmouth: portrait of a resort.* Buckingham; Barracuda Books; 1978. Pp 148.

84. Fieldhouse, R.; Jennings, B. *A history of Richmond and Swaledale.* Chichester; Phillimore; 1978. Pp xiv, 520.

85. Fenton, A. *The northern isles: Orkney and Shetland.* Eginburgh; Donald; 1978. Pp x, 721.

86. Allott, S. *Friends in York: the Quaker story in the life of a Meeting.* York; Sessions; 1978. Pp xii, 127.

87. Law, A.D.; Barry, S.; (ed.) Tonkin, W.G.S. *The forest of Walthamstow and Chingford.* London; Chingford Historical Soc.; 1978. Pp 32.

88. Sellers, I., 'The Risley case,' *T. of the Unitarian Historical Soc.* 16 (1978), 176—87.

89. Phythian-Adams, C. *Continuity, fields and fission: the making of a Midland parish.* Leicester UP; 1978. Pp vi, 53.

90. Burnby, J.G.L.; Parker, M. *The navigation of the River Lee (1190—1790).* Enfield; Edmonton Hundred Historical Soc.; 1978. Pp 26.

91. Messenger, M.J. *Caradon and Looe: the canal, railways and mines.* Truro; Twelveheads Press; 1978. Pp 128.

92. Bailey, J. *Country wheelwright.* London; Batsford; 1978. Pp 120.

93. Pilkington, F. *Ashburton: the Dartmoor town.* Ashburton; the author; 1978. Pp 136.

94. Hamilton-Edwards, G. *Perthshire marriage contracts, 1687—1809.* Oxford; the compiler; 1978. Pp ii; 25 leaves.

95. Bettey, J.H. *Rural life in Wessex, 1500—1900.* Bradford-on-Avon; Moonraker Press; 1977. Pp 151.

96. Howse, V.M. *Shellingford: a parish record.* Faringdon; the author; 1978. Pp 120.

97. Corina, M. *Fine silks and oak counters: Debenhams, 1778—1978.* London; Hutchinson; 1978. Pp 200.

98. Millward, R.; Robinson, A. *The Welsh borders.* London; Eyre Methuen; 1978. Pp 256.

99. Liverpool Heritage Bureau. *Buildings of Liverpool.* Liverpool; The Bureau; 1978. Pp x, 278.

100. Everitt, A.M., 'The making of the agrarian landscape of Kent,' *Archaeologia Cantiana* 92 (1977 for 1976), 1—31.

101. Horn, P., 'The Dorset dairy system,' *Agricultural History R.* 26 (1978), 100—7.

102. Altick, R.D. *The shows of London* [public entertainment]. Cambridge, Mass.; Belknap Press; 1978. Pp 553.

103. Hiscock, R.H., 'The proprietary chapel of St John, Gravesend,' *Archaeologia Cantiana* 93 (1978 for 1977), 1—24.

104. Perriam, D.R., 'The dating of the county gaol,' *T. of the Cumberland & Westmorland Antiquarian & Arch. Soc.* 78 (1978), 129—40.

105. Parkin, E.W., 'Ratling Court, Aylesham,' *Archaeologia Cantiana* 92 (1977 for 1976), 53—64.

106. Huelin, G., 'Christmas in the city,' *Guildhall Studies in London History* 3 (1978), 164—74.

107. Lloyd, D.J. *County grammar school: a history of Ludlow Grammar School through eight centuries against its local background.* Ludlow; Ludlow College; 1977. Pp 192.

108. Jackson, S. *The Old Bailey*. London; W.H. Allen; 1978. Pp 234.
109. Cryer, L.R. *A history of Rochford*. London; Phillimore; 1978. Pp 190.
110. Brander, M. *Portrait of a hunt: the history of the Puckeridge and Newmarket and Thurlow Combined Hunt*. London; Hutchinson; 1976. Pp xvi, 192.
111. Buck, A., 'Middlemen in the Bedfordshire lace industry,' Bc10, 31–58.
112. French, W.L. (ed.). *The registers of Kirkby St Chad's Chapelry in the parish of Walton-on-the-Hill. Baptisms, 1610–1839*. Liverpool; Knowsley Borough Libraries; 1977. Pp 207.
113. O'Connell, M. *Historic towns in Surrey*. Guildford; Surrey Arch. Soc.; 1977. Pp vi, 50.
114. Rowan, E. (ed.). *Art in Wales, 2000 BC – AD 1850: an illustrated history*. Cardiff; University of Wales Press; 1978. Pp 127.
115. Thomas, I. *Methodism in Mullion*. Mullion Methodist Church; 1978. Pp 104.
116. Harvey, M. *The morphological and tenurial structure of a Yorkshire township: Preston in Holderness 1066–1750*. London; Queen Mary College; 1978. Pp 32.
117. Jones, D.T., 'Excavations at the site of the medieval hall-house at North Cray,' *Archaeologia Cantiana* 93 (1978 for 1977), 187–94.
118. Alexander, M.J.; Roberts, B.K., 'The deserted village of Low Buston, Northumberland: a study in soil phosphate analysis,' *Archaeologia Aeliana* 5th ser. 6 (1978), 107–16.

(c) *Collective volumes*

1. Holmes, C. (ed.). *Immigrants and minorities in British society*. London; Allen & Unwin; 1978. Pp 208.
2. Chaloner, W.H.; Ratcliffe, B.M. *Trade and transport: essays in economic history in honour of T.S. Willan*. Manchester UP; 1977. Pp x, 293.
3. Douglas, D.C. *Time and the hour: some collected papers*. London; Eyre Methuen; 1977. Pp 252.
4. Walker, D.; Sheils, W.J.; Kent, J. (ed.). *An ecclesiastical miscellany*. Bristol and Gloucestershire Arch. Soc.; 1976. Pp ix, 156.
5. Baker, J.H. (ed.). *Legal records and the historian: papers presented to the Cambridge Legal History Conference, 7–10 July 1975, and in Lincoln's Inn Old Hall on 3 June 1974*. London; Royal Historical Society; 1978. Pp xiii, 233.
6. Apted, M.R.; Gilyard-Beer, R.; Saunders, A.D. (ed.). *Ancient monuments and their interpretation: essays presented to A.J. Taylor*. London; Phillimore; 1977. Pp xix, 371.
7. Baker, D. (ed.). *Religious motivation: biographical and sociological problems for the Church historian*. Studies in Church History, 15. Oxford; Blackwell; 1978. Pp xvi, 516.

8. Runte, R. (ed.). *Studies in eighteenth-century culture, vol. 7.* Madison/London; University of Madison Press; 1978. Pp xv, 512.
9. Moody, T.W. (ed.). *Nationality and the pursuit of national independence.* Belfast; Appletree Press; 1978. Pp xvi, 178.
10. *Worthington George Smith and other studies presented to Joyce Godber.* Bedfordshire Historical Record Society, vol. 57; 1978. Pp 243.
11. Not used.
12. Baker, D. (ed.). *Mediaeval women: dedicated and presented to Professor Rosalind M.T. Hill.* Studies in Church History, Subsidia 1. Oxford; Blackwell; 1978. Pp xii, 399.
13. Cowling, M. (ed.). *Conservative essays.* London; Cassell; 1978. Pp viii, 198.
14. Andrews, K.R.; Canny, N.P.; Hair, P.E.H. (ed.). *The westward enterprise: English activities in Ireland, the Atlantic and America, 1480–1560.* [Essays for D.B. Quinn]. Liverpool UP; 1978. Pp xvi, 326.
15. Hepburn, A.C. (ed.). *Minorities in history.* London; Arnold; 1978. Pp vii, 251.

(d) *Genealogy and heraldry*

1. Mitchell, A. *Pre-1855 gravestone inscriptions from Speyside.* Edinburgh; Scottish Genealogy Soc.; 1977. Pp 137.
2. Marks, R.; Payne, A. *British heraldry from its origins to c. 1800.* London; British Museum Publications Ltd.; 1978. Pp 136.
3. Hamilton-Edwards, G. *In search of army ancestry.* London; Phillimore; 1977. Pp 106.
4. Pontifex, C.E.C. *The family of Pontifex of West Wycombe, Co. Buckingham, 1500–1977.* Hassocks; the author; 1977. Pp 50.
5. Humphery-Smith, C.R. *A genealogist's bibliography.* London; Phillimore; 1976. Pp 93.
6. Felgate, T.M. *Suffolk heraldic brasses.* Ipswich; East Anglia Magazine; 1978. Pp 152.
7. Rayment, J.L. *Notes on the recording of monumental inscriptions.* Ongar; Essex Soc. for Family History; 1977. Pp 19.
8. Kuhlicke, F.W., 'Bedfordshire heraldry: a conspectus,' Bc10, 21–30.
9. Graham, N.H. *The genealogist's consolidated guide to parish registers in the Outer London area, 1538 to 1837.* Orpington; the compiler; 1977. Pp 79.

C. ROMAN BRITAIN

(a) *Archaeology*

1. Philip, B.J., 'The forum of Roman London, 1968–9,' *Britannia* 8 (1977), 1–64.
2. Miles, H., 'The Honeyditches villa, Seaton,' ibid. 107–48.
3. Potter, T.W., 'The Biglands milefortlet, Cumberland,' ibid. 149–83.
4. Wilson, D.R., 'The first-century fort near Gosbecks,' ibid. 185–7.
5. Riley, D.N., 'Roman defended sites at Kirmingham, S. Humberside, and Farnsfield, Notts., recently found from the air,' ibid. 189–92.
6. Boon, G.C., 'Gold-in-glass beads from the ancient world,' ibid. 193–207.
7. Knowles, A.K., 'Brampton, Norfolk: interim report,' ibid. 209–21.
8. Phillips, B.; Walters, B., 'A mansion at Wanborough,' ibid. 223–7.
9. Peacock, D.P.S., 'Bricks of the *classis Britannica*,' ibid. 235–48.
10. Williams, D., 'Viticulture in Roman Britain,' ibid. 327–34.
11. Lloyd-Morgan, G., 'Two Roman mirrors from Corbridge,' ibid. 335–8.
12. Money, J.H., 'The iron age hill-fort and Romano-British ironworking settlement at Garden Hill, Sussex,' ibid. 339–50.
13. Millett, M., 'A marble head from Crondall, Hampshire,' ibid. 351–2.
14. Browne, D.M., 'An unusual sherd from Cambridgeshire.' ibid. 352–4.
15. Frere, S.S., 'Roman Britain in 1976: I, Sites,' ibid. 356–425.
16. St Joseph, J.K., 'Air reconnaisance in Roman Britain, 1973–76,' *J. of Roman Studies* 67 (1977), 125–61.
17. Down, A. *Chichester excavations, 3.* Chichester; Phillimore; 1978. Pp x, 375.
18. Forde-Johnston, J. *Hadrian's Wall.* London; Joseph; 1978. Pp 205.
19. Gillam, J.P., 'The Roman forts at Corbridge,' *Archaeologia Aeliana* 5th ser. 5 (1977), 47–74.
20. Sheil, N., 'Carausian and Allectan coin evidence from the northern frontier,' ibid. 75–80.
21. Shorer, P.H.T., 'An unusual dragonesque brooch from South Shields,' ibid. 197–8.
22. Boon, G.C., 'A Graeco-Roman anchor-stock from North Wales,' *Antiquaries J.* 57 (1977), 10–30.
23. Hobley, B.; Schofield, J., 'Excavations in the city of London: first interim report, 1974–1975,' ibid. 31–66.
24. Hartley, B.R.; Fitts, R.L., 'Comments on some Roman material from Stanwick,' ibid. 93–4.

25. Brown, D., 'The significance of the Londesborough ring brooch,' ibid. 95—7.
26. Jones, M.J., 'Archaeological work at Brough under Stainmore 1971—2: the Roman discoveries,' *T. of the Cumberland and Westmorland Antiquarian and Arch. Soc.* 77 (1977), 17—45.
27. Potter, T.W., 'Excavations at the Roman fort of Watercrook, 1975,' ibid. 49—52.
28. Richardson, G.G.S., 'A Romano-British farmstead at Fingland,' ibid. 53—9.
29. Shotter, D.C.A.; White, A.J., 'Two hoards of Roman coins from the Lancaster area,' ibid. 173—8.
30. Shotter, D.C.A., 'A Roman as from Carlisle,' ibid. 178.
31. Burkett, M.E., 'Rescue dig in Ambleside,' ibid. 179—80.
32. Leech, R.H., 'Late iron age and Romano-British briquetage sites at Quarrylands Lane, Badworth,' *Somerset Archaeology and Natural History* 121 (1977), 89—96.
33. Aston, M., 'Somerset archaeology 1976,' ibid. 107—28.
34. Boon, G.C., 'A Romano-British wooden carving from Llanio,' *B. of the Board of Celtic Studies* 27 (1978), 619—24.
35. Boon, G.C., 'A list of Roman hoards in Wales — second supplement 1977,' ibid. 625—32.
36. Griffiths, J.G., 'Mithras or Attis? Remarks on a Caerlon sculpture,' ibid. 633—7.
37. Toms, G., 'Archaeological discoveries on the East Shropshire border,' *T. of the Shropshire Arch. Soc.* 59 (1978 for 1973/4), 209—13.
38. Houghton, A.W.J., 'The last mile of Watling Street east of Wroxeter,' ibid. 214—24.
39. Day, W., 'Temporary Roman camp at Perry Farm, Whittington,' ibid. 280—2.
40. Houghton, A.W.J., 'Personal observations at and near Wroxeter,' ibid. 283—5.
41. Corbet, J.; Toms, G., 'The site of Rutunium,' ibid. 286—8.
42. Keppie, L.J.F., 'Some rescue excavation on the line of the Antonine Wall, 1973—6,' *P. of the Soc. of Antiquaries of Scotland* 107 (1978 for 1975/6), 61—80.
43. Elliot, J.W., 'A Roman terra-cotta head and a bronze weight from Newstead, Roxburghshire,' ibid. 314—6.
44. Smith, C.A., 'Late prehistoric and Romano-British enclosed homesteads in north-west Wales: an interpretation of their morphology,' *Archaeologia Cambrensis* 126 (1978 for 1977), 38—52.
45. Knight, J.K.; Thomas, W.G.; Ward, A.H.; Lynch, F.; White, R.B., 'New finds of early Christian monuments,' ibid. 60—73.
46. Dool, J.; Hughes, R.G., 'Two Roman pigs of lead from Derbyshire,' *Derbyshire Arch. J.* 96 (1978 for 1976), 15—16.
47. Dool, J., 'Roman material from Rainster Rocks, Brassington,' ibid. 17—22.

48. O'Brien, C.F.; Todd, M., 'A section across Ryknield Street at New Tupton,' ibid. 23—5.
49. Darling, M.J. *A group of late Roman pottery from Lincoln.* London; Council for British Archaeology; 1977. Pp 42.
50. Burke, J. *Life in the villa in Roman Britain.* London; Batsford; 1978. Pp 120.
51. Todd, M. (ed.). *Studies in the Romano-British villa.* Leicester UP; 1978. Pp 244.
52. Rahtz, P.A.; Greenfield, E. *Excavations at Chew Valley Lake, Somerset.* London; HMSO; 1977. Pp xix, 392.
53. Guido, M. *The glass beads of the prehistoric and Roman periods in Britain and Ireland.* London; Soc. of Antiquaries; 1978. Pp xxxi, 250.
54. Wilkes, J.J.; Elrington, C.R. (ed.). *A history of the county of Cambridgeshire, vol. 7: Roman Cambridgeshire.* Oxford UP (for Victoria County History); 1978. Pp xvi, 98.
55. Ramm, H.G. *The Parisi.* London; Duckworth; 1978. Pp viii, 160.
56. Boon, G.C. (ed.). *Monographs and collections, relating to excavations financed by H.M. Department of the Environment in Wales.* Cardiff; Cambrian Arch. Association; 1978. Pp ix, 129.
57. Robinson, J.F. *The archaeology of Malton and Norton.* Leeds; Yorkshire Arch. Soc.; 1978. Pp xi, 42.
58. Detsicas, A.P., 'Excavations at Exeter, 1975,' *Archaeologia Cantiana* 92 (1977 for 1976), 157—63.
59. Tatton-Brown, T.W.T., 'Excavations in 1976 by the Canterbury Archaeological Trust,' ibid. 235—44.
60. Detsicas, A.P., 'Excavations at Eccles, 1976: final interim report,' *Archaeologia Cantiana* 93 (1978 for 1977), 55—9.
61. Tatton-Brown, T.W.T., 'Excavations in 1977 by the Canterbury Archaeological Trust,' ibid. 212—8.
62. King, C.E., 'The Woodeaton (Oxfordshire) hoard and the problem of Constantinian imitations, A.D. 330—41,' *Numismatic Chronicle* 7th ser. 18 (1978), 38—65.
63. Boon, G.C., 'A counterstamped and defaced As of Nero from Exeter,' ibid. 178—80.
64. Jobey, G., 'Iron age and Romano-British settlements on Kennel Hall Knowe, North Tynedale, Northumberland (1976),' *Archaeologia Aeliana* 5th ser. 6 (1978), 1—28.
65. Greene, K., 'Apperley Dene "Roman fortlet": a re-examination 1975—5,' ibid. 29—59.
66. Charlton, D.B.; Day, J.C., 'Excavations and field survey in upper Redesdale,' ibid. 61—86.
67. Dennis, W., 'A bronze lamp from the North Tyne at Chesters,' ibid. 161—2.
68. Gilson, A., 'A doctor at Housesteads,' ibid. 162—5.
69. Savage, M., 'A fourth century coin hoard from Washington (Tyne and Wear),' ibid. 166—9.

70. Bell, R.C., 'Games played at Corstopitum,' ibid. 174—6.
71. White, A.J., 'Archaeology in Lincolnshire and South Humberside,' *Lincolnshire History and Archaeology* 13 (1978), 75—89.
72. Bell, M., 'Excavations at Bishopstone,' *Sussex Arch. Collections* 115 (1977).
73. Henig, M., 'A Roman signet-ring from Sheerness,' *Archaeologia Cantiana* 93 (1978 for 1977), 207.
74. Hayward, L.C. *The Romans at Ilchester, Lufton, Yeovil and district.* Yeovil Arch. and Local History Soc.; 1978. Pp 32.
75. Wainwright, G.J., 'New light on neolithic habitation sites and early Iron Age settlements in southern Britain,' Bc6, 1—12.
76. Charlesworth, D., 'The turrets on Hadrian's Wall,' Bc6, 13—26.
77. Neal, D.S., 'Witcomb Roman villa,' Bc6, 27—40.
78. Butcher, S.A., 'Enamels from Roman Britain,' Bc6, 41—70.

(b) *History*

1. Crummy, P., 'Colchester, fortress and colonia,' *Britannia* 8 (1977), 65—105.
2. Hind, J.G.F., 'The "Genouian" part of Britain,' ibid. 229—34.
3. Kennedy, D., 'The *ala I* and *cohors I Britannica*,' ibid. 249—55.
4. Davies, J.L., 'Arrowheads from Dinorben and the *sagittarii*,' ibid. 257—70.
5. Davies, R.W., 'Ateco of Old Carlisle,' ibid. 271—4.
6. Bogaers, J.E., 'Tile-stamps from Lincoln and Legion V Alaudae,' ibid. 275—8.
7. Wright, R.P., 'A Roman veterinary physician from the Thames valley,' ibid. 279—82.
8. Casey, P.J., 'Carausius and Allectus — rulers in Gaul?,' ibid. 283—301.
9. Thompson, E.A., 'Britain A.D. 406—10,' ibid. 303—18.
10. Todd, M., '*Famosa pastis* and fifth-century Britain,' ibid. 319—25.
11. Hassall, M.W.C.; Tomlin, R.S.O., 'Roman Britain 1976: II, Inscriptions,' ibid. 426—49.
12. Breeze, D., 'Review article: *Birrena* and Kastell *Künzing-Quintana*,' ibid. 451—60.
13. Johnson, S. *Roman fortification on the 'Saxon shore'.* London; HMSO; 1977. Pp 28.
14. Davies, R.W., 'Cohors I Hispaniorum and the garrisons of Maryport,' *T. of the Cumberland and Westmorland Antiquarian and Arch. Soc.* 77 (1977), 7—16.
15. Shotter, D.C.A., 'Coin evidence and the northern frontier in the second century AD,' *P. of the Soc. of Antiquaries of Scotland* 107 (1978 for 1975/6), 81—91.
16. Reed, N., 'The Scottish campaigns of Septimius Severus,' ibid. 92—102.

17. Branigan, K., 'Britain after Boudicca,' *Archaeologia Cambrensis* 126 (1978 for 1976), 53–9.
18. Frere, S. *Britannia: a history of Roman Britain* (revd. ed.). London; Routledge; 1978. Pp 487.
19. Thornhill, P., 'A lower Thames ford and the campaigns of 54 B.C. and A.D. 43,' *Archaeologia Cantiana* 92 (1977 for 1976), 119–28.
20. Higham, N.J., 'Continuity studies in the first millenium A.D. in North Cumbria,' *Northern History* 14 (1978), 1–18.
21. Ellis, P.B. *Caesar's invasion of Britain.* London; Orbis Books; 1978. Pp 144.
22. Hawkes, C., 'Britain and Julius Caesar,' *P. of the British Academy* 63 (1978 for 1977), 125–92.
23. Rutherford, W. *The druids and their heritage.* London; Gordon & Cremonesi; 1978. Pp 179.

D. ENGLAND 450–1066

See also Cb20

(a) *General*

1. Taylor, A. *Anglo-Saxon Cambridgeshire.* Cambridge; Oleander Press; 1978.
2. Brown, D. *Anglo-Saxon England.* London; Bodley Head; 1978. Pp 112.
3. Loyn, H.R. *The Vikings in Britain.* London; Batsford; 1977. Pp 176.
4. Taylor, H.M. and J. *Anglo-Saxon architecture*, vol. 3. Cambridge UP; 1978. Pp xx, [735–] 1118.
5. Clemoes, P. (ed.). *Anglo-Saxon England, vol. 7.* Cambridge UP; 1978. Pp x, 303.
6. Sawyer, P.H. *From Roman Britain to Norman England.* London; Methuen; 1978. Pp x, 294.
7. Winterbottom, M. (ed.). *The ruin of Britain, and other works, by Gildas.* London; Phillimore; 1978. Pp 162.

(b) *Politics and Institutions*

1. Campbell, M.W., 'The rise of an Anglo-Saxon "kingmaker"; Earl Godwin of Wessex,' *Canadian J. of History* 13 (1978), 17–33.
2. Wilson Smith, T., 'King Alfred: an eleventh centenary,' *History Today* 28 (1978), 423–8.
3. Whitlock, R. *The warrior kings of Saxon England.* Bradford-on-Avon; Moonraker Press; 1977. Pp 160.

4. Stafford, P., 'Sons and mothers: family politics in the early middle ages,' Bc12, 79—200.

(c) *Religion*

1. Harrison, K., 'Easter cycles and the equinox in the British Isles,' Da5, 1—8.
2. Rollason, D.W., 'Lists of saints' resting-places in Anglo-Saxon England,' Da5, 61—94.
3. Sheerin, D., 'The dedication of the Old Minster, Westminster, in 980,' *Revue Bénédictine* 88 (1978), 261—73.
4. Ralegh Radford, C.A., 'The church of Saint Alkmund, Derby,' *Derbyshire Arch. J.* 96 (1978 for 1976), 26—61.

(d) *Economic Affairs and Numismatics*

1. Barker, E.E., 'The Bromley charters,' *Archaeologia Cantiana* 93 (1978 for 1977), 1—24.
2. Brown, A.E.; Key, T.R., 'The Badby and Newnham (Northamptonshire) charters,' *English Place-Name Society J.* 10 (1977—8), 1—6.
3. Higham, M.C., 'The "erg" place-names of northern England,' ibid. 7—17.
4. Atkin, M., 'Viking race-courses? The distribution of Skeid place-name elements in northern England,' ibid. 26—39.
5. Fellows Jensen, G., 'A Gaelic-Scandinavian loan-word in English place-names,' ibid. 18—25.
6. Gelling, M., 'Recent work on Anglo-Saxon charters,' *Local Historian* 13 (1978), 209—15.
7. Fellows Jensen, G., 'Place-names and settlement in the North Riding of Yorkshire,' *Northern History* 14 (1978), 19—46.
8. Keynes, S., 'An interpretation of the *Pacx*, *Pax* and *Paxs* pennies,' Da5, 165—73.
9. Rigold, S.E., 'The principal series of English *sceattas*,' *British Numismatic J.* 47 (1978 for 1977), 21—30.
10. Rigold, S.E.; Metcalf, D.M., 'A check-list of English finds of sceattas,' ibid. 31—52.
11. Dolley, M.; Talvio, T., 'The regional pattern of die-cutting exhibited by the first hand pennies of Aethelred II preserved in the British Museum,' ibid. 53—65.
12. Burrows, O., 'An unnoticed parcel from the 1872 Queen Victoria Street hoard,' ibid. 66—76.
13. Blunt, C.E.; Dolley, M., 'Coins from the Winchester excavations 1961—1973,' ibid. 135—8.

(e) *Intellectual and Cultural*

1. Alexander, J.J.G. (ed.). *A survey of manuscripts illuminated in the British Isles; vol. 1: Insular manuscripts, 6th to the 9th century.* London; Harvey Miller; 1978. Pp 219.
2. Needham, G.I. (ed.). *Aelfric's Lives of three English saints.* Exeter; The University; 1876. Pp viii, 119.
3. Miller, M., 'Bede's Roman dates,' *Classica et Mediaevalia* 31 (1976 for 1970), 239–52.
4. Aronstam, R.A., 'The Blickling Homilies: a reflection of popular Anglo-Saxon belief,' *Law, Church and Society: essays in honour of Stephan Kuttner* (ed. K. Pennington and R. Somerville; Philadelphia; University of Pennsylvania Press; 1977), 271–80.
5. Kitson, P., 'Lapidary traditions in Anglo-Saxon England; part I: the background; the Old English lapidary,' Da5, 9–60.
6. Blake, N.F., 'The genesis of *The Battle of Maldon*,' Da5, 119–29.
7. Brownrigg, L.L., 'Manuscripts containing English decoration 871–1066, catalogued and illustrated: a review,' Da5, 239–66.
8. Chaplais, P., 'The letter from Bishop Wealdhere of London to Archbishop Brihtwold of Canterbury: the earliest original "letter close" in the west,' Bc11, 3–23.
9. Mahler, A.E., '*Ligum domini* and the opening vision of *The Dream of the Rood*: a viable hypothesis?,' *Speculum* 53 (1978), 441–59.
10. Nicholson, J., '*Feminae gloriosae*: women in the age of Bede,' Bc12, 15–29.
11. Braswell, B.K., '*The Dream of the Rood* and Aldhelm on sacred prosopopoeia,' *Mediaeval Studies* 40 (1978), 461–7.
12. Bishop, T.A.M., 'The prototype of *Liber glossarum*,' Ei40, 69–86.
13. Cope, J.P., 'Palaeography and poetry: some solved and unsolved problems of the Exeter Book,' Ei40, 25–65.
14. Gneuss, H., 'Dunstan and the Hrabanus Maurus: zur Hs, Bodleian Auctarium G.4.32,' *Anglia* 96 (1978), 136–48.

(f) *Society and Archaeology*

1. Morris, C.D., 'Northumbria and the Viking settlement: the evidence for land-holding,' *Archaeologia Aeliana* 5th ser. 5 (1977), 81–103.
2. Foard, G., 'Systematic fieldwalking and the investigation of Saxon settlement in Northamptonshire,' *World Archaeology* 9 (1978), 357–74.
3. Myres, J.N.L. *A corpus of Anglo-Saxon pottery of the pagan period.* Cambridge UP; 1977. 2 vols. Pp xxxvi, 358; 376.
4. Hills, C. *The Anglo-Saxon cemetery at Spong Hill, North Elmham, part 1: catalogue of cremations, nos. 20–64 and 1000–1690.* East Anglian Archaeology, Report no. 6 (Suffolk). Ipswich; Suffolk Planning Department; 1978. Pp xii, 242.

5. Hill, D.H., 'Continuity from Roman to medieval Britain,' *European towns: their archaeology and early history* (ed. M.W. Barley; London; Academic Press; 1977), 293—302.
6. Brooks, N.P., 'The ecclesiastical topography of early medieval Canterbury,' ibid. 487—98.
7. Addyman, P.V., 'York and Canterbury as ecclesiastical centres,' ibid. 499—509.
8. Avent, R.; Leigh, D., 'A study of cross-hatched gold foils in Anglo-Saxon jewellery,' *Medieval Archaeology* 21 (1977), 1—46.
9. Hill, D., 'Offa's and Wat's Dykes: some aspects of recent work, 1972—1976,' *T. of the Lancashire and Cheshire Antiquarian Soc.* 79 (1977), 21—33.
10. Carver, M.O.H., 'Early Shrewsbury: an archaeological definition in 1975,' *T. of the Shropshire Arch. Soc.* 59 (1978 for 1973—4), 225—63.
11. Webster, L.E., 'Pre-conquest,' *Medieval Archaeology* 21 (1977), 204—22.
12. Carter, A., 'The Anglo-Saxon origins of Norwich; the problems and approaches,' Da5, 175—204.
13. Hewett, C.A., 'Anglo-Saxon carpentry,' Da5, 205—29.
14. Hawkes, S.C., 'Orientation in Finglesham: sunrise dating of death and burial in an Anglo-Saxon cemetery,' *Archaeologia Cantiana* 92 (1977 for 1976), 33—51.
15. Kennett, D.H., *Anglo-Saxon pottery.* Aylesbury; Shire Publications; 1978. Pp 56.
16. Devenish, D.C.; Champion, T.C., 'A sixth-century Anglo-Saxon grave at Meonstoke, Hampshire,' *P. of the Hampshire Field Club and Arch. Soc.* 34 (1978 for 1977), 37—42.
17. Myres, J.N.L., 'The origin of the Jersey parishes: some suggestions,' *Société Jersiaise Annual B.* 22 (1978), 163—75.

E. ENGLAND 1066—1500

(a) *General*

1. Chibnall, M. (ed.). *The ecclesiastical history of Ordericus Vitalis.* Vol. 6: Books 11, 12 and 13. Oxford; Clarendon; 1978. Pp xxviii, 611.
2. Morris, J. (ed.). *Domesday Book.* Vol. 26: Cheshire (ed. P. Morgan from translation by A. Rumble). Chichester; Phillimore; 1978. Pp 176. — Vol. 13: Buckinghamshire (ed. from a translation by E. Teague and V. Sankaran). Ibid. 1978. Pp 183. — Vol. 14: Oxfordshire (ed. from a translation by C. Caldwell). Ibid. 1978. Pp 160.

3. Platt, C. *Medieval England: a social history and archaeology from the Conquest to A.D. 1600.* London; Routledge; 1978. Pp xix, 292.
4. Miller, E.; Hatcher, J. *Medieval England: rural society and economic change, 1086–1348.* London; Longman; 1978. Pp xviii, 302.
5. Russell, J.C. *Twelfth century studies.* New York; AMS Press; 1978. Pp 268.

(b) *Politics*

1. Hicks, M.A., 'The case of Sir Thomas Cook, 1468,' *English Historical R.* 93 (1978), 82–96.
2. Davis, R.H.C., 'The *Carmen de Hastingae Proelio*,' *English Historical R.* 93 (1978), 241–61.
3. Haines, R.M. *The church and politics in fourteenth-century England: the career of Adam Orleton, c. 1275–1345.* Cambridge UP; 1978. Pp xiv, 303.
4. Given-Wilson, C.J., 'Richard II and his grandfather's will,' *English Historical R.* 93 (1978), 320–37.
5. Post, J.B., 'A privately drafted common petition of 1398–9,' *J. of the Soc. of Archivists* 6 (1978), 10–17.
6. Myers, A.R., 'A parliamentary debate of 1449,' *B. of the Institute of Historical Research* 51 (1978), 78–83.
7. Teunis, H.B., 'The coronation charter of 1100: a postponement of decision. What did not happen in Henry I's reign,' *J. of Medieval History* 4 (1978), 135–44.
8. Barber, R. *Edward, prince of Wales and Aquitaine: a biography of the Black Prince.* London; Allen Lane; 1978. Pp 298.
9. Russell, J.C., 'Tall kings: the height of medieval English kings,' Ea5, 62–75.
10. Russell, J.C., 'Death along the deer trails,' Ea5, 76–82.
11. Russell, J.C., 'Allegations of poisoning in the Norman world,' Ea5, 83–93.
12. Russell, J.C., 'The canonization of opposition to the king in Angevin England,' Ea5, 248–60.
13. Henderson, G., 'Romance and politics on some medieval English seals,' *Art History* 1 (1978), 26–42.
14. Young, A., 'William Cumin: border politics and the bishopric of Durham,' *Borthwick Papers* 54 (1978); pp. 37.
15. Meade, M. *Eleanor of Aquitaine: a biography.* London; Muller; 1978. Pp xiii, 389.
16. Gillingham, J.B. *Richard the Lionheart.* London; Weidenfeld & Nicolson; 1978. Pp viii, 318.
17. Warren, W.L. *King John* (2nd ed.). London; Eyre Methuen; 1978. Pp xi, 350.

18. Denton, J.H., 'The crisis of 1297 from the Evesham Chronicle,' *English Historical R.* 93 (1978), 560—79.
19. Denton, J.H., 'A Worcester text of the Remonstrances of 1297,' *Speculum* 53 (1978), 511—21.
20. Cuttino, G.P.; Lyman, T.W., 'Where is Edward III?,' ibid. 522—43.
21. Salter, E., 'The timeliness of *Wynnere and Wastoure*,' *Medium Aevum* 47 (1978), 40—65.
22. Bird, B.; Stephenson, D., 'Who was John Ball?,' *Essex Archaeology and History* 3rd ser. 8 (1978 for 1976), 287—8.
23. Palmer, J.J.N., 'The authorship, date and historical value of the French chronicles on the Lancastrian revolution, I,' *B. of the John Rylands University Library of Manchester*, 61 (1978), 145—81.
24. Sutton, A.F., 'Sir Thomas Cook and his "troubles",' [cf Eb1], *Guildhall Studies in London History* 3 (1978), 85—108.
25. Hicks, M.A., 'Dynastic change and northern society: the career of the fourth earl of Northumberland, 1470—89,' *Northern History* 14 (1978), 78—107.

(c) *Constitution, Administration and Law*

1. Bates, D.R., 'The land pleas of William I's reign: Penenden Heath revisited,' *B. of the Institute of Historical Research* 51 (1978), 1—19.
2. Hollister, C.W., 'The origins of the English treasury,' *English Historical R.* 93 (1978), 262—75.
3. Rogers Forbes, T., 'Crowner's quest,' *T. of the American Philosophical Soc.* 68 (1978); pp. 52.
4. Hammer, jr., C.I., 'Patterns of homicide in a medieval university town: fourteenth-century Oxford,' *Past & Present* 78 (1978), 3—23.
5. Maddicott, J.R., 'The birth and setting of the ballads of Robin Hood,' *English Historical R.* 93 (1978), 276—99.
6. Cameron, A., 'Complaint and reform in Henry VII's reign: the origins of the statute of 3 Henry VII, c.2,' *B. of the Institute of Historical Research* 51 (1978), 83—9.
7. Hollister, C.W.; Baldwin, J.W., 'The rise of administrative kingship: Henry I and Philip Augustus,' *American Historical R.* 83 (1978), 867—905.
8. Turner, R.V., 'The *miles literatus* in twelfth- and thirteenth-century England: how rare a phenomenon?,' ibid. 928—45.
9. Thorne, S.E., 'Henry I's coronation charter, ch. 6,' *English Historical R.* 93 (1978), 794.
10. Russell, J.C., 'The date of Henry I's charter to London,' Ea5, 94—102.
11. Russell, J.C., 'The triumph of dignity over order in England,' Ea5, 190—202.

12. Russell, J.C., 'Social status at the court of King John,' Ea5, 203—18.
13. Russell, J.C., 'Attestation of charters in the reign of John,' Ea5, 219—47.
14. Russell, J.C., 'Ranulf de Glanville,' Ea5, 126—41.
15. Falls, J.S., 'Ranulf de Glanville's formative years c. 1120—79: the family background and his ascent to the justiciarship,' *Mediaeval Studies* 40 (1978), 312—27.
16. Studd, J.R., 'Chancellors of the Lord Edward: a supplementary note,' *B. of the Institute of Historical Research* 51 (1978), 181—3.
17. Douglas, A.W., 'Frankalmoin and the jurisdictional immunity; Maitland revisited,' *Speculum* 53 (1978), 26—48.
18. Thorne, S.E. (ed.). *Bracton on the Laws and Customs of England,* vols. 3 and 4. Cambridge, Mass.; Belknap Press; 1977. Pp liii, 412 (bis); xiii, 378 (bis).
19. Keeton, G.W. *Harvey the Hasty: a mediaeval chief justice.* [Chichester; Rose; 1978]. Pp 178.
20. Pugh, R.B. (ed.). *Wiltshire gaol delivery and trailbaston trials, 1275—1306.* Wiltshire Record Soc., vol. 33; 1977; pp. 273.
21. Pugh, R.B., 'England's earliest gazeteer? [*Nomina Villarum*, 1316],' *B. of the Institute of Historical Research* 51 (1978), 113—23.
22. Given-Wilson, C., 'The merger of Edward III's and Queen Philippa's household, 1360—9,' ibid. 183—7.
23. Maddicott, J.R., 'The county community and the making of public opinion in fourteenth-century England,' *T. of the Royal Historical Soc.* 5th ser. 28 (1978), 27—43.
24. Roskell, J.S., 'John Doreward of Bocking: Speaker in 1399 and 1413,' *Essex Archaeology and History* 3rd ser. 8 (1976), 209—23.
25. Robertson, C.A., 'Local government and the king's "affinity" in fifteenth-century Leicestershire and Warwickshire,' *T. of the Leicestershire Arch. and Historical Soc.* 52 (1978 for 1976/7), 37—45.
26. Kellaway, W., 'John Carpenter's *Liber albus,*' *Guildhall Studies in London History* 3 (1978), 67—84.
27. Sutton, A.F.; Hammond, P.W., 'The problems of dating and the dangers of redating: the Acts of Court of the Mercer's Company of London, 1453—1527,' *J. of the Soc. of Archivists* 6 (1978), 87—91.
28. Drury, J.L., 'Durham Palatinate forest law and administration, specially in Weardale up to 1440,' *Archaeologia Aeliana* 5th ser. 6 (1978), 87—105.
29. Winchester, A.J.L., 'The medieval vill in the western Lake District: some problems of definition,' *T. of the Cumberland and Westmorland Antiquarian & Arch Soc.* 78 (1978), 55—69.

30. Sayles, G.O., 'The Royal Marriages Act 1428,' *Law Quarterly R.* 74 (1978), 188—92.
31. Not used.
32. Hunnisett, R.F.; Post, J.B. (ed.). *Medieval legal records, in memory of C.A.F. Meekings.* London; HMSO; 1978. Pp 560.
33. Nicol, A., 'Changes in the assize *utrum* between the Constitutions of Clarendon and Bracton,' Ec32, 17—24.
34. Clanchy, M.T., 'Highway robbery and trial by battle in the Hampshire eyre of 1249,' Ec32, 25—61.
35. Brand, P.A., 'Oldcotes *v.* d'Arcy,' Ec32, 63—113.
36. Pegues, F.J., 'Letters to John Mettingham, 1296,' Ec32, 115—28.
37. Hunnisett, R.F., 'A coroner's roll of the liberty of Wye, 1299—1314,' Ec32, 129—41.
38. Harding, A., 'Early trailbaston proceedings from the Lincoln roll of 1305,' Ec32, 143—68.
39. Hall, G.D.G., 'Three courts of the hundred of Penwith, 1333,' Ec32, 169—96.
40. Fryde, N., 'A medieval robber baron: Sir John Molyns of Stoke Poges, Bucks.,' Ec32, 197—221.
41. Hector, L.C., 'Reports, writs and records in the common bench in the reign of Richard II,' Ec32, 267—88.
42. Post, J.B., 'Courts, councils and arbitrators in the Ladbroke Manor dispute, 1382—1400,' Ec32, 289—339.
43. Storey, R.L., 'Clergy and common law in the reign of Henry IV,' Ec32, 341—408.
44. Condon, M.M., 'A Wiltshire sheriff's notebook, 1464—5,' Ec32, 409—28.
45. Barnes, P.M., 'the Chancery *corpus cum causa* file, 10—11 Edward IV,' Ec32, 429—76.
46. Owen, D.M., 'White Annays and others,' Bc12, 331—46.
47. Brand, P.A., 'The control of mortmain alienation in England, 1200—1300,' Bc5, 29—40.
48. Guth, D.J., 'Enforcing late-medieval law: patterns of litigation during Henry VII's reign,' Bc5, 80—96.
49. Owen, D.M., 'An episcopal Audience court,' Bc5, 140—9.
50. Prest, J.B., 'Ravishment of women and the Statutes of Westminster,' Bc5, 150—64.
51. Walker, S.S., 'The action of waste in the early common law,' Bc5, 185—206.

(d) *External affairs*

1. Pistono, S.P., 'Henry IV and Charles VI: the confirmation of the twenty-eight-year truce [1399—1400] ,' *J. of Medieval History* 3 (1977), 353—65.
2. Noble, P., 'Some traces of Anglo-Norman influence in early fifteenth-century Agenais,' *Medium Aevum* 46 (1977), 241—44.

3. Nony, D., 'Deux sceaux-matrices aquitains de l'administration du Prince Noir (XIVe siècle),' *Annales du Midi* 90 (1978), 67—9.

4. Jones, M., 'The diplomatic evidence for Franco-Breton relations, c. 1370—1372,' *English Historical R.* 93 (1978), 300—19.

5. Stevenson, W.B., 'English rule in the Channel Islands in a period of transition, 1204—1259,' *La Société Guernesiaise: Report and T.* 20 (1977), 234—58.

6. Cassard, J.-C., 'Vins et marchands de vins gascons au début du XIVe siècle,' *Annales du Midi* 90 (1978), 121—40.

7. Clarke, M.L., 'English visitors to Rome in the middle ages,' *History Today* 28 (1978), 643—9.

8. Pistono, S.P., 'The diplomatic mission of Jean de Hangest, lord of Hugueville (October, 1400),' *Canadian J. of History* 13 (1978), 193—207.

(e) *Religion*

1. Clarke, J.P.H., 'Walter Hilton and "liberty of spirit",' *Downside R.* 96 (1978), 61—78.

2. Harper-Bill, C., 'Archbishop John Morton and the province of Canterbury, 1486—1500,' *J. of Ecclesiastical History* 29 (1978), 1—21.

3. Wilson, C. *The shrines of St William of York: an account written to commemorate the 750th anniversary of the canonisation of Saint William.* [York; Yorkshire Museum] ; 1977. Pp 28.

4. Cooper, R.G., 'New light on Aelred's immersion,' *Harvard Theological R.* 69 (1976), 416—19.

5. Postles, D., 'The bursary of Oseney Abbey: a note,' *J. of the Soc. of Archivists* 6 (1978), 28—30.

6. Denton, J.H., 'The "communitas cleri" in the early fourteenth century,' *B. of the Institute of Historical Research* 51 (1978), 72—8.

7. Davies, R.G., 'A contested appointment to the bishopric of Bath and Wells, 1400—1,' *Somerset Archaeology and Natural History* 121 (1977), 67—76.

8. Erickson, C., 'The fourteenth-century Franciscans and their critics: II, poverty, jurisdiction and internal change,' *Franciscan Studies* 36 (1976), 108—47.

9. Hudson, A. (ed.). *Selection from English Wycliffite writings.* Cambridge UP; 1978. Pp xii, 234.

10. Hudson, A., 'A neglected Wycliffite text,' *J. of Ecclesiastical History* 29 (1978), 257—79.

11. Burson, M.C., ' " . . . For the sake of my soul": the activities of a medieval executor,' *Archives* 13 (1978), 131—6.

12. Hicks, S.B., 'The Anglo-Papal bargain of 1125: the legatine mission of John of Crema,' *Albion* 8 (1976), 301—10.

13. Fairley, F., 'Adrian IV: England's only pope,' *History Today* 28 (1978), 530—6.

14. Harper-Bill, C., 'The priory and parish of Folkestone in the fifteenth century,' *Archaeologia Cantiana* 93 (1978 for 1977), 195—200.

15. Hill, R.M.T. (ed.). *The register of William Melton, archbishop of York, 1317—1340, vol. 1.* Canterbury and York Soc. vol. 70; 1977. Pp xi, 178.

16. Martin, J.D., 'The cartularies and registers of Peterborough Abbey,' *Northamptonshire Record Soc.* 28 (1978); pp. 52.

17. Tanner, N.P. (ed.). *Heresy trials in the diocese of Norwich, 1428—31.* London; Royal Historical Soc. (Camden 4th ser. 20); 1977. Pp 233.

18. Sheehan, M.M., 'Marriage theory and practice in the conciliar legislation and diocesan statutes of medieval England,' *Mediaeval Studies* 40 (1978), 408—60.

19. Horner, P.J., 'A sermon on the anniversary of the death of Thomas Beauchamp, earl of Warwick,' *Traditio* 34 (1978), 381—401.

20. Richards, M.P., 'MS Cotton Vespasian A.XXII: the Vespasian homilies,' *Manuscripta* 22 (1978), 96—103.

21. Hill, B., 'British Library MS Egerton 613,' *Notes and Queries* 223 (1978), 492—501.

22. Ackerman, R.W., 'The liturgical day in *Ancrene Riwle*,' *Speculum* 53 (1978), 734—44.

23. Bestul, T.H., 'A note on the contents of the Anselm manuscript, Bodleian Library Laud MS. 508,' *Manuscripta* 21 (1977), 167—70.

24. Bestul, T.H., 'The collection of Anselm's prayers in British Library MS Cotton Vespasian D.XXVI,' *Medium Aevum* 47 (1978), 1—5.

25. Boyer, R., 'The companions of St Bruno in Middle English verses on the foundation of the Carthusian order [B.L. Add. MS. 27049],' *Speculum* 53 (1978), 784—5.

26. Johnston, J., 'The points of Thomas Becket,' *Notes and Queries* 223 (1978), 296—99.

27. Wilson, E., 'An unpublished Passion Poem in B.L. Ms Harley 4012,' *Notes and Queries* 222 (1977), 485—8.

28. Orme, N., 'The transept altars of Exeter Cathedral,' *Devon and Cornwall Notes and Queries* 34 (1978), 1—3.

29. Harper-Bill, C., 'Herluin abbot of Bec and his biographer,' Bc7, 15—25.

30. Mason, E., 'Timeo barones et dona ferentes [lay patronage],' Bc7, 61—75.

31. Mortimer, R., 'Religious and secular motives for some English monastic foundation,' Bc7, 77—85.

32. Cazel, F.A., 'Religious motivation in the biography of Hubert de Burgh,' Bc7, 109—19.

31

33. Greatrex, J.G., 'Some statistics of religious motivation,' Bc7, 179—86.
34. Holdsworth, C.J., 'Christina of Markyate,' Bc12, 185—204.
35. Constable, G., 'Ailred of Rievaulx and the nun of Watton: an episode in the early history of the Gilbertine order,' Bc12, 205—26.
36. Thompson, S., 'The problem of the Cistercian nuns in the twelfth and early thirteenth centuries,' Bc12, 227—52.
37. Cross, C., ' "Great reasoner in scripture": the activities of women Lollards, 1380—1530,' Bc12, 359—80.
38. Goodman, A., 'The piety of John Brunham's daughter, of Lynn [Margery Kemp],' Bc12, 347—58.
39. Walker, D. (ed.). 'A register of the churches of the monastery of St Peter's, Gloucester,' Bc4, 3—58.

(f) *Economic affairs*

1. Blanchard, I., 'Labour productivity and work psychology in the English mining industry, 1400—1600,' *Economic History R.* sec. ser. 31 (1978), 1—24.
2. Britnell, R.H., 'English markets and royal administration before 1200,' *Economic History R.* 2nd ser. 31 (1978), 183—96.
3. Mate, M., 'Coping with inflation: a fourteenth-century example [Canterbury Cathedral Priory, 1290—1330] ,' *J. of Medieval History* 4 (1978), 95—107.
4. Lomas, R.A., 'The priory of Durham and its demesnes in the fourteenth and fifteenth centuries,' *Economic History R.* 2nd ser. 31 (1978), 339—53.
5. Butcher, A.F., 'Sandwich in the thirteenth century,' *Archaeologia Cantiana* 93 (1978 for 1977), 25—31.
6. Archibald, M.M.; Connolly, P.A., 'The Meopham hoard of fourteenth century gold coins,' ibid. 47—53.
7. Mate, M., 'The role of gold coinage in the English economy, 1338—1400,' *Numismatic Chronicle* 7th ser. 18 (1978), 126—41.
8. Stewart, I., 'A lead striking of William II's last coin-type,' ibid. 185—7.
9. Davis, R.L., 'Class II coins of the long cross coinage 1247—1248,' *British Numismatic J.* 47 (1978 for 1977), 138—41.
10. Wood, C.J., 'Preliminary results of a die-analysis of approximately one hundred early Edward I pence of the mint of Berwick-on-Tweed,' ibid. 141—4.
11. Peters, I.-M. *Hansekaufleute als Gläubiger der englischen Krone (1294—1350).* Quellen und Darstel lungen zur hansischen Geschichte, neue Folge, Bd. 24. Köln/Wien; Böhlau; 1978. Pp xi, 323.
12. Childs, W.R. *Anglo-Castilian trade in the later middle ages (1254—1485).* Manchester UP; 1978. Pp 264.

13. Isaac, J., 'Two medieval accounts for the town of Lichfield,' *T. of the South Staffordshire Arch. and Historical Soc.* 18 (1976–7), 59–67.
14. Donkin, R.A. *The Cistercians: studies in the geography of medieval England and Wales.* Toronto; Pontifical Institute of Mediaeval Studies; 1978. Pp 242.
15. Postles, D., 'Problems in the administration of small manors: three Oxfordshire glebe-demesnes, 1278–1345,' *Midland History* 4 (1978), 1–14.
16. Fryde, E., 'The tenants of the bishops of Coventry and Lichfield and of Worcester after the plague of 1348–9,' Ec32, 223–66.
17. Bridbury, A.R., 'The farming out of manors'; Postan, M.M., 'A note on the farming out of manors,' *Economic History R.* 2nd ser. 31 (1978), 503–20, 521–5.
18. Birrell, J. (ed.). 'The *status maneriorum* of John Catesby, 1385 and 1386,' *Miscellany I* (ed. R. Bearman: Publications of the Dugdale Soc. 31; 1978), 15–28.
19. Styles, D. (ed.)., 'A financial account of St Mary's, Warwick, Michaelmas 1410–Michaelmas 1411,' ibid. 138–58.
20. Brand, J.D.; Duplessy, J., 'A parcel from the Montpellier (1934) hoard,' *British Numismatic J.* 47 (1978 for 1977), 77–91.
21. Stewart, I., 'Edwardian sterlings in the 1900 Berscar (Closeburn) find,' ibid. 92–101.

(g) *Social Structure and Population*

1. Rawcliffe, C. *The Staffords, earls of Stafford and dukes of Buckingham, 1394–1521.* Cambridge UP; 1978. Pp xiii, 279.
2. Yonekawa, Sh., 'Champion and woodland Norfolk: the development of regional differences,' *J. of European Economic History* 6 (1977), 163–76.
3. Hindle, B.P., 'Seasonal variations in travel in medieval England,' *J. of Transport History* new ser. 4 (1977–8), 170–8.
4. Taylor, C.C., 'Polyfocal settlement and the English village,' *Medieval Archaeology* 21 (1977), 189–93.
5. Aston, M.A., 'Deserted settlements in Mudford parish, Yeovil,' *Somerset Archaeology and Natural History* 121 (1977), 41–53.
6. Mazur, M.P., 'The dispersion of holdings in the open fields: an interpretation in terms of property rights,' *J. of European Economic History* 6 (1977), 461–71.
7. Pimsler, M., 'Solidarity in the medieval village? The evidence of personal pledging at Elton, Huntingdonshire,' *J. of British Studies* 17 (1977), 1–11.
8. Gottfried, R.S., 'Population, plague and the sweating sickness: demographic movements in the late fifteenth century,' ibid. 12–37.
9. McClure, P., 'Surnames from English placenames as evidence for mobility in the Middle ages,' *Local Historian* 13 (1976), 80–6.

10. Clark, C., 'Women's names in post-conquest England: observations and speculations,' *Speculum* 53 (1978), 223–51.

11. Ditmas, E.M.R., 'Breton settlers in Cornwall after the Norman Conquest,' *T. of the Honourable Soc. of Cymmrodorion*, 1977, 11–39.

12. Miskimin, H.A., 'The legacies of London 1259–1330,' *The medieval city* (ed. H.A. Miskimin, D. Herlihy, A.J. Udovich; New Haven/London, Yale UP, 1977), 209–27.

13. Bullock-Davies, C. *Menestrollorum multitudo: minstrels at a royal feast.* Cardiff; University of Wales Press; 1978. Pp xli, 188.

14. Phythian-Adams, C., 'Urban decay in late medieval England,' *Towns in Societies: essays in economic history and historical sociology* (ed. P. Abrams, E.A. Wrigley; Cambridge UP; 1978), 159–85.

15. Palliser, D.M., 'A crisis in English towns? The case of York,' *Northern History* 14 (1978), 108–25.

16. Butcher, A.F., 'Rent, population and economic change in late-medieval Newcastle,' ibid. 67–77.

17. Fraser, C.M.; Emsley, K., 'Newcastle merchant adventurers from west Yorkshire,' *Archaeologia Aeliana* 5th ser. 6 (1978), 117–29.

18. Russell, J.C., 'The short dark folk of England,' Ea5, 21–37.

19. Russell, J.C., 'A quantitative approach to medieval population change,' Ea5, 38–61.

20. Gottfried, R.S. *Epidemic disease in fifteenth century England: the medical response and the demographic consequences.* Leicester UP; 1978. Pp xiii, 262.

21. Sherman, R.M., 'The continental origins of the Ghent family of Lincolnshire,' *Nottingham Mediaeval Studies* 22 (1978), 23–35.

22. Swanson, R., 'Saunford and Vere [Christ's College Cambridge MS 8],' *P. of the Cambridge Antiquarian Soc.* 67 (1978 for 1977), 103–9.

23. Sparks, J.A. *In the shadow of the Blackdowns: life at the Cistercian abbey of Dunkeswell and on its manors and estates, 1201–1539.* Bradford-on-Avon; Moonraker Press; 1978. Pp viii, 133.

24. Burke, J. *Life in the castle in medieval England.* London; Batsford; 1978. Pp 120.

(h) *Naval and Military*

1. Strayer, J.R., 'The costs and profits of war: the Anglo-French conflict of 1294–1303,' *The medieval city* (ed. H.A. Miskimin, D. Herlihy, A.J. Udovich; New Haven/London, Yale UP, 1977), 269–91.

2. Seymour, W., 'Simon de Montfort as a soldier,' *History Today* 28 (1978), 455–62.

3. Mann, E.L. *The battle of Lewes, 1264.* Lewes; M. Harman; 1976. Pp 32.
4. Holmer, P.J., jr., 'A sea-fight in 1480,' *Mariner's Mirror* 64 (1978), 233—4.
5. Howard, G.F., 'The date of the Hastings Manuscript ship [Pierpont Morgan MS M.775],' ibid. 313—14.
7. Saunders, A.D.; Barton, K.J.; Holden, E.W.; Sladden, S.R.; Dunning, G.C.; Barker, P.A.; Renn, D.F.; Perrin, J.R.; Holdsworth, J.; Davison, B.K.; Pirie, E.J.E.; Addyman, P.V.; Priestley, J.; Rigold, S.E.; Rackham, J., 'Five castle excavations: reports on the Institute's research project into the origins of the castle in England,' *Archaeological J.* 134 (1978 for 1977), 1—156.
8. Weir, M., 'The use of paid cavalry by Edward I,' *Studies in Medieval Culture* 6 (1977), 105—10.

(i) *Intellectual and Cultural*

1. Smallwood, T.M., 'The text of Langtoft's Chronicle,' *Medium Aevum* 46 (1977), 219—30.
2. Gransden, A., 'Silent meanings in Ranulf Higden's *Polychronicon* and in Thomas Elmham's *Liber Metricus de Henrico Quinto*,' ibid. 231—40.
3. Howlett, D.R., 'The date and authorship of the Middle English verse translation of Palladius' *De re rustica*,' ibid. 245—52.
4. Patterson, S., 'An attempt to identify Matthew Paris as a flourisher, *The Library* 5th ser. 32 (1977), 367—70.
5. Adams, M.McC., 'Ockham on identity and distinction,' *Franciscan Studies* 36 (1977 for 1976), 5—74.
6. Boler, J., 'Ockham on evident cognition,' ibid. 85—98.
7. Etzwiler, J.P., 'John Baconthorpe, "prince of the Averroists",' ibid. 148—76.
8. Gray, C.B., 'Freedom and necessity in St Anselm's *Cur deus homo*,' ibid. 177—91.
9. Walton, D., 'St Anselm and the logical syntax of agency,' ibid. 298—312.
10. Evans, G.R., 'St Anselm and St Bruno of Segni: the common ground,' *J. of Ecclesiastical History* 29 (1978), 129—44.
11. Nelson, V.C., 'Problems of transcription in the "Speculum vitae" mss.,' *Scriptorium* 31 (1977), 254—9.
12. Dumville, D.N., 'Celtic-Latin texts in northern England, c. 1150— c. 1250,' *Celtica* 12 (1977), 19—49.
13. Foster, B.; Short, I. (ed.). *The Anglo-Norman 'Alexander': Le roman de toute chevalerie.* Vol. 2: Introduction, notes and glossary. London; Anglo-Norman Text Soc.; 1977. Pp vii, 161.
14. Merrilees, S. (ed.). *La vie Set Dormanz, by Chardri.* London; Anglo-Norman Text Soc.; 1977. Pp vii, 99.

15. Benhan, H. *Latin church music in England, c. 1460–1575.* London; Barrie & Jenkins; 1977. Pp xiii, 247.

16. Evans, G.R., 'The development of some textbooks on the "useful arts" c. 1000–c. 1250,' *History of Education* 7 (1978), 85–94.

17. Edwards, A.S.G., 'Hoccleve's *Regiment of Princes*: a further manuscript,' *Edinburgh Bibliographical Soc. T.* 5/1 (1978); pp. 32.

18. Ashley, K.M., 'Divine power in Chester Cycle and late medieval thought,' *J. of the History of Ideas* 39 (1978), 387–404.

19. Jambeck, T.J., '*Everyman* and the implications of Bernardine humanism in the character "Knowledge",' *Medievalia et Humanistica* new ser. 8 (1977), 103–23.

20. Martin, J.S., 'History and paradigm in the Towneley Cycle,' ibid. 125–45.

21. Thomson, R.M., 'William of Malmesbury and the letters of Alcuin,' ibid. 147–61.

22. Olsson, K.O., 'Rhetoric, John Gower and the late medieval exemplum,' ibid. 185–200.

23. Clogan, P.M., 'The narrative style of the Man of Law's Tale,' ibid. 217–33.

24. Russell, J.C., 'The writing of history in the twelfth century,' Ea5, 1–20.

25. Russell, J.C., 'Hereford and Arabic science in England about 1175–1200,' Ea5, 142–54.

26. Russell, J.C., 'Alexander Neckam in England,' Ea5, 155–66.

27. Russell, J.C., 'The early schools of Oxford and Cambridge,' Ea5, 167–80.

28. Russell, J.C., 'The patrons of the *The Owl and the Nightingale*,' Ea5, 181–9.

29. Thomson, R.M., 'William of Malmesbury as historian and man of letters,' *J. of Ecclesiastical History* 29 (1978), 387–413.

30. Carley, J.P., 'an identification of John of Glastonbury and a new dating of his chronicle,' *Mediaeval Studies* 40 (1978), 478–83.

31. Carley, J.P. (ed.). *John of Glastonbury: Cronica sive Antiquitates Glastoniensis Ecclesie.* Oxford; British Arch. Reports, 47; 1978. Pp lii, 417.

32. Hull, P.L., 'Thomas Chiverton's book of obits, part VII,' *Devon and Cornwall Notes & Queries* 34/1 (1978), 5–11.

33. Orme, N., 'Education in the west of England 1066–1548: additions and corrections,' ibid. 22–5.

34. Aston, T.H., 'The date of John Rous's list of the colleges and academic halls of Oxford,' *Oxoniensia* 42 (1977), 226–36.

35. Garrod, H.W.; Highfield, J.R.L., 'An indenture between William Rede, bishop of Chichester, and John Bloxham and Henry Stapilton, fellows of Merton College Oxford,' *Bodleian Library Record* 10 (1978), 9–19.

36. Temple, E., 'A note on the University College life of St Cuthbert,' ibid. 320–2.

37. Lapidge, M., 'Dominic of Evesham's *Vita S. Ecgwini episcopi et confessoris*,' *Analecta Bollandiana* 96 (1978), 65–104.
38. Thomson, R. (ed.). *The Life of Gundulf bishop of Rochester.* Toronto; Pontifical Institute of Medieval Studies; 1977. Pp 88.
39. Smetana, C. (ed.). *The Life of St. Norbert by John Capgrave.* Ibid; 1977. Pp 179.
40. Parkes, M.B.; Watson, A.G. (ed.). *Medieval scribes, manuscripts and libraries: essays presented to N.R. Ker.* London; Scolar Press; 1978. Pp xv, 395.
41. Alexander, J.J.G., 'Scribes as artists: the arabesque initial in twelfth-century English manuscripts,' Ei40, 87–116.
42. Thomson, R.M., 'The "scriptorium" of William of Malmesbury,' Ei40, 117–42.
43. Pollard, G., 'The *pecia* system in the medieval universities,' Ei40, 145–61.
44. Doyle, A.I.; Parkes, M.B., 'The production of copies of the *Canterbury Tales* and the *Confessio Amantis* in the early fifteenth century,' Ei40, 163–210.
45. Piper, A.J., 'The libraries of the monks of Durham,' Ei40, 213–49.
46. Hunt, R.W., 'The library of the abbey of St Albans,' Ei40, 251–77.
47. Rigg, A.G., 'Antiquaries and authors: the supposed works of Robert Baston, O. Carm.,' Ei40, 317–31.
48. Patterson, R.B., 'Vassals and the Norman earldom of Gloucester's scriptorium,' *National Library of Wales J.* 20 (1978), 342–4.
49. McLachlan, E.P., 'The scriptorium of Bury St Edmunds in the third and fourth decades of the twelfth century: books in three related hands and their decoration,' *Mediaeval Studies* 40 (1978), 328–48.
50. Grant, J., 'A new *Passio beati Edmundi regis (et) martyris*,' ibid. 81–95.
51. Horrall, S.M., 'An Old French source for the *Genesis* section of *Cursor Mundi*,' ibid. 361–73.
52. Principe, W.H., 'Richard Fishacre's use of Averroes with respect to motion and the human soul of Christ,' ibid. 349–60.
53. Long, R.J., 'Richard Fishacre's *Quaestio* on the Ascension of Christ: an edition,' ibid. 30–55.
54. Spade, P.V., 'Robert Fland's *Insolubilis*: an edition, with comments on the dating of Fland's works,' ibid. 56–80.
55. Spade, P.V., 'Roger Swyneshed's *Obligationes*: edition and comment,' *Archives d'histoire doctrinale et littéraire du Moyen Age* 44 (1977), 243–85.
56. Braakhuis, H.A.G., 'The views of William of Sherwood on some semantical topics and their relation to those of Roger Bacon,' *Vivarium* 15 (1977), 111–42.
57. Fredborg, K.M.; Nielsen, L.; Pinborg, J., 'An unedited part of

Roger Bacon's *Opus maius: De signis*,' *Traditio* 34 (1978), 75–136.

58. Courtenay, W.J., 'The *Sentences*-commentary of Stukle: a new source for Oxford theology in the fourteenth century,' ibid. 435–8.

59. Adams, R., 'The nature of Need in *Piers Plowman* XX,' ibid. 273–301.

60. Patterson, L.W., 'The *Parson's Tale* and the quitting of the *Canterbury Tales*,' ibid. 331–80.

61. Evans, G.R., 'Unstudied arguments in the early letters of St Anselm,' *Reading Medieval Studies* 4 (1978), 19–36.

62. Thorpe, L., 'Walter Map and Gerald of Wales,' *Medium Aevum* 47 (1978), 6–21.

63. Linder, A., 'The knowledge of John of Salisbury in the late middle ages,' *Studi Medievali* 3rd ser. 18 (1977), 315–66.

64. Middleton, A., 'The idea of public poetry in the reign of Richard II,' *Speculum* 53 (1978), 94–114.

65. Peck, R.A., 'Chaucer and the Nominalist questions,' ibid. 745–60.

66. Green, R.F., 'Notes on some manuscripts of Hoccleve's *Regiment of Princes*,' *British Library J.* 4 (1978), 37–41.

67. Horner, P.J., 'The use and knowledge of spoken French in early fifteenth-century England [MS Laud. misc. 706],' *Notes & Queries* 222 (1977), 488.

68. Edwards, A.S.G., 'Notes on the *Polychronicon*,' *Notes & Queries* 223 (1978), 2–3.

69. Eldredge, L., 'Imagery of roundness in William Woodford's *De Sacramento Altaris* and its possible relevance to the Middle English *Pearl*,' ibid. 3–5.

70. Power, K.H., 'A newly identified prose version of the Trevisa version of the *Gospel of Nicodemus* [Winchester College MS 33],' ibid. 5–6.

71. Whitfield, D.W., 'A contemporary reference in a fourteenth-century carol [B.L. Add. MS 47214],' ibid. 203–4.

72. Green, R.F., 'The date of Gilbert Banester's translation of the Tale of Guiscardo and Ghismonda,' ibid. 299–300.

73. Colledge, E., 'South Netherlands books of hours made for England,' *Scriptorium* 32 (1978), 55–7.

74. De la Mare, A.C.; Hellinga, L., 'The first book printed in Oxford: the *Expositio Symboli* of Rufinus,' *T. of the Cambridge Bibliographical Soc.* 7 (1978), 184–244.

75. Bennett, J., 'The *Mary Magdalene* of Bishop's Lynn,' *Studies in Philology* 75 (1978), 1–10.

76. Parfitt, G., 'Early Robin Hood plays: two fragments and a bibliography,' *Renaissance and Modern Studies* 22 (1978), 3–12.

77. Wightman, C.L., 'The genesis and function of the English mystery plays,' *Studies in Medieval Culture* 11 (177), 133–6.

(j) *Visual Arts*

1. Hurst, J.G., 'Spanish pottery imported into medieval Britain,' *Medieval Archaeology* 21 (1977), 68—105.

2. Everson, P., 'Pottery with roller-stamped linked circle decoration from Lincolnshire,' ibid. 197—202.

3. Bismanis, M.R., 'An aisled hall at Withington, Herefordshire,' ibid. 202—3.

4. Neal, D.S., 'Excavations at the palace of Kings Langley, Hertfordshire, 1974—1976,' ibid. 124—65.

5. Moran, M., 'The medieval parts of Plowden Hall,' *T. of the Shropshire Arch. Soc.* 59 (1978 for 1973/4), 264—71.

6. Williams, E.H.D.; Gilson, R.G., 'Base crucks in Somerset, I: Glastonbury Abbey farm and the priory of St John, Wells,' *Somerset Archaeology and Natural History* 121 (1977), 55—66.

7. Hawkyard, A.D.K., 'Thornbury Castle,' *T. of the Bristol and Gloucestershire Arch. Soc.* 95 (1978 for 1977), 51—8.

8. Barker, S., 'A collection of pilgrim signs and other badges in Bristol City Museum,' ibid. 47—50.

9. Smith, T.P., 'The English medieval windmill,' *History Today* 28 (1978), 256—63.

10. Cowie, L.W., 'York Minster before the Reformation,' ibid. 331—7.

11. Harthan, J.P., 'The Salisbury book of hours,' ibid. 406—10.

12. Glasscoe, M.; Swanton, M. *Medieval woodwork in Exeter Cathedral.* Exeter Cathedral; 1978. Pp 35.

13. Eames, P. *Furniture in England, France and the Netherlands from the twelfth to the fifteenth century.* London; The Furniture History Soc.; 1977. Pp xxiv, 303.

14. Cavines, M.H. *The early stained glass of Canterbury Cathedral, circa 1175—1220.* Princeton/Guildford; Princeton UP; 1977. Pp xix, 191.

15. Adams, L. *Medieval pottery from Broadgate East, Lincoln, 1973.* London; Council for British Archaeology; 1977. Pp 54.

16. Draper, P., 'The retrochoir of Winchester Cathedral,' *Architectural History* 2 (1978), 1—17.

17. Morris, R.K., 'The developments of later Gothic mouldings in England, c. 1250—1400,' ibid. 18—57.

18. Goodall, J.A., 'Two medieval drawings,' *Antiquarian J.* 58 (1978), 159—62.

19. Rigold, A.E., 'The St Nicholas or "boy bishop" tokens,' *P. of the Suffolk Institute of Archaeology and History*, 34/2 (1978), 87—101.

20. Henig, M., 'The seal of William de Melcombe,' *P. of the Dorset Natural History and Arch. Soc.* 98 (1978 for 1977), 67—8.

21. Haslam, J. *Medieval pottery in Britain.* Aylesbury; Shire Publications; 1978. Pp 64.

22. Lowe, B.J. *Medieval floor tiles of Keynsham Abbey*. Keynsham; the author; 1978. Pp iii, 151.

23. Emden, A.B. *Medieval decorated tiles in Dorset*. Chichester; Phillimore; 1977. Pp 100.

24. Wander, S.H., 'The Westminster Abbey sanctuary pavement,' *Traditio* 34 (1978), 137—56.

25. Angus-Butterworth, L.M., 'Early Lancashire brasses,' *T. of the Ancient Monuments Soc.* new ser. 22 (1977—8), 90—103.

26. Emmerson, R., 'Monumental brasses: London design c. 1420—85,' *J. of the British Arch. Association* 131 (1978), 50—78.

27. Marks, R., 'The glazing of Fotheringhay church and college,' ibid. 79—109.

28. Cherry, B., 'Romanesque architecture in eastern England,' ibid. 1—29.

29. Leedy, W.C., jr., 'The origin of fan vaulting,' *Art B.* 60 (1978), 207—13.

30. Rigold, S.E., 'Romanesque bases, in and south-east of the limestone belt,' Bc6, 99—137.

31. Curnow, P.E.; Moorhouse, S.; Thorn, J., 'The Wakefield Tower, Tower of Lonfon,' Bc6, 155—89.

32. Gilyard, Beer, R., 'De Ireby's tower in Carlisle Castle,' Bc6, 191—210.

33. Thompson, M.W., 'Three stages in the construction of the hall at Kenilworth Castle, Warwickshire,' Bc6, 211—18.

34. Hurst, J.G., 'Langerwehe stoneware of the fourteenth and fifteenth centuries,' Bc6, 219—38.

35. Borne, P.; Dixon, P., 'Halton Castle reconsidered,' *Archaeologia Aeliana* 5th ser. 6 (1978), 131—9.

36. Beresford, G., 'Excavations of a moated house at Wintringham in Huntingdonshire,' *Archaeological J.* 134 (1978 for 1977), 194—286.

37. Bismanis, M.R., 'Bidcombe Court, Wraxall, Avon: a fifteenth-century house,' ibid. 303—6.

38. Machin, R., 'Barnston Manor, Dorset, and Aydon Castle, Northumberland: a reassessment of two late thirteenth-century houses,' ibid. 297—302.

39. Hewett, C.A., 'Scarf jointing during the later thirteenth and fourteenth centuries and a reappraisal of the origin of spurred tenons,' ibid. 287—96.

40. Gee, E.A., 'The chronology of crucks,' *T. of the Ancient Monuments Soc.* new ser. 22 (1977—8), 9—27.

41. Castle, S.A., 'A late medieval timber-framed building in Watford,' *Hertfordshire Archaeology* 5 (1977), 176—85.

42. Jones, S.R.; Penn, V.F., 'A medieval cruck-trussed house in High Street, Aldridge,' *T. of the South Staffordshire Arch. and Historical Soc.* 18 (1978 for 1976/7), 1—23.

43. Gould, J., 'Observations at Aldridge Church, Staffs.,' ibid. 47—52.

44. Williams, J.H., et al., 'Excavations at Greyfriars, Northampton, 1972,' *Northamptonshire Archaeology* 13 (1978), 96—160.
45. Hinton, D.A., 'Excavations at Beaulieu Abbey, 1977,' *P. of the Hampshire Field Club and Arch. Soc.* 34 (1978 for 1977), 49—52.
46. Tester, P.J., 'Excavations on the site of Leeds priory; part I: the church,' *Archaeologia Cantiana* 93 (1978 for 1977), 33—45.
47. Bishop, H., 'Excavations at the church of SS Peter and Paul, Healing, South Humberside,' *Lincolnshire History and Archaeology* 13 (1978), 25—32.

(k) *Topography*

1. Magilton, J.R.; Roberts, P. *The Doncaster district: an archaeological survey.* Doncaster Museums and Arts Service; 1977. Pp viii, 102.
2. Dunning, R.W., 'Croft Castle,' *Somerset Archaeology and Natural History* 121 (1977), 129—30.
3. Dent, J.S., 'Recent excavations on the site of Stockport Castle,' *T. of the Lancashire and Cheshire Antiquarian Soc.* 79 (1977), 1—13.
4. Cherry, J., 'Post-conquest [résumé of recent work] ,' *Medieval Archaeology* 21 (1977), 222—62.
5. Clarke, H.; Carter, A. *Excavations in King's Lynne, 1963—1970.* London; Soc. for Medieval Archaeology; 1977. Pp xvi, 483.
6. Harden, G. *Medieval Boston and its archaeological implications.* Sleaford; South Lincolnshire Arch. Unit; 1978. Pp 40.
7. McDonnell, K.G.T. *Medieval London suburbs.* London; Phillimore; 1978. Pp viii, 196.
8. Parkin, E.W., 'Wingham, a medieval town,' *Archaeologia Cantiana* 93 (1978 for 1977), 61—79.
9. Taylor, A.; Hall, D., ' "Roman Bank": a medieval sea-wall. I: a culvert beneath the sea-bank at Newton, near Wisbech. II: the sea-bank in Cambridgeshire,' *P. of the Cambridge Antiquarian Soc.* 67 (1977), 63—8.
10. Wilson, J.D., 'The medieval deer-parks of Dorset, XV,' *P. of the Dorset Natural History and Arch Soc.* 98 (1978 for 1976), 6—10.
11. Palliser, D.M., 'The medieval street-names of York,' *York Historian* 2 (1978), 2—16.
12. Armstrong, P. et al., 'Hull Old Town Report Series no. 1: excavations in Sewer Lane, Hull, 1974,' *East Riding Archaeologist* 3 (1977), pp. 82.
13. Harbottle, B., 'An early cemetery at Tynemouth,' *Archaeologia Aeliana* 5th ser. 6 (1978), 159.
14. Weare, T.J., 'Excavations at Wallingford, 1974,' *Oxoniensia* 42 (1977), 204—15.

15. Chambers, R.A., 'Observations at Somerton, Oxon., 1973,' ibid. 216—25.
16. Wrathmell, S. and S., 'Excavations at the Moat Site, Walsall,' *T. of the South Staffordshire Arch. and Historical Soc.* 18 (1978 for 1976—7), 29—45.
17. Hinton, D.A., 'Excavations at 58 French Street, Southampton, 1977,' *P. of the Hampshire Field Club and Arch. Soc.* 34 (1977), 43—7.
18. Leach, P.J. et al., 'Excavations at North Petherton 1975,' *Somerset Archaeology and Natural History* 121 (1977), 9—39.
19. Hanworth, R.; Tomalin, D.J. *Brooklands, Weybridge: the excavation of an iron age and medieval site, 1964—5 and 1970—71.* Guildford; Surrey Arch. Soc.; 1977. Pp 88.
20. Owen, D.M., 'Bedfordshire chapelries: an essay in rural settlement history,' Bc10, 9—20.

F. ENGLAND AND WALES 1500—1714

See also Hi5

(a) *General*

1. Usherwood, S., 'Honi soit qui mal y pense, 1585,' *History Today* 28 (1978), 53—8.
2. Miller, J. *James II: a study in kingship.* Hove; Wayland; 1978. Pp x, 281.
3. Kenyon, J.P. *Stuart England.* London; Allen Lane; 1978. Pp 384.
4. Clarke, M.L., 'The education of a prince in the sixteenth century: Edward VI and James VI and I,' *History of Education* 7 (1978), 7—19.
5. Ives, E.W.; Knecht, R.J.; Scarisbrick, J.J. (ed.). *Wealth and power in Tudor England: essays presented to S.T. Bindoff.* London; Athlone; 1978. Pp xxi, 248.
6. Virgoe, R., 'The recovery of the Howards in East Anglia,' Fa5, 1—20.
7. Ives, E.W., ' "Against the taking away of women": the inception and operation of the Abduction Act of 1487,' Fa5, 21—44.
8. Scarisbrick, J.J., 'Cardinal Wolsey and the common weal,' Fa5, 45—67.
9. Elton, G.R., 'The sessional printing of statutes, 1484—1547,' Fa5, 68—86.
10. Miller, H., 'Henry VIII's unwritten will: grants of lands and honours in 1574,' Fa5, 87—105.
11. Alexander, G., 'Victim or spendthrift? the bishop of London and his income in the sixteenth century,' Fa5, 128—45.

12. Hembry, P., 'Episcopal palaces, 1535 to 1660,' Fa5, 146—66.
13. Power, M.J., 'The east and west in early-modern London,' Fa5, 167—85.
14. Dietz, B., 'Antwerp and London: the structure and balance of trade in the 1560s,' Fa5, 186—203.
15. Goring, J.J., 'Wealden ironmasters in the age of Elizabeth,' Fa5, 204—27.
16. Land, S.K. *Kett's rebellion: the Norfolk rising of 1549.* Ipswich; Boydell Press; 1977. Pp 165.
17. Wilson, D.A. *England in the age of Thomas More.* London; Hart-Davis, Macgibbon; 1978. Pp vii, 261.
18. Forster, M., 'Walter Montague, courtier, diplomat and abbot, 1603—77; part I,' *Downside R.* 96 (1978), 85—102.
19. Wrigley, E.A., 'A simple model of London's importance in changing English society and economy 1650—1700,' *Towns in Societies: essays in economic history and historical sociology,* ed. P. Abrams, E.A. Wrigley (Cambridge UP; 1978), 215—43.
20. Ravenhill, W., 'Joel Gascoyne's Stepney: his last years in pastures old yet new,' *Guildhall Studies in London History* 2/4 (1977), 200—12.
21. Sjögren, G., 'Helena, marchioness of Northampton,' *History Today* 28 (1978), 597—604.
22. Mann, J.E. *Clay tobacco pipes from excavations in Lincoln, 1970—74.* Council for British Archaeology; 1977. Pp 60.
23. Alvey, T.C.; Laxton, R.R., 'A note on the chemical analysis of some Nottingham clay tobacco pipes,' *Archaeometry* 20 (1978), 189—96.
24. Dainton, C., 'Barts Hospital,' *History Today* 28 (1978), 810—16.
25. Johnson, R.R., 'Politics redefined: an assessment of recent writings on the late Stuart period of English history, 1660 to 1714,' *William and Mary Q.* 3rd ser. 35 (1978), 691—732.
26. Warhurst, M., 'Tudor and Stuart coins from the wreck of the Mary,' *British Numismatic J.* 47 (1978 for 1977), 144—6.
27. Lessen, M., 'The Cromwell Lord Protector medal by Simon,' ibid. 114—26.
28. Sharp, M.B., 'The Tower shillings of Charles I and their influence on the Aberystwyth issue,' ibid. 102—13.
29. Gabrieli, V., 'Thomas Cromwell (1485—1540) nella letteratura e nella storia,' *La Cultura* 16 (1978), 376—408.
30. Fosso, E.F., 'Signs and signatures: William Caxton, possessor of lead,' *B. of Research in the Humanities* 81 (1978), 139—45.
31. Tricomi, A.H., 'The provenance of John Marston's letter to Lord Kimbolton,' *Papers of the Bibliographical Soc. of America* 72 (1978), 213—19.
32. Mawson, J.W., 'Another important copy of John Denton's manuscript,' *T. of the Cumberland & Westmorland Antiquarian & Arch. Soc.* 78 (1978), 97—103.

33. Berry, G. *Taverns and tokens of Pepys' London.* London; Seaby; 1978. Pp 144.
34. Lindsay, J. *The monster city: Defoe's London, 1688–1730.* London; Hart-Davis MacGibbon; 1978. Pp viii, 220.
35. Jones, J.R. *Country and Court: England 1658–1714.* London; Arnold; 1978. Pp vi, 377.
36. Blackwood, B.G. *The Lancashire gentry and the great rebellion.* Manchester; Chetham Soc.; 1978. Pp 192.
37. Pennington, D.H.; Thomas, K.V. (ed.). *Puritans and revolutionaries: essays in seventeenth-century history presented to Christopher Hill.* Oxford; Clarendon; 1978. Pp xii, 419.
38. Styles, P. *Studies in seventeenth century West Midlands history.* Kineton; Roundwood Press; 1978. Pp xvii, 325.
39. Sawada, P.A. *Thomas More in Japan.* Tokyo; Sophia University, Renaissance Institute; 1978. Pp 127.

(b) *Politics*

1. [Anon.], 'Letter from Sir Francis Windebank to Charles I, 2 September 1640,' *Bodleian Library Record* 9 (1977–8), 370–4.
2. Davies, G.A., 'Sir Richard Fanshaw, hispanist cavalier,' *University of Leeds R.* 20 (1977), 87–119.
3. Gruenfelder, J.K., 'The electoral patronage of Sir Thomas Wentworth, earl of Strafford, 1614–1640,' *J. of Modern History* 49 (1977), 557–74.
4. Christianson, P., 'The peers, the people and parliamentary management in the first six months of Long Parliament,' ibid. 575–99.
5. Roberts, C., 'The earl of Bedford and the coming of the English Revolution,' ibid. 600–16.
6. Kishlansky, M., 'The emergence of adversary politics in the Long Parliament,' ibid. 617–40.
7. Smuts, R.M., 'The puritan followers of Henrietta Maria in the 1630s,' *English Historical R.* 93 (1978), 26–45.
8. Ashley, M. *James II.* London; Dent; 1978. Pp 328.
9. Clark, P., 'Thomas Scot and the growth of urban opposition to the early Stuart regime,' *Historical J.* 21 (1978), 1–26.
10. Balleine, G.R. *All for the king: the life story of Sir George Carteret.* St Helier: Société Jersiaise; 1976. Pp xiv, 188.
11. Grosvenor, I.D., 'Catholics and politics: the Worcestershire election of 1604,' *Recusant History* 14 (1978), 149–62.
12. Gruenfelder, J.K., 'The parliamentary election for Shrewsbury in 1604,' *T. of the Shropshire Arch. Soc.* 59 (1978 for 1973/4), 272–7.
13. Robinson, W.R.B., 'Patronage and hospitality in early Tudor Wales: the role of Henry, earl of Worcester, 1526–49,' *B. of the Institute of Historical Research* 51 (1978), 20–36.
14. Heath-Agnew, E. *Roundhead to royalist: a biography of Colonel*

John Birch, 1615–1691. Hereford; Express Logic; 1977. Pp xxiii, 246.

15. Rupp, E.G. *Thomas More; the king's good servant.* London; Collins; 1978. Pp 63.

16. Roberts, C.; Duncan, O., 'The parliamentary undertaking of 1614,' *English Historical R.* 93 (1978), 481–98.

17. Gentles, I., 'London Levellers in the English Revolution: the Chidleys and their circle,' *J. of Ecclesiastical History* 29 (1978), 281–309.

18. Miller, A.C., 'Sir William Morgan of Pencoed: "A man to be much accounted of",' *Welsh History R.* 9 (1978), 1–31.

19. Hirst, D., 'Unanimity in the Commons, aristocratic intrigues, and the origins of the English civil war,' *J. of Modern History* 50 (1978), 51–71.

20. Hexter, J.H., 'Power struggle, parliament and liberty in early Stuart England,' ibid. 1–50.

21. Gruenfelder, J.K., 'Two Midland parliamentary elections of 1604,' *Midland History* 3/4 (1976), 241–55.

22. Engstrom, H.R., 'Sir Arthur Hesilrige: the forgotten knight of the Long Parliament,' *Albion* 8 (1976), 320–32.

23. O'Malley, L.C., 'The whig prince: Prince Rupert and the court vs. country factions during the reign of Charles II,' ibid. 333–50.

24. Hill, L.M., 'Continuity and discontinuity: Professor Neale and the two worlds of Elizabethan government,' *Albion* 9 (1977), 343–58.

25. Durant, D.N. *Arabella Stuart: a rival to the queen.* London; Weidenfeld & Nicolson; 1978. Pp xiv, 242.

26. Slavin, A.J., 'Cromwell, Cranmer and Lord Lisle: a study in the politics of reform,' *Albion* 9 (1977), 316–36.

27. Seaver, P.S., 'Community control and puritan politics in Elizabethan Suffolk,' ibid. 297–315.

28. Horwitz, H., 'The East India trade: the politicians and the constitution 1689–1702,' *J. of British Studies* 17/2 (1978), 1–18.

29. Smart, I.M., 'Francis Quarles: professed royalist and "puritanical poet",' *Durham University J.* (1978), 187–92.

30. Gruenfelder, J.K., 'The Wynns of Gwydir and parliamentary elections in Wales, 1604–40,' *Welsh History R.* 9 (1978), 121–41.

31. Gruenfelder, J.K., 'Boston's early Stuart elections, 1604–40,' *Lincolnshire History and Archaeology* 13 (1978), 47–50.

32. Gruenfelder, J.K., 'Dorsetshire elections, 1604–40,' *Albion* 10/1 (1978), 1–13.

33. Munden, R.C., 'The defeat of Sir John Fortescue: court versus country at the hustings,' *English Historical R.* 93 (1978), 811–16.

34. Cotton, A.N.B., 'John Dillingham, journalist of the middle group,' ibid. 817–34.

35. Greene, D.G., 'The authenticity of the art of Anglesey's *Memoirs*,' *Bodleian Library Record* 9 (1977–8), 351–7.

36. Beckett, J.V.; Downie, J.A.,'Letters from Sir Christopher Mus-
grave to the earl of Dartmouth, 1711—15: new light on the
politics of opposition in Cumberland and Westmorland,' *T. of
the Cumberland and Westmorland Antiquarian & Arch. Soc.* 78
(1978), 121—7.

37. Hill, C., 'From Lollards to Levellers,' *Rebels and their causes:
essays in honour of A.L. Morton*, ed. M. Cornforth (London;
Lawrence & Wishart; 1978), 49—67.

38. Lutaud, O. (ed.). *Les deux révolutions d'Angleterre: documents
politiques, sociaux, religieux.* Paris; Aubier-Montaigne; 1978.
Pp 400.

39. Phillips, C.B., 'The royalist north: the Cumberland and Westmorland gentry, 1642—1660,' *Northern History* 14 (1978), 169—92.

40. Johnson, R.C. et al. (ed.). *Commons debates, 1628* (4 vols.). New
Haven/London; Yale UP; 1977 and 1978. Pp xv, 136, 584, 641.

41. Ludlow, E. (ed. B. Worden). *A Voyce from the Watch Tower,
part five: 1660—1662.* London; Royal Historical Soc. (Camden
4th Series, 21); 1978. Pp xi, 370.

42. Sharpe, K. (ed.). *Faction and parliament: essays in early Stuart
history.* Oxford; Clarendon; 1978. Pp ix, 292.

43. Sharpe, K., 'Introduction: parliamentary history 1603—1629: in
or out of perspective?,' Fb42, 1—42.

44. Munden, R.C., 'James I and the "growth of mutual distrust":
king, Commons and reform 1603—4,' Fb42, 43—72.

45. Harriss, G.L., 'Medieval doctrines in the debates on supply,
1610—1629,' Fb42, 73—104.

46. Hirst, D., 'Court, country and politics before 1629,' Fb42, 105—
38.

47. Adams, S.L., 'Foreign policy and the parliaments of 1621 and
1624,' Fb42, 139—72.

48. Ball, J.N., 'Sir John Eliot and parliament,' Fb42, 173—208.

49. Sharpe, K., 'The earl of Arundel, his circle and the opposition to
the duke of Buckingham, 1618—1628,' Fb42, 209—44.

50. Thompson, C., 'The divided leadership of the House of Commons,'
Fb42, 246—84.

51. Williams, C.M., 'The anatomy of a radical gentleman: Henry
Marten,' Fa37, 118—38.

52. Underdown, D.E., ' "Honest" radicals in the counties, 1642—
1649,' Fa37, 186—205.

53. Johnson, A.M., 'Wales during the Commonwealth and Protectorate,'
Fa37, 233—56.

54. Roots, I., 'The tactics of the Commonwealthsmen in Richard
Cromwell's parliament,' Fa37, 283—309.

55. Charlton, J., 'The Lady Anne Clifford (1590—1676),' Bc6, 303—
14.

56. Bennett, G.V., 'The seven bishops: a reconsideration,' Bc7, 267—
87.

57. Kishlansky, M., 'The creation of the New Model Army,' *Past and Present* 81 (1978), 51–74.

(c) *Constitution, administration and law*

1. Farnell, J.E., 'The social and intellectual basis of London's role in the English civil wars,' *J. of Modern History* 49 (1977), 641–60.
2. Connor, W.J. (ed.). *The Southampton mayor's book of 1606–1608.* Southampton UP; 1978. Pp ix, 127.
3. Sherwood, R.E. *The court of Oliver Cromwell.* London; Croom Helm; 1977. Pp 194.
4. Axton, M. *The queen's two bodies: drama and the Elizabethan succession.* London; Royal Historical Soc.; 1978. Pp xiv, 174.
5. Cope, E.S., 'John Rushworth and the Short Parliament of 1640,' *B. of the Institute of Historical Research* 51 (1978), 94–8.
6. Stourzh, G., 'Staatsformenlehre und Fundamentalgesetze in England und Nordamerika im 17. und 18. Jahrhundert,' *Herrschaftsverträge, Wahlkapitulationen, Fundamentalgesetze* (ed. R. Vierhaus; Göttingen; Vanderhoeck & Ruprecht; 1977), 294–328.
7. Underwood, M., 'The structure and operation of the Oxford chancellor's court, from the sixteenth to the early eighteenth century,' *J. of the Soc. of Archivists* 6 (1978), 18–27.
8. Shipley, N.R., 'The city lands committee, 1592–1642,' *Guildhall Studies in London History* 2/4 (1977), 161–78.
9. Leonard, H.H., 'Distraint of knighthood: the last phase, 1625–41,' *History* 63 (1978), 23–37.
10. Timmis, J.H., 'Evidence and 1 Eliz. I, cap. 6: the basis of the Lords' decision in the trial of Strafford,' *Historical J.* 21 (1978), 677–83 [virtually identical with next item].
11. Timmis, H.J., 'The basis of the Lords' decision in the trial of Strafford: contravention of the two-witness rule,' *Albion* 8 (1976), 311–19.
12. Steckley, G.F., 'Merchants and the Admiralty Court during the English Revolution,' *American J. of Legal History* 22 (1978), 137–75.
13. Ward, P.L. (ed.). *William Lambarde's notes on the procedures and privileges of the House of Commons* [House of Commons Library Document No. 10]. London; HMSO; 1977. Pp 96.
14. Langbein, J.H., 'The criminal trial before the lawyers,' *University of Chicago Law R.* 45 (1978), 263–316.
15. Fraser, C.M.; Emsley, K. (ed.). *The court rolls of the manor of Wakefield, from October 1639 to September 1640.* Leeds; The Wakefield Court Rolls Series no. 1; 1977. Pp xxviii, 196.
16. Zell, M.J., 'Early Tudor J.P.s at work,' *Archaeologia Cantiana* 93 (1978 for 1977), 125–43.
17. Baker, J.H. (ed.). *The reports of Sir John Spelman* (2 vols.). London; Selden Soc.; 1977/8. Pp li, 238; *396*, 239–468.

18. Stevens Cox, J. (ed.). *Ilchester borough records of the 17th century*. St Peter Port; Toucan Press; 1978. Ilchester . . . Occasional Papers 10, 160—74.

19. Haynes, A., 'Supplying the Elizabethan court,' *History Today* 28 (1978), 729—39.

20. Cust, R., 'A list of commissioners for the forced loan of 1625—7,' *B. of the Institute of Historical Research* 51 (1978), 199—206.

21. Harriss, G.L., 'Thomas Cromwell's "new principle" of taxation,' *English Historical R.* 93 (1978), 721—38.

22. Samaha, J.B., 'Hanging for felony: the rule of law in Elizabethan Colchester,' *Historical J.* 21 (1978), 763—82.

23. Warden, G.B., 'Law reform in England and New England 1620 to 1660,' *William and Mary Q.* 3rd ser. 35 (1978), 668—90.

24. Prest, W.R., 'Counsellors' fees and earnings in the age of Sir Edward Coke,' Bc5, 165—84.

25. Blatcher, M. *The court of King's Bench 1450—1550: a study in self-help*. London; Athlone Press; 1978. Pp xv, 181.

26. Foster, F.F. *The politics of stability: a portrait of the rulers of Elizabethan London*. London; Royal Historical Soc.; 1977. Pp x, 209.

27. Yale, D.E.C. (ed.). *Sir Matthew Hale's The prerogatives of the king*. London; Selden Soc.; 1976. Pp lxxxiv, 353.

28. Yale, D.E.C. *Hale as a legal historian*. London; Selden Soc.; 1976 (i.e. 1978). Pp 18.

29. Habakkuk, H.J., 'The land settlement and the restoration of Charles II,' *T. of the Royal Historical Soc.* 5th ser. 28 (1978), 201—22.

30. Prest, W.R., 'The art of law and the law of God: Sir Henry Finch,' Fa37, 94—117.

31. Pennington, D.H., 'The making of the war 1640—1642,' Fa37, 161—85.

32. Barnes, T.G., 'Star chamber litigants and their counsel, 1596—1641,' Bc5, 7—28.

33. Brooks, C.W., 'Litigants and attorneys in the King's Bench and Common Pleas, 1560—1640,' Bc5, 41—59.

34. Cockburn, J.S., 'Trial by the book? Fact and theory in the criminal process, 1558—1625,' Bc5, 60—79.

35. Billings, W.L., 'The transfer of English law to Virginia, 1606—50,' Bc14, 215—44.

(d) *External affairs*

1. Skilliter, S.A. *William Harborne and the trade with Turkey, 1578—1582: a documentary study of the first Anglo-Ottoman relations*. Oxford UP (for British Academy); 1977. Pp xxiii, 291.

2. Cassavetti, E. *The lion and the lilies: the Stuarts and France*. London; Macdonald and Janes's; 1977. Pp xiii, 332.
3. Clarke, M.L., 'British travellers to Rome in Tudor and Stuart times,' *History Today* 28 (1978), 746—52.
4. Baron, S.H., 'Ivan the Terrible, Giles Fletcher and the Muscovite merchantry: a reconsideration,' *Slavonic and East European R.* 56 (1978), 563—85.
5. Parry, J.H., 'Introduction: the English in the New World,' Bc14, 1—16.
6. Andrews, K.R., 'The English in the Caribbean, 1560—1620,' Bc14, 103—23.

(e) *Religion*

1. Gordon, W.M., 'A scholastic problem in Thomas More's controversy with John Frith,' *Harvard Theological R.* 69 (1976), 131—49.
2. Bauckham, R., 'Hooker, Travers and the Church of Rome in the 1580s,' *J. of Ecclesiastical History* 29 (1978), 37—50.
3. Lake, P., 'The dilemma of the establishment puritan: the Cambridge heads and the case of Francis Johnson and Cuthbert Bainbrigg,' ibid. 23—35.
4. Dowley, T.E., 'A London congregation during the great persecution: Petty France particular Baptist church,' *Baptist Q.* 27 (1978), 233—9.
5. Luoma, J.K., 'Who owns the Fathers? Hooker and Cartwright on the authority of the primitive Church,' *Sixteenth Century J.* 8/3 (1977), 45—59.
6. MacGregor, J.F., 'Ranterism and the development of early Quakerism,' *J. of Religious History* 9 (1977), 349—63.
7. Morey, A. *The Catholic subjects of Elizabeth I*. London; Allen & Unwin; 1978. Pp 240.
8. Green, I.M. *The re-establishment of the Church of England, 1660—1663*. Oxford UP; 1978. Pp x, 263.
9. Watts, M.R. *The dissenters; vol. 1: from the Reformation to the French Revolution*. Oxford; Clarendon; 1978. Pp xviii, 543.
10. Blethen, H.T., 'Bishop John Williams's recantation of his *Holy Table, Name and Thing*, 1638,' *J. of Theological Studies* 29 (1978), 157—60.
11. Wallis, A.E., 'Who was "Colonel Wallis"?,' *J. of the Friends' Historical Soc.* 54 (1976), 12—14.
12. Morland, S.C., 'John Whiting and Sarah Hurd,' ibid. 28—32.
13. MacGrade, A.S., 'Repentance and spiritual power: Book VI of Richard Hooker's *Of the Laws of Ecclesiastical Polity*,' *J. of Ecclesiastical History* 29 (1978), 163—76.
14. Foster, M., 'Sir Richard Forster (?1585—1661),' *Recusant History* 14 (1978), 163—74.

15. Joyce, M.B., 'The Haggerstons: the education of a Northumberland family,' ibid. 175—92.
16. Evans, S.J.A.; Eward, S., 'Dr Abraham Gregory, prebendary of Gloucester cathedral,' *T. of the Bristol and Gloucestershire Arch. Soc.* 95 (1978 for 1977), 59—67.
17. Martin, J.W., 'Elizabethan Familists and other separatists in the Guildford area,' *B. of the Institute of Historical Research* 51 (1978), 90—3.
18. Flaningham, J., 'The Occasional Conformity controversy: ideology and party politics, 1697—1711,' *J. of British Studies* 17 (1977—8), 38—62.
19. Holeczek, H. *Humanistische Bibelphilosophie als Reformproblem bei Erasmus von Rotterdam, Thomas More und William Tyndale.* Leiden; Brill; 1975. Pp viii, 414.
20. White, B.R. (ed.). *Association records of the Particular Baptists of England, Wales and Ireland to 1660.* London; Baptist Historical Soc.; 1977. 22 leaves.
21. Ball, B.W. *A great expectation: eschatological thought in English protestantism to 1660.* Leiden; Brill; 1975. Pp xiv, 282.
22. Haigh, C., 'The fall of a Church or the rise of a sect? Post-Reformation Catholicism in England,' *Historical J.* 21 (1978), 181—6.
23. Reay, B., 'The Quakers, 1659, and the restoration of the monarchy,' *History* 63 (1978), 193—213.
24. Hargrave, O.T., 'The predestinarian controversy among the Marian protestant prisoners,' *Historical Magazine of the Protestant Episcopal Church* 47 (1978), 131—51.
25. Loomie, A.J. (ed.). *Spain and the Jacobean catholics; vol. 2: 1613—1624.* London; Catholic Record Soc.; 1978. Pp xxiv, 191.
26. Clark, P., 'The prophesying movement in Kentish towns during the 1570s,' *Archaeologia Cantiana* 93 (1978 for 1977), 81—90.
27. Almasy, R., 'The purpose of Richard Hooker's polemic,' *J. of the History of Ideas* 39 (1978), 251—70.
28. Dietz Moss, J., 'Variations on a theme: the Family of Love in Renaissance England,' *Renaissance Q.* 31 (1978), 186—95.
29. McLean, A.M., ' "A noughtye and a false lyeng boke": William Barlow and the Lutheran factions,' ibid. 173—85.
30. O'Rourke Boyle, M., 'Erasmus' prescription for Henry VII; logotherapy,' ibid. 161—72.
31. Daw, C.P., 'The occasion of Swift's *Excellency of Christianity*,' *Huntingdon Library Q.* 41 (1978), 251—9.
32. Chinchen, B. (ed.). *Hampshire papist recusants, 1680.* Eastleigh, Hants.; the editor; 1977. 10 leaves.
33. Lupton, L. *A history of the Geneva bible.* Vol. 9: Love: a supplementary background volume showing the effect of biblical ideals on the life of Katherine Willoughby de Eresby, duchess of Suffolk. London; Olive Tree; 1977. Pp 192.

34. Fienberg, S.P., 'Thomas Goodwin's scriptural hermeneutics and the dissolution of puritan unity,' *J. of Religious History* 10 (1978), 32—49.

35. Wallace, D.D., 'George Gifford, puritan propaganda and popular religion in Elizabethan England,' *Sixteenth Century J.* 9 (1978), 27—50.

36. Mutter, R.A., 'Perkins' *A Golden Chaine*: predestinarian system and or schematic *ordo salutis*,' ibid. 69—81.

37. Blethen, H.T., 'Bishop Williams, the altar controversy, and the royal supremacy, 1627—41,' *Welsh History R.* 9 (1978), 142—54.

38. Briggs, E.R., 'Reflexions upon the first century of Huguenot churches in England,' *P. of the Huguenot Soc. of London* 23 (1978), 99—119.

39. Hallam, E.M., 'Henry VIII's monastic refoundations of 1536—7 and the course of the Dissolution,' *B. of the Institute of Historical Research* 51 (1978), 124—31.

40. Auksi, P., ' "So rude and simple style": William Tyndale's polemical prose,' *J. of Medieval and Renaissance Studies* 8 (1978), 235—56.

41. Hurwich, J.J., ' "A Fanatick Town": the political influence of dissenters in Coventry, 1660—1720,' *Midland History* 4 (1978), 15—47.

42. Fisher, R.M., 'Simon Fishe, Cardinal Wolsey and John Roo's play at Gray's Inn, Christmas 1526,' *Archiv für Reformationsgeschichte* 69 (1978), 293—8.

43. Wallace, D.D., 'Puritan and anglican: the interpretation of Christ's descent into hell in Elizabethan theology,' ibid. 248—87.

44. Hodge, R., 'Satan and the revolution of the saints,' *Literature and History* 7 (1978), 20—33.

45. Smith, D.M., 'The York institution act books: diocesan registration in the sixteenth century,' *Archives* 13 (1978), 171—9.

46. Anselment, R.A., ' "The Church Militant": George Herbert and the metamorphoses of Christian history,' *Huntington Library Q.* 41 (1978), 299—316.

47. Watson, R., 'Some early printed receipts for clerical taxation,' *J. of the Soc. of Archivists* 6 (1978), 96—8.

48. Elton, G.R., 'England und die oberdeutsche Reform,' *Zeitschrift für Kirchengeschichte* 89 (1978), 3—11.

49. Buckingham, C., 'The movement of clergy in the diocese of Canterbury, 1552—62,' *Recusant History* 14 (1978), 219—41.

50. Miller, J., 'The correspondence of Edward Coleman, 1674—78,' ibid. 261—75.

51. Anderson, M.W., 'Royal idolatry: Peter Martyr and the reformed tradition,' *Archiv für Reformationsgeschichte* 69 (1978), 157—201.

52. Jabex-Smith, A.R., 'A 17th-century version of Thomas Tonge's

visitation of 1530,' *T. of the Cumberland & Westmorland Antiquarian & Arch. Soc.* 78 (1978), 85—96.

53. Wilson, E.M., 'Ralph Tyrer, B.D., vicar of Kendal 1592—1627,' ibid. 71—84.

54. Leatherbarrow, J.S. *Churchwardens' presentments in the diocese of Worcester, c. 1660—1760.* Worcestershire Historical Soc.; 1977. Pp 20.

55. Christianson, P. *Reformers and Babylon: English apocalyptic visions from the Reformation to the eve of the Civil War.* Toronto/Buffalo/London; University of Toronto Press; 1978. Pp x, 285.

56. Kohler, C. *A quartet of Quakers: Isaac and Mary Penington, John Bellers, John Woolman.* London; Friends Home Service Committee; 1978. Pp 60.

57. Wright, A.D., 'Catholic history, north and south,' *Northern History* 14 (1978), 126—51.

58. Aylmer, G.E., 'Unbelief in seventeenth-century England,' Fa37, 1—21.

59. Tyacke, N.R.N., 'Science and religion at Oxford before the Civil War,' Fa37, 73—93.

60. Manning, B.S., 'Puritanism and democracy,' Fa37, 139—160.

61. Thomas, K.V., 'The puritans and adultery: the act of 1650 reconsidered,' Fa37, 257—82.

62. Haley, K.D.H., 'Sir Johannes Rothe: English knight and Dutch Fifth Monarchist,' Fa37, 310—32.

63. Sheils, W.J.; Percival, A.C. (ed.), 'A survey of the diocese of Gloucester, 1603,' Bc4, 59—102.

64. Trevor-Roper, H.R., 'The Church of England and the Greek Church in the time of Charles I,' Bc7, 213—40.

65. Patterson, W.B., 'The peregrinations of Marco Antonio de Dominis, 1616—24,' Bc7, 241—57.

66. Fletcher, A., 'The religious motivation of Cromwell's major-generals,' Bc7, 259—66.

67. Parker, J., 'Religion and the Virginia colony, 1609—10,' Bc14, 245—70.

68. Dunn, R.S., 'Experiments holy and unholy, 1630—1,' Bc14, 271—89.

(f) *Economic affairs*

1. Horsefield, J.K., 'The beginnings of paper money in England,' *J. of European Economic History* 6 (1977), 117—32.

2. Cooper, F.R., 'The silver crowns of Truro and Exeter under Charles I,' *British Numismatic J.* 46 (1976), 51—4.

3. Gaspar, P.P., 'Simon's Cromwell crown dies in the Royal Mint Museum and Blondeau's method for the production of lettered edges,' ibid. 55—63.

4. Barker, A.J. *The African link: British attitudes to the negro in the era of the Atlantic slave trade, 1550—1807.* London; Cass; 1978. Pp xi, 263.

5. Melton, F.T., 'Absentee land management in seventeenth-century England,' *Agricultural History* 52 (1978), 147—59.

6. Melton, F.T., 'Goldsmith's notes, 1654—1655,' *J. of the Soc. of Archivists* 6 (1978), 30—1.

7. Coleman, D.C., 'Texts for pre-industrial times,' *Historical J.* 21 (1978), 187—91.

8. Challis, C.E. *The Tudor coinage.* Manchester UP; 1978. Pp xii, 348.

9. Melton, F.T., 'Sir Robert Clayton's building projects in London, 1666—72,' *Guildhall Studies in London History* 3/1 (1977), 37—41.

10. Thirsk, J. *Economic policy and projects: the development of a consumer society in early modern England.* Oxford; Clarendon; 1978. Pp viii, 199.

11. McVeagh, J., 'Defoe and the romance of trade,' *Durham University J.* (1978), 141—7.

12. Leutic, J., 'English mariners and ships in seventeenth-century Dubrovnik,' *Mariner's Mirror* 64 (1978), 276—84.

13. Lamarchand, G., 'Un cas de transition du féodalisme au capitalisme: l'Angleterre,' *Revue d'histoire moderne et contemporaine* 25 (1978), 275—305.

14. Blackman, M.E. (ed.). *Ashley House (Walton-on-Thames) building accounts, 1602—1607.* Guildford; Surrey Record Soc.; 1977. Pp xxix, 84.

15. Sewell, J.R., 'A "Short View" of some Northumberland manors, 1629,' *Northern History* 14 (1978), 152—63.

16. Jones, A.C.; Harrison, C.J., 'The Cannock Chase ironworks, 1590,' *English Historical R.* 93 (1978), 795—810.

17. Rowlands, M., 'Society and industry in the West Midlands at the end of the seventeenth century,' *Midland History* 4 (1978), 48—60.

18. Davies, M.G., 'Country gentry and falling rents in the 1660s and 1670s,' ibid. 86—96.

19. Osborne, B., 'Glamorgan agriculture in the seventeenth and eighteenth centuries,' *National Library of Wales J.* 20 (1978), 387—407.

20. Appleby, J.O. *Economic thought and ideology in seventeenth-century England.* Princeton/Guildford; Princeton UP; 1978. Pp x, 287.

21. Cobb, H.S., 'Cloth exports from London and Southampton in the later fifteenth and early sixteenth centuries: a revision,' *Economic History R.* 2nd ser. 31 (1978), 601—9.

22. Ramsay, G.D., 'The recruitment and fortunes of some London freemen in the mid-sixteenth century,' ibid. 526—40.

23. [Anon.], 'Andrew Yarranton, ironmaster and pioneer economist, 1616–1684,' *Industrial Archaeology* 13 (1978), 67–80.
24. Woodward, D.M., 'Cattle droving in the seventeenth century: a Yorkshire example,' Bc2, 35–58.
25. Phillips, C.B., 'The Cumbrian iron industry in the seventeenth century,' Bc2, 1–34.
26. Bratchel, M.E., 'Italian merchant organization and business relationships in early Tudor London,' *J. of European Economic History* 7 (1978), 5–32.
27. McGrath, P., 'Bristol and America, 1480–1631,' Bc14, 81–102.
28. Lorimer, J., 'The English contraband trade from Trinidad and Guiana, 1590–1617,' Bc14, 124–50.
29. Shammas, C., 'English commercial development and American colonization, 1560–1620,' Bc14, 151–74.

(g) *Social history (general)*

1. Hollis, D.W., 'A mid-seventeenth century view of East Dereham manor,' *Norfolk Archaeology* 36 (1977), 342–54.
2. Machin, R., 'The great rebuilding: a reassessment,' *Past and Present* 77 (1977), 33–56.
3. [Debate]: Hadwin, J.F., 'Deflating philanthropy'; Coleman, D.C., 'Philanthropy deflated: a comment'; Gould, J.D., 'Bittle and Lane on charity: an uncharitable comment'; Bittle, W.G., Lane, R.T., 'A re-assessment reiterated,' *Economic History R.* 2nd ser. 31 (1978), 105–28.
4. Power, M.J., 'Shadwell: the development of a London suburban community in the seventeenth century,' *London J.* 4 (1978), 29–46.
5. Herlan, R.W., 'Poor relief in the London parish of Antholin's Budge Row, 1638–1664,' *Guildhall Studies in London History* 2/4 (1977), 179–99.
6. Herlan, R.W., 'Poor relief in the London parish of Dunstan in the West during the English Revolution,' ibid. 3/1 (1977), 13–36.
7. Dow, F.D., 'The early modern family [review article],' *History* 63 (1978), 239–45.
8. Michel, R.H., 'English attitudes towards women, 1640–1700,' *Canadian Journal of History* 13 (1978), 35–60.
9. Emmison, F.G. *Elizabethan Life.* Vol. 4: Wills of Essex gentry and merchants proved in the Prerogative Court of Canterbury. Chelmsford; Essex County Council; 1978. Pp x, 36.
10. Najzyk, H., 'Some little-known ladies of Lincolnshire 1603–1640,' *Lincolnshire History and Archaeology* 13 (1978), 39–43.
11. Beier, A.L., 'Social problems in Elizabethan London,' *J. of Interdisciplinary History* 9 (1978), 203–21.
12. McIntosh, M.K., 'The fall of a Tudor gentle family: the Cookes of

Gidea Hall, Essex, 1579–1629,' *Huntington Library Q.* 41 (1978), 279–97.

13. Morgan, P. *Warwickshire apprentices in the Stationers' Company of London, 1563–1700.* Stratford-upon-Avon; Dugdale Soc.; 1978. Pp 46.

14. Williams, G. *The general and common sort of people, 1540–1640.* University of Exeter; 1977. Pp 32.

15. Cliffe, J.T., 'The royalist composition papers and the landed income of the gentry: a rejoinder,' *Northern History* 14 (1978), 164–8.

16. Clark, P., 'The alehouse and the alternative society,' Fa37, 22–46.

17. Pearl, V., 'Puritans and poor relief: the London workhouse, 1649–1660,' Fa37, 206–32.

18. Saunders, A.D., 'The building of Upnor Castle, 1559–1601,' Bc6, 263–83.

19. Weaver, O.J., 'Heath Old Hall, Yorkshire,' Bc5, 285–301.

20. Apted, M.R., 'The seventeenth-century buildings at Tredegar House, Newport,' Bc6, 315–34.

(h) *Social structure and population*

1. Swain, S.A. (ed.). *The parish registers of St Giles, Sheldon, Warwickshire; vol. 1: 1558–1683.* Birmingham and Midland Soc. for Genealogy and Heraldry; 1977. Pp 97.

2. Burchall, M.J. (ed.). *A catalogue of Sussex quarter sessions settlement orders and cases, 1661–1700.* Brighton; Sussex Family History Group; 1977. Pp 60.

3. Finlay, R.A.P., 'The accuracy of the London parish registers, 1580–1653,' *Population Studies* 32 (1978), 95–112.

4. Wrightson, K., 'Aspects of social differentiation in rural England c. 1580–1660,' *J. of Peasant Studies* 5 (1977), 33–47.

5. Stoate, T.L. (ed.). *Dorset Tudor muster rolls, 1539, 1542, 1569.* Bristol; the author; 1978. Pp xxiv, 199.

6. *The plague reconsidered: a new look at its origins and effects in 16th and 17th century England.* Matlock; Local Population Studies; 1977. Pp 144.

7. Aylmer, G.E., 'Office-holding, wealth, and social structure in England, c. 1580–c. 1720,' *Domanda e consumi* (Istituto internazionale di storia economica; Datini; Firenze; 1978), 247–59.

8. Skipp, V.H.T. *Crisis and development: an ecological case study of the Forest of Arden, 1570–1674.* Cambridge UP; 1978. Pp xii, 132.

9. Morrow, R.B., 'Family limitation in pre-industrial England: a reappraisal,' *Economic History R.* 2nd ser. 31 (1978), 419–28. With: Wrigley, E.A., 'Marital fertility in seventeenth-century Colyton: a note,' ibid. 429–36.

10. Chinchen, B. *Southampton Protestation returns, 1641.* Eastleigh; the author; 1977. 14 leaves.
11. Dyer, A., 'Northampton in 1524,' *Northamptonshire Past and Present* 6 (1979), 73—80.
12. Appleby, A.B. *Famine in Tudor and Stuart England.* Liverpool UP; 1978. Pp 250.
13. Bromley, R. (ed.). *The register of Rufford parish church, 1632—1812.* Manchester; Lancashire Parish Register Soc.; 1976. Pp vii, 197.
14. Grassby, R., 'Social mobility and business enterprise in seventeenth century England,' Fa37, 355—81.

(i) *Naval and military*

1. Gray, R., 'Spinola's galleys in the narrow seas, 1599—1603,' *Mariner's Mirror* 64 (1978), 71—83.
2. Sewell, J.R. *The artillery ground and fields in Finsbury: two maps of 1641 and 1705, with a commentary.* London Topographical Soc.; 1977. Pp 15.
3. Earle, P. *Monmouth's rebels: the road to Sedgemoor, 1685.* London; Weidenfeld & Nicolson; 1977. Pp xi, 236.
4. Newman, P.R., 'Marston Moor, 2 July 1644: the sources and the site,' *Borthwick Papers* 53 (1978). Pp 46.
5. Usherwood, S., 'Sir Peter Carew, 1514—1575: "Valiantness in service",' *History Today* 28 (1978), 249—55.
6. Le Fevre, P., 'Arthur Herbert and his scheme for establishing convoys in the Mediterranean,' *Mariner's Mirror* 64 (1978), 134.
7. Smith, G.R.; Toynbee, M. *Leaders of the civil wars, 1642—1648.* Kineton; Roundwood Press; 1977. Pp xxiii, 222.
8. Malcolm, J.L., 'A king in search of soldiers: Charles I in 1642,' *Historical J.* 21 (1978), 251—73.
9. Ireland, J. de C. 'Ragusa and the Spanish Armada in 1588,' *Mariner's Mirror* 64 (1978), 251—62.
10. McKee, A. *The queen's corsair: Drake's journey of circumnavigation 1577—1580.* London; Souvenir Press; 1978. Pp 320.
11. Greenall, R.L., 'The demolition of Northampton's walls, July 1662,' *Northamptonshire Past and Present* 6 (1979), 83—4.
12. Gaier, C., 'L'invincibilité et le grand arc après la guerre de cent ans: un mythe tenace,' *Tijdschrift voor Geschiedenis* 91 (1978), 379—85.
13. Gooch, L., 'Catholic officers in the navy of James II,' *Recusant History* 14 (1978), 276—80.
14. Young, P.; Emberton, W. *Sieges of the great civil war.* London; Bell & Hyman; 1978. Pp xv, 159.
15. Roy, I., 'England turned Germany? The aftermath of the Civil War in its European context,' *T. of the Royal Historical Soc.* 5th ser. 28 (1978), 127—44.

(j) *Political thought and history of ideas*

1. Missner, M., 'Hobbes' method in *Leviathan*,' *J. of the History of Ideas* 38 (1977), 635—49.
2. Morrison, J.C., 'Philosophy and history in Bacon,' ibid. 585—606.
3. Danner, D.G., 'Christopher Goodman and the English Protestant tradition of civil disobedience,' *Sixteenth Century J.* 8/3 (1977), 61—73.
4. Backhouse, J., 'An Elizabethan schoolboy's exercise book,' *Bodleian Library Record* 9 (1977—8), 323—32.
5. Downie, J.A., 'Defoe and *The Advantage of Scotland by an Incorporate Union with England*: an attribution reviewed,' *Papers of the Bibliographical Society of America* 71 (1977), 489—93.
6. Franklin, J.H. *John Locke and the theory of sovereignty: mixed monarchy and the right of resistance in the political thought of the English Revolution.* Cambridge UP; 1978. Pp xi, 146.
7. Nelson, J.M., 'Unlocking Locke's legacy; a comment,' *Political Studies* 26 (1978), 101—8.
8. Anglim, J., 'On Locke's state of nature,' ibid. 78—90, 99—100.
9. Hampster-Monk, I., 'Critique of Locke's state of nature,' ibid. 78—90.
10. Carabelli, G. *Tolandiana: materiali bibliografici per lo studio dell'opera e della fortuna de John Toland (1670—1722).* Florence; La Nuova Italia Editrice; 1975. Pp xii, 407.
11. Harris, J., 'Swift's *The Publick Spirit of the Whigs*: a partly censored state of the Scottish paragraphs,' *Papers of the Bibliographical Soc. of America* 72 (1978), 92—4.
12. Pocock, J.G.A. *The Machiavellian moment: Florentine political thought and the Atlantic republican tradition.* Princeton UP; 1975.
13. Zagorin, P., 'Thomas Hobbes's departure from England in 1640: an unpublished letter,' *Historical J.* 21 (1978), 157—60.
14. Tarlton, C.D., 'A rope of sand: interpreting Locke's *First Treatise of Government*,' ibid. 43—73.
15. Sacksteder, W., 'Hobbes: teaching philosophy to speak English,' *J. of the History of Philosophy* 16 (1978), 33—45.
16. Daly, J., 'The idea of absolute monarchy in seventeenth-century England,' *Historical J.* 21 (1978), 227—50.
17. Wende, P., 'Vernunft und Tradition in der englischen Staatslehre der frühen Neuzeit,' *Historische Zeitschrift* 226 (1978), 317—48.
18. Mulligan, W.J., 'The British Constantine: an English historical myth,' *J. of Medieval and Renaissance Studies* 8 (1978), 257—79.
19. Sandler, F., 'Thomas Fuller's *Pisgah-Sight of Palestine* as a comment on the politics of its time,' *Huntington Library Q.* 41 (1978), 317—43.
20. Hopes, J., 'Politics and morality in the writings of Jeremy Collier,' *Literature and History* 8 (1978), 159—74.

21. Eccleshall, R. *Order and reason in politics: theories of absolute and limited monarchy in early modern England*. Oxford UP (for Univ. of Hull); 1978. Pp 197.

(k) *Cultural and history of science*

1. Campbell, W.A., 'The chemical library of Thomas Britton,' *Ambix* 24 (1977), 143–8.
2. Hudson, E.K., 'An identification of a controversial English publication of Castellio's *De fide*,' *Harvard Theological R.* 69 (1976), 197–206.
3. Smith, A.H.; MacCulloch, D., 'The authorship of the chorographies of Norfolk and Suffolk,' *Norfolk Archaeology* 36 (1977), 327–41.
4. Tucker, E.F.J., 'Ruggle's *Ignoramus* and humanistic criticism of the language of the common law,' *Renaissance Q.* 30 (1977), 341–50.
5. Gardiner, R.A., 'William Roy, surveyor and antiquary,' *Geographical J.* 143 (1977), 439–50.
6. Bevan, J., 'Izaak Walton and his publisher,' *The Library* 5th ser. 32 (1977), 344–58.
7. Waller, G.F., 'Sir Walter Alexander and Renaissance court culture,' *Aevum* 51 (1977), 505–15.
8. Stoker, D., 'The establishment of printing in Norwich: causes and effects 1660–1760,' *T. of the Cambridge Bibliographical Soc.* 7 (1977), 94–111.
9. Clark, S., 'Wisdom literature of the seventeenth century: a guide to the contents of the "Bacon-Tottel" commonplace books, Part II,' ibid. 46–73.
10. O'Kill, B., 'The printed works of William Patten (c. 1510–c. 1600),' ibid. 28–45.
11. Gabrieli, V. (ed.), 'Tomaso Moro: "Le Quattro Cose Ultime",' *La Cultura* 15 (1977), 447–503.
12. Jenkins, G.H. *Literature, religion and society in Wales, 1660–1730*. Cardiff; University of Wales Press; 1978. Pp 351.
13. Fisher, R.M., 'The origins of divinity lectureships at the Inns of Court, 1569–1585,' *J. of Ecclesiastical History* 29 (1978), 145–62.
14. Holman, J.R., 'Higher education in Bristol and Gloucestershire, 1650–1750,' *T. of the Bristol and Gloucestershire Arch. Soc.* 95 (1978 for 1977), 86–97.
15. Albury, W.R., 'Halley's ode on the Principia of Newton and the Epicurean revival in England,' *J. of the History of Ideas* 39 (1978), 24–43.
16. Cohen, M. *Sensible words: linguistic practice in England, 1640–1785*. Baltimore/London; Johns Hopkins UP; 1977. Pp xxvii, 188.

17. Cowling, T.G. *Isaac Newton and astrology.* Leeds UP; 1977. Pp 21.
18. Shapiro, M. *Children of the revels: the boy companies of Shakespeare's time and their plays.* New York/Guildford; Columbia UP; 1977. Pp xvii, 313.
19. Hall, A.R.; Tilling, L. (ed.). *The correspondence of Sir Isaac Newton, vol. 7: 1718–1727.* Cambridge UP; 1977. Pp xlvii, 522.
20. Vale, M. *The gentleman's recreations: accomplishments and pastimes of the English gentleman, 1580–1630.* Ipswich; Brewer; 1977. Pp ix, 182.
21. Salmon, V., 'John Brinsley and his friends [a 17th century educationalist] ,' *T. of the Leicestershire Arch. and Historical Soc.* 51 (1977 for 1975–6), 1–14.
22. Fox, A., 'Richard III's Pauline oath: Shakespeare's response to Thomas More,' *Moreana* 57 (1978), 13–23.
23. Saslow, E.L., 'Dryden as historiographer royal, and the authorship of *His Majesties Declaration Defended,*' *Modern Philology* 75 (1978), 261–72.
24. Gaunt, J.L., 'Popular fiction and the ballad market in the second half of the seventeenth century,' *Papers of the Bibliographical Soc. of America* 72 (1978), 1–13.
25. Jones, J.G., 'Sir John Wynn of Gwydir and John Speed: aspects of antiquarian activities,' *National Library of Wales J.* 20 (1978), 253–64.
26. Williams, F.B. jr., 'Lost books of Tudor England,' *The Library* 5th ser. 33 (1978), 1–14.
27. Höltgen, K.J., 'Richard Haydocke: translator, engraver, physician,' ibid. 15–32.
28. Leath Mills, J., 'Prince in *The Faerie Queene*, Book II,' *Huntington Library Q.* 41 (1978), 83–101.
29. Airs, M., 'The designing of five East Anglian country houses, 1505–1637,' *Architectural History* 21 (1978), 58–67.
30. Čapková, D., 'The educational plans of J.A. Comenius in 1646: from a diary sent to English colleagues,' *History of Education* 7 (1978), 95–103.
31. McGuire, J.E., 'Existence, actuality and necessity: Newton on space and time,' *Annals of Science* 35 (1978), 463–508.
32. Rechlin, J.G., 'John Foxe's *Comprehensive Collection of Commonplaces,*' *Sixteenth Century J.* 9/1 (1978), 83–9.
33. Hattaway, M., 'Bacon and "Knowledge Broken": limits for scientific method,' *J. of the History of Ideas* 39 (1978), 183–97.
34. Gray, R., 'Hobbes' system and his early philosophical views,' ibid. 199–215.
35. Rogers, G.A.J., 'Locke's *Essay* and Newton's *Principia,*' ibid. 217–32.
36. McKitterick, D.J. (ed.). *The library of Sir Thomas Knyvet of Ashwellthrope, c. 1539–1618.* Cambridge University Library; 1978. Pp v, 186.

37. Hahn, T., 'Indians east and west: primitivism and savagery in English discovery narratives of the sixteenth century,' *J. of Medieval and Renaissance Studies* 8 (1978), 77—114.
38. Waage, F.O., 'Touching the compass: empiricism in popular scientific writing of Bacon's time,' *Huntington Library Q.* 41 (1978), 201—16.
39. Bentley, G.E., 'The troubles of a Caroline acting troupe: Prince Charles's Company,' ibid. 217—49.
40. Sandon, N., 'The Henrician partbooks at Peterhouse, Cambridge,' *P. of the Royal Musical Association* 103 (1976—7), 106—40.
41. Shearing, D.K., 'Kettering schoolmasters in the Tudor and Stuart period,' *Northamptonshire Past and Present* 6 (1978), 81—2.
42. Gordon, W.M., 'The Platonic dramaturgy of Thomas More's *Dialogues*,' *J. of Medieval and Renaissance Studies* 8 (1978), 193—215.
43. Downie, J.A., 'Mr. Review and his scribbling friends: Defoe and the critics 1705—1706,' *Huntington Library Q.* 41 (1978), 345—65.
44. Brown, K., 'The artist of the Leviathan title-page,' *British Library J.* 4 (1978), 24—36.
45. Burdon, P., 'Marvell after Cambridge,' ibid. 42—8.
46. Fletcher, J., 'The date of the portrait of Elizabeth I in her coronation robes,' *Burlington Magazine* 120 (1978), 753.
47. Marly, D. de, 'Undress in the oeuvre of Lely,' ibid. 749—50.
48. Talley, K., 'Extracts from the executors' account book of Sir Peter Lely, 1679—1691: an account of the contents of Sir Peter's studio,' ibid. 745—9.
49. Rogers, M., 'The meaning of Van Dyck's portrait of Sir John Suckling,' ibid. 741—5.
50. Arnold, J., 'The "Coronation" portrait of Queen Elizabeth I,' ibid. 727—41.
51. Campbell, L.; Phillips, M.M.; Herbrüggen, H.S.; Trapp, J.B., 'Quentin Matsys, Desiderius Erasmus, Pieter Gillis and Thomas More,' ibid. 716—24.
52. Wilson, F.P. (ed. R.F. Hill). *Dramatic records in the Declared Accounts of the Office of Work*. London; Malone Soc.; 1977. Pp xxiv, 59.
53. De Beer, E.S. (ed.). *The correspondence of John Locke: vol. 3, Letters nos. 849—1241*. Oxford; Clarendon; 1978. Pp vii, 801.
54. Ormsby-Lennon, H., 'Radical physicians and conservative poets in Restoration England: Dryden among the doctors,' Bc8, 389—411.
55. Watson, A.G., 'Thomas Allen of Oxford and his manuscripts,' Bc11, 279—314.
56. Barton, A., 'London comedy and the ethos of the city,' *London J.* 4 (1978), 158—80.

57. Guerlac, H., 'Amicus Plato and other friends [concerning Isaac Newton] ,' *J. of the History of Ideas* 39 (1978), 627–33.
58. Hutton, S., 'Thomas Jackson, Oxford platonist, and William Twisse, aristotelian,' ibid. 635–52.
59. Pennington, L.E., 'The Amerindian in English promotional literature, 1575–1625,' Bc14, 175–94.
60. Hulton, P., 'Images of the New World: Jacques le Moyne de Morgues and John White,' Bc14, 195–214.

G. BRITAIN 1715–1814

See also Fh13, k12, 14, 16, 19, 20; Hi5

(a) *General*

1. Murphy, M., 'Blanco White: an anglicised Spaniard,' *History Today* 28 (1978), 40–6.
2. Camp, A.J. (ed.). *An index to the wills proved in the Prerogative Court of Canterbury, 1750–1800; vol. 2: Bi–Ce.* London; Society of Genealogists; 1977. Pp 428.
3. Baber, J. *Commonly called Rob Roy.* London; New Horizon; 1977. Pp 134.
4. Berry, C.L. *The Young Pretender's mistress: Clementine Walking-shaw (Comtesse d'Albestroff), 1720–1802.* Edinburgh; Skilton; 1977. Pp xvii, 228.
5. Calder-Marshall, A. *The two duchesses* [of Devonshire] . London; Hutchinson; 1978. Pp 208.
6. Gould, W. (ed.). *Lives of the Georgian age, 1714–1837.* Compiled by Laurence Urdang Associates, London; Osprey Publishing; 1978. Pp xi, 516.
7. Ribeiro, A., 'The macaronis,' *History Today* 28 (1978), 463–8.
8. Thorne, R.G., 'Herbert Lloyd of Carmarthen,' *T. of the Honourable Society of Cymmrodorion* (1977), 103–30.
9. Austin, F., 'London life in the 1790's,' *History Today* 28 (1978), 738–46.
10. Kramnick, I. *The rage of Edmund Burke: portrait of an ambivalent conservative.* New York; Basic Books; 1977. Pp xiii, 225.
11. Tolstoy, N. *The half-mad lord: Thomas Pitt, 2nd Baron Camelford (1775–1804).* London; Cape; 1978. Pp xiv, 239.
12. Thomas, P.D.G., 'The St George's Fields "massacre" of 10 May 1768: an eye witness report,' *London J.* 4 (1978), 221–4.
13. Mitchison, R., 'Patriotism and national identity in eighteenth-century Scotland,' Bc9, 73–95.

Gb1

(b) *Politics*

1. Brown, P.D. *William Pitt, earl of Chatham: the Great Commoner.* London; Allen & Unwin; 1978. Pp 448.
2. Marshall, P. *Bristol and the American War of Independence.* Bristol Branch of the Historical Association; 1977. Pp 27.
3. Probyn, C.T., 'William Preston: an eye witness of the Jacobite invasion,' *T. of the Cumberland and Westmorland Antiquarian and Arch. Soc.* 77 (1977), 145–7.
4. Lowe, B.; Marshall, P.J.; Woode, J.A. (ed.). *The Correspondence of Edmund Burke, vol. 10: Index volume.* Cambridge UP; 1978. Pp ix, 507.
5. Cannon, J. (ed.). *The letters of Junius.* Oxford; Clarendon; 1978. Pp xxxiii, 643.
6. Christie, I.R., 'British politics and the American Revolution,' *Albion* 9 (1977–8), 205–26.
7. Avery, M.E., 'Toryism in the age of American revolution: John Lind and John Shebbeare,' *Historical Studies* 18 (1978), 24–36.
8. Bonwick, C. *English radicals and the American Revolution.* Chapel Hill; University of North Carolina Press; 1977. Pp xxii, 362.
9. Christie, I.R., 'William Pitt and American taxation, 1766: a problem of parliamentary reporting,' *Studies in Burke and His Time* 17 (1976), 167–79.
10. Clark, J.C.D., 'Whig tactics and parliamentary precedent: the English management of Irish politics, 1754–1756,' *Historical J.* 21 (1978), 275–301.
11. Clark, J.C.D., 'The decline of party, 1740–1760,' *English Historical R.* 93 (1978), 499–527.
12. Emsley, C., 'The London "Insurrection" of December 1792: fact, fiction, or fantasy?,' *J. of British Studies* 17/2 (1978), 66–86.
13. Kaplanoff, M., 'England, America and the American revolution,' *Historical J.* 21 (1978), 409–27.
14. Rogers, N., 'Popular protest in early Hanoverian London,' *Past and Present* 79 (1978), 70–100.
15. Sainsbury, J., 'The pro-Americans of London, 1769 to 1782,' *William and Mary Q.* 35/3 (1978), 423–54.
16. Belchem, J.C., 'Henry Hunt and the evolution of the mass platform,' *English Historical R.* 93 (1978), 739–73.
17. Cannon, J.; Speck, W.A., 'Re-election on taking office, 1706–90,' *B. of the Institute of Historical Research* 51 (1978), 206–9.
18. Davies, K.G. (ed.). *Documents of the American Revolution, 1770–1783; Colonial Office series, vol. 18: Transcripts, 1780.* Dublin; Irish UP; 1978. Pp vi, 289. — *Vol. 19: Calendar 1781–1783, and Addenda, 1770–1780.* Dublin; Irish UP; 1978. Pp vii, 541.
19. Jones, C., 'Seating arrangements of the House of Lords in the early eighteenth century: the evidence of the manuscript

minutes,' *B. of the Institute of Historical Research* 51 (1978), 132–45.

20. Milne, M., 'The Tyne Mercury and parliamentary reform 1802–1846,' *Northern History* 14 (1978), 227–42.

21. Huch, R.K. *The radical Lord Radnor: the public life of Viscount Folkestone, third earl of Radnor (1779–1869).* Minneapolis; University of Minnesota Press; 1977. Pp xii, 204.

22. Dickinson, H.T., 'The politics of Edward Gibbon,' *Literature & History* 8 (1978), 175–96.

23. Reilly, R. *Pitt the Younger, 1759–1806.* London; Cassell; 1978. Pp ix, 390.

(c) *Constitution, Administration and Law*

1. Surry, N.W.; Thomas, J.H. (ed.). *Book of original entries, 1731–1751* [in the Portsmouth City Record Office]. Portsmouth; The City; 1976. Pp lxii, 149.

2. Torrance, J., 'Social class and bureaucratic innovation: the Commissioners for Examining the Public Accounts, 1780–1787,' *Past & Present* 78 (1978), 56–81.

3. Usherwood, S., ' "A mere lawyer? No, Sir," Lord Mansfield 1705–1793,' *History Today* 28 (1978), 390–6.

4. Gilbert, A.N., 'Military and civilian justice in eighteenth-century England: an assessment,' *J. of British Studies* 17/2 (1978), 41–65.

5. Meek, R.L.; Raphael, D.D.; Stein, P.G. (ed.). *Adam Smith: Lectures on jurisprudence.* Oxford; Clarendon; 1977. Pp viii, 610.

6. Ellis, J., 'The poisoning of William Cotesworth, 1725,' *History Today* 28 (1978), 752–7.

7. Harvey, A.D., 'Prosecutions for sodomy in England at the beginning of the nineteenth century,' *Historical J.* 21 (1978), 939–48.

8. McIntyre, S., 'The Scarborough Corporation quarrel, 1736–1760,' *Northern History* 14 (1978), 208–26.

9. Pugh, R.B., 'Newgate between two fires (part I),' *Guildhall Studies in London History* 3/3 (1978), 137–63.

10. Rudé, George. *Protest and punishment: the story of the social political protesters transported to Australia, 1788–1868.* Oxford; Clarendon; 1978. Pp xi, 270.

11. Wells, R., 'Counting riots in eighteenth century England,' *Soc. for the Study of Labour History* 37 (1978), 68–72.

(d) *External affairs*

1. Cross, A. *Anglo-Russian relations in the eighteenth century* [catalogue of an exhibition]. [Norwich; the author; 1977]. Pp 59.

2. Mahajani, U., 'Slavery, Indian labour and British colonialism: a review article,' *Pacific Affairs* 50 (1977), 263–71.
3. Woodcock, G., 'Captain Cook at Nootka: the political aftermath,' *History Today* 28 (1978), 97–104.
4. Balderston, M.; Syrett, D. (ed.). *The lost war: letters from British officers during the American Revolution.* New York: Horizon, 1975. Pp xi, 237.
5. Knight, D. *Gentlemen of fortune: the men who made their fortunes in Britain's slave colonies.* London; Muller; 1978. Pp xvi, 135.
6. Mooney, G., 'British diplomatic relations with the Holy See, 1793–1830,' *Recusant History* 14 (1978), 193–210.
7. William, G.A., 'John Evans's mission to the Madogwys,' *B. of the Board of Celtic Studies* 27 (1978), 569–601.
8. Caffrey, K. *The lion and the Union: the Anglo-American War, 1812–1815.* London; Deutsch; 1978. Pp 340.
9. Chapman, M., 'Thomas Gordon of Cairness,' *Aberdeen University R.* 159 (1978), 238–48.
10. Harvey, A.D., 'European attitudes to Britain during the French Revolutionary and Napoleonic era,' *History* 63 (1978), 356–65.
11. Middleton, C.R. *The administration of British foreign policy, 1782–1846.* Durham, N.C.; Duke UP; 1977. Pp ix, 364.

(e) *Religion*

1. Ditchfield, G.M., 'Dissent and toleration: Lord Stanhope's bill of 1789,' *J. of Ecclesiastical History* 29 (1978), 51–73.
2. Garlick, K.B. *Mr Wesley's preachers: an alphabetical arrangement of Wesleyan Methodist preachers and missionaries and the stations to which they were appointed, 1739–1818.* London; Pinhorns; 1977. Pp 54.
3. Guy, J.R., 'Bishop Richard Watson and his Lakeland friends: a study in patronage,' *T. of the Cumberland and Westmorland Antiquarian and Arch. Soc.* 77 (1977), 139–44.
4. Hayes, A.J., 'The extinct Methodist societies of south-east Scotland: 3. Musselburgh,' *P. of the Wesley Historical Soc.* 41 (1977), 77–85.
5. Hayes, A.J., 'The extinct Methodist societies of south-east Scotland: 4. Dalkeith,' ibid. 104–16.
6. Martin, R.H., 'United conversionist activities among the Jews in Great Britain 1795–1815: pan-evangelicalism and the London Society for Promoting Christianity,' *Church History* 46 (1977), 437–52.
7. Roberts, G.M., 'Y Morafiaid yn Beheudir Cymru [History of the Moravian Church in South Wales],' *National Library of Wales J.* 20 (1978), 273–99.

8. Salter, J.I., 'The books of an early eighteenth-century curate,' *The Library* 5th ser. 33 (1978), 33—46.
9. Abercrombie, N.J., 'The early life of Charles Butler (1750—83),' *Recusant History* 14 (1978), 281—92.
10. Morgan, R., 'Divine philanthropy: John Howard reconsidered,' *History* 62 (1977), 388—410.
11. Payne, E.A., 'The Venerable John Stanger of Bessels Green,' *Baptist Q.* 27 (1978), 300—20.
12. Stern, M., ' "Returning from the gates of death": revelations of a participant in four generations of anniversary death, Catherine Maria Fanshawe, 1765—1834,' *Archives of the Foundation of Thanatology* 6 (1977).
13. Foreman, H., 'Baptist provision for ministerial education in the 18th century,' *Baptist Q.* 27 (1978), 358—69.
14. Sharratt, M., 'Alban Butler, Newtonian in part,' *Downside R.* 96 (1978), 103—11.
15. Stransk, C.J., 'John Sharp at Bamborough Castle 1758—92,' *Archaeologia Aeliana* 5th ser. 6 (1978), 141—50.
16. Williams, A.H., 'John Wesley, incumbent?,' *P. of the Wesley Historical Soc.* 41 (1978), 133—8.
17. Kent, J., 'Wesleyan membership in Bristol, 1783,' Bc4, 103—32.
18. Royal, S.J., 'John Wesley on war and peace,' Bc8, 329—44.
19. Mossner, E.C., 'The religion of David Hume,' *J. of the History of Ideas* 39 (1978), 653—63.
20. Tibbutt, H.G., 'Joshua Symonds, an eighteenth-century Bedford dissenting minister,' Bc10, 59—73.
21. Duffy, E., ' "Poor protestant flies": conversions to Catholicism in early eighteenth century England,' Bc7, 289—304.

(f) Economic affairs

1. Beckett, J.V., 'Westmorland's "Book of Rates",' *T. of the Cumberland and Westmorland Antiquarian and Arch. Soc.* 77 (1977), 127—37.
2. Burt, R. *John Taylor: mining entrepreneur and engineer, 1779—1863.* Buxton; Moorland Publishing Co.; 1977. Pp 91.
3. Cope, S.E., 'The stock exchange revisited: a new look at the market in securities in London in the eighteenth century,' *Economica* 45 (1978), 1—21.
4. Davies, A.C., 'A Welsh waterway in the industrial revolution: the Aberdare canal, 1793—1900,' *J. of Transport History* new ser. 4 (1977—8), 147—69.
5. Dodgshon, R.A., 'Land improvement in Scottish farming: marl and lime in Roxburghshire and Berwickshire in the eighteenth century,' *Agricultural History R.* 26 (1978), 1—14.
6. Hausman, W.J., 'Size and profitability of English colliers in the eighteenth century,' *Business History R.* 51 (1977), 460—73.

7. Klein, H.S., 'The English slave trade to Jamaica, 1782–1808,' *Economic History R.* 2nd ser. 31 (1978), 25–45.
8. Lowe, J.B. *Welsh industrial workers' housing, 1775–1875.* Cardiff; National Museum of Wales; 1977. Pp 65.
9. Merrett, L.H., 'The Grand Western Canal — an expensive gamble,' *Transport History* 8 (1977), 99–105.
10. Mokyr, J., 'Demand *vs.* supply in the industrial revolution,' *J. of Economic History* 37 (1977), 981–1008.
11. Tylecote, R.F., 'Lead smelting and refining during the industrial revolution 1720–1850,' *Industrial Archaeology* 12 (1977), 102–10.
12. Whatley, C.A., 'The introduction of the Newcomen engine to Ayrshire,' *Industrial Archaeology R.* 2 (1977–8), 69–77.
13. Williams, D.M., 'The shipping and organization of the Atlantic slave trade: a review article,' *J. of Transport History* new ser. 4 (1977–8), 179–84.
14. Crowhurst, P. *The defence of British trade, 1689–1815.* Folkestone; Dawson; 1977. Pp 281.
15. Higgins, L.S., 'The Brogden pioneers of the early industrial development of mid-Glamorgan,' *National Library of Wales J.* 20 (1978), 240–52.
16. Hobsbawm, E.J., 'Capitalisme et agriculture: les réformateurs écossais au XVIIIe siècle,' *Annales* 33 (1978), 580–601.
17. Hunt, E.N., 'The anti-slave trade agitation in Manchester,' *T. of the Lancashire and Cheshire Antiquarian Soc.* 79 (1977), 46–72.
18. Lloyd, L. (ed.). *The 'Unity' of Barmouth.* [Caernarfon County Offices;] Gwynedd Archives Service; 1977. Pp 236.
19. Phillips, C.B., 'William Wright: Cumbrian ironmaster,' *T. of Lancashire and Cheshire Antiquarian Soc.* 79 (1977), 34–45.
20. Wells, R.A.E. *Dearth and distress in Yorkshire, 1793–1802.* York; Borthwick Institute; 1977. Pp 49.
21. Yogev, G. *Diamonds and coral; Anglo-Dutch Jews and eighteenth-century trade.* Leicester UP; 1978. Pp 360.
22. Cope, S.R., 'The stock-brokers find a home: how the Stock Exchange came to be established in Sweetings Alley in 1773,' *Guildhall Studies in London History* 2/4 (1977), 213–19.
23. Craton, M., 'Hobbesian or Panglossian? The two extremes of slave conditions in the British Caribbean, 1783 to 1834,' *William and Mary Q.* 32/2 (1978), 324–56.
24. Daunton, M.J., 'Towns and economic growth in eighteenth-century England,' *Towns in Society: essays in economic history and historical sociology* (ed. P. Abrams, E.A. Wrigley; Cambridge UP; 1978), 245–77.
25. Drescher, S. *Econocide: British slavery in the era of abolition.* Pittsburgh; University of Pittsburgh Press; 1977. Pp xiv, 279.
26. Jones, S.R.H., 'The development of needle manufacturing in the

West Midlands before 1750,' *Economic History R.* 2nd ser. 31 (1978), 354—68.

27. Lamb, D.P., 'Re-landing and trans-shipping of slaves by British vessels in the 1790s: a note,' *Business History* 20 (1978), 100—4.
28. McKichan, F., 'A burgh's response to the problems of urban growth: Stirling, 1780—1880,' *Scottish Historical R.* 57 (1978), 68—86.
29. Michie, R.C., 'The transfer of shares in Scotland 1700—1820,' *Business History* 20 (1978), 153—64.
30. Molinier, J., 'L'évolution de l'agriculture en Angleterre et en France au XVIIIe siècle et au début du XIXe siècle,' *Revue d'Economie Politique* 88 (1978), 449—54.
31. Musson, A.E. *The growth of British industry.* London; Batsford; 1978. Pp 396.
32. Owen, D. *Canals to Manchester.* Manchester UP; 1977. Pp viii, 133.
33. Pope, D.J., 'The eighteenth century Liverpool newspapers as a source for maritime history (Part I),' *Maritime History* 5 (1977), 116—34.
34. Smith, D.J., 'The Chesterfield, Brimington and High Moors Turnpike Trust,' *Transport History* 8 (1977), 195—208.
35. Chapman, S.D. (ed.). *The Devon cloth industry in the eighteenth century: Sun Fire Office inventories of merchants' and manufacturers' property, 1726—1770.* Exeter; Devon and Cornwall Record Soc.; 1978. Pp xxvi, 159.
36. Sussex, V.J.; Shelton, S.S. *Continental mail service, 1793—1815: especially by Yarmouth packet boat.* London; East Anglia Postal History Study Circle; 1978. Pp 95.
37. Tann, J., 'Marketing methods in the international steam engine market: the case of Boulton and Watt,' *J. of Economic History* 38/2 (1978), 363—91.
38. Ward, J.R., 'Speculative building at Bristol and Clifton,' *Business History* 20 (1978), 3—18.
39. West, E.G., 'Literacy and the industrial revolution,' *Economic History R.* 2nd ser. 31 (1978), 369—83.
40. Williams, D.E., 'Midland hunger riots in 1766,' *Midland History* 3 (1978 for 1976), 256—97.
41. Acaster, E.J.T., 'Benjamin Heywood, Sons & Co.: bankers in Manchester 1788—95,' *Three Banks R.* 119 (1978), 47—57.
42. Appleby, J., 'Modernization theory and the formation of modern social theories in England and America,' *Comparative Studies in Society and History* 20 (1978), 259—85.
43. Chapman, J., 'Some problems in the interpretation of enclosure awards,' *Agricultural History R.* 26 (1978), 108—14.
44. Gough, B.M., 'James Cook and the origins of the maritime fur trade,' *American Neptune* 38 (1978), 217—24.
45. Craigen, G.D., 'Forrest Alexander,' *Three Banks R.* 118 (1978), 46—64.

46. Crafts, N.F.R., 'Entrepreneurship and a probabilistic view of the British industrial revolution,' *Economic History R.* 2nd ser. 31 (1978), 613–14.

47. Cromar, P., 'The coal industry on Tyneside 1715–1750,' *Northern History* 14 (1978), 193–207.

48. Gray, M. *The fishing industries of Scotland, 1790–1914: a study in regional adaptation.* Oxford UP; 1978. Pp x, 230.

49. Griffin, C.P., 'Transport change and the development of the Leicestershire coalfield in the canal age: a re-interpretation,' *J. of Transport History* 4 (1978), 227–38.

50. Major, J.K., 'Gunton Park sawmill, Norfolk,' *Industrial Archaeology* 13 (1978), 3–8.

51. Marton, J., 'Private enterprise versus manorial rights: mineral property disputes in mid-eighteenth-century Glamorgan,' *Welsh History R.* 9 (1978), 155–75.

52. Murray, N. *The Scottish handloom weavers, 1790–1850: a social history.* Edinburgh; Donald; 1978. Pp viii, 269.

53. Rostow, W.E., 'No random walk: a comment on "why was England first?",' *Economic History R.* 2nd ser. 31 (1978), 610–12.

54. Tann, J.; Breckin, M.J., 'The international diffusion of the Watt engine, 1775–1825,' ibid. 541–64.

55. Tyson, B., 'The Cragg, Troutbeck and the Otley family: a building project and its social setting in 18th-century Westmorland,' *T. of the Cumberland & Westmorland Antiquarian and Arch. Soc.* 78 (1978), 105–20.

56. Farrant, S., 'John Ellman of Glynde in Sussex,' *Agricultural History R.* 26 (1978), 77–88.

57. Grant, R. *The great canal.* London; Gordon & Cremonesi; 1978. Pp 156.

58. Anderson, B.L., 'The Lancashire bill system and its Liverpool practitioners: the case of a slave merchant,' Bc2, 59–97.

(g) *Social structure and population*

1. Trumback, R., 'London's sodomites: homosexual behaviour and western culture in the eighteenth century,' *J. of Social History* 11 (1977–8), 1–33.

2. Itzkowitz, D.C. *Peculiar privilege: a social history of English fox-hunting 1753–1885.* Hassocks; Harvester; 1977. Pp 248.

3. Thompson, E.P., 'Eighteenth-century English society: class struggle without class?,' *Social History* 3 (1978), 133–65.

4. Wells, R.V., *The population of the British colonies in America before 1776: a survey of census data.* Princeton UP; 1975. Pp xii, 342.

5. Klein, H.S.; Engerman, S.L., 'Fertility differentials between slaves in the United States and the British West Indies: a note on lactation practices,' *William and Mary Q.* 35 (1978), 357–74.

6. Martin, J.M., 'The rich, the poor and the migrant in eighteenth century Stratford-on-Avon,' *Local Population Studies* 20 (1978), 38—48.
7. Gibson, J.S.W. (ed.). *Baptism and burial register of Banbury, Oxfordshire; part 3: 1723—1812*. Banbury Historical Soc.; 1978. Pp x, 190.
8. Trumbach, R. *The rise of the egalitarian family: aristocratic kinship and domestic relations in eighteenth-century England.* New York; Academic Press; 1978. Pp xviii, 324.
9. Wrigley, E.A., 'English mortality in the industrial revolution period,' *Human Implications of Scientific Advance* (P. of the XVth International Congress of the History of Science, ed. E.G. Forbes; Edinburgh UP; 1978), 203—13.
10. Voyce, C.; Page, A.; Haden, Mr and Mrs H.J. *The parish registers of Oldswinford, Worcestershire, vol. 3: 1719—1735*. Birmingham and Midland Soc. for Genealogy and Heraldry; [1977]. Pp 120.
11. Malmgreen, G. *Neither bread nor roses: utopian feminists and the English working class, 1800—1850*. Brighton; Noyce; 1978. Pp 41.

(h) *Naval and military*

1. Bennett, G. *The battle of Trafalgar*. London; Batsford; 1977. Pp 256.
2. Glover, M. *A very slippery fellow: The life of Sir Robert Wilson, 1777—1849*. Oxford UP; 1978. Pp xvi, 224.
3. Gradish, S.F., 'Wages and manning: the Navy Act of 1758,' *English Historical R.* 93 (1978), 46—67.
4. Lawford, J.P. *Britain's army in India, from its origins to the conquest of Bengal.* London; Allen & Unwin; 1978. Pp 342.
5. Neal, L., 'The cost of impressment during the Seven Years' War,' *Mariner's Mirror* 64 (1978), 45—56.
6. Syrett, D., 'H.M. Armed Ship *Vigilant*, 1777—1780,' ibid. 57—62.
7. Stamp, T. and C. *James Cook, maritime scientist.* Whitby; Caedmon Press; 1978. Pp xiv, 159.
8. Barnett, R.C., 'The view from below deck: the British Navy, 1777—1781,' *American Neptune* 38 (1978), 92—100.
9. Buckley, R.N., 'The destruction of the British Army in the West Indies 1793—1815: a medical history,' *J. of the Soc. for Army Medical Research* 56 (1978), 79—92.
10. Glover, M., 'The courtesies of war,' *History Today* 28 (1978), 469—75.
11. Haas, J.M., 'Methods of wage payments in the Royal Dockyards 1775—1865,' *Maritime History* 5 (1977), 99—115.
12. Hackmann, W.K., 'The British raid on Rocheford, 1757,' *Mariner's Mirror* 64 (1978), 263—75.
13. Lloyd, C., 'The defence of Acre, 1799,' *History Today* 28 (1978), 500—6.

14. Phillips, I.L., 'Lord Barham at the Admiralty,' *Mariner's Mirror* 64 (1978), 217—33.
15. Reid, A., 'Broughton's schooner,' ibid. 241—4.
16. Stuart, V.; Eggleston, G.T. *His Majesty's sloop-of-war 'Diamond Rock'*. London; Hale; 1978. Pp 206.
17. Thompson, D.; Smith, V., 'The excavation of the Gravesend blockhouse, 1975—76,' *Archaeologia Cantiana* 93 (1978 for 1977), 153—77.
18. Walder, D. *Nelson*. London; Hamilton; 1978. Pp xxii, 538.
19. Bailey, de W.; Nie, D.A. *English gunmakers: the Birmingham and provincial gun trade in the 18th and 19th century*. London; Arms and Armour Press; 1978. Pp 128.
20. Bryant, G., 'Officers of the East India Company's army in the days of Clive and Hastings,' *J. of Imperial and Commonwealth History* 6 (1978), 203—27.
21. Chandler, D., 'The battle of Corunna,' *History Today* 28 (1978), 758—60.
22. Eaton, H.B., 'Lieutenant-General Patrick Sinclair: an account of his military career,' *J. of the Soc. for Army Historical Research* 56 (1978), 128—42.
23. Hayter, T. *The army and the crown in mid-Georgian England*. London; Macmillan; 1978. Pp xi, 239.
24. Kennedy, G. *Bligh*. London; Duckworth; 1978. Pp xii, 420.
25. Kennedy, G. *The death of Captain Cook*. London; Duckworth; 1978. Pp vii, 103.
26. Emsley, C.; Hill, A.M.; Ashcroft, M.Y. (ed.). *North Riding naval recruits: the Quota Acts and the quota men, 1795—1979*. [Northallerton] ; North Yorkshire County Record Office Publications, no. 18; 1978. Pp 151.
27. Russell, P.E. *Redcoats in the wilderness: British officers and irregular warfare in Europe and America, 1740 to 1760,'* William and Mary A. 3rd ser. 35 (1978), 629—52.
28. Bradford, E. *Nelson: the essential hero*. London; Macmillan; 1978. Pp 368.

(i) *Intellectual and cultural*

1. Brownley, M.W., 'Appearance and reality in Gibbon's History,' *J. of the History of Ideas* 38 (1977), 651—66.
2. Bryant, H. *Theatre Royal Bath: a calendar of performances at the Orchard Street theatre, 1750—1805*. Bath; Kingsmead; 1977. Pp xix, 249.
3. Cowie, L.W., 'Carlton House,' *History Today* 28 (1978), 113—20.
4. Dickinson, H.T. *Liberty and property: political ideology in eighteenth-century Britain*. London; Weidenfeld & Nicolson; 1977. Pp x, 369.

5. Evans, H. *The man who drew the drunkard's daughter.* London; Muller; 1978.

6. Hunt, C.J.; Isaac, P.C.G., 'The regulation of the booktrade in Newcastle upon Tyne at the beginning of the nineteenth century,' *Archaeologia Aeliana* 5th ser. 5 (1977), 163–78.

7. Joy, E.T. *English furniture, 1800–1851.* London; Ward Lock; 1977. Pp 318.

8. Leary, D.E., 'Berkeley's social theory: context and development,' *J. of the History of Ideas* 38 (1977), 635–49.

9. Thomas, D., 'Press prosecutions of the eighteenth and nineteenth centuries,' *The Library* 5th ser. 32 (1977), 315–32.

10. Trevor-Roper, H.R., 'Another unpublished letter of Edward Gibbon,' *Bodleian Library Record* 9 (1977–8), 374–5.

11. Valenze, D.M., 'Prophecy and popular literature in eighteenth-century England,' *J. of Ecclesiastical History* 29 (1978), 75–92.

12. Morice, G.P. (ed.). *David Hume: bicentenary papers.* Edinburgh UP; 1977. Pp 232.

13. Mossner, E.C., 'Hume and the legacy of the *Dialogues,*' Gi12, 1–22.

14. Raphael, D.D., ' "The true old Humean philosophy" and its influence on Adam Smith,' Gi12, 23–48.

15. Forbes, D., 'Hume's science of politics,' Gi12, 39–50.

16. Ardal, P.S., 'Convention and value,' Gi12, 51–68.

17. Davie, D., 'Edmund Husserl and "the as yet in its most important respect, unrecognized greatness of Hume",' Gi12, 69–76.

18. Passmore, J.A., 'Hume and the ethics of belief,' Gi12, 77–92.

19. Berlin, I., 'Hume and the sources of German anti-rationalism,' Gi12, 93–116.

20. Brandt, R., 'The beginnings of Hume's philosophy,' Gi12, 117–27.

21. Gawlick, G., 'Hume and the Deists: a reconsideration,' Gi12, 128–28.

22. Demé, N., 'La méthode Newtonienne et les lois empiriques de l'anthropologie dans *Traité II,*' Gi12, 139–45.

23. Khamara, E.J.; Mcnabb, D.G.C., 'Hume and his predecessors on the causal maxim,' Gi12, 146–55.

24. Robinson, W.L., 'Hume's causal scepticism,' Gi12, 156–66.

25. Bricke, J., 'Hume on self-identity, memory and causality,' Gi12, 167–74.

26. Davis, J.W., 'Hume on qualitative content,' Gi12, 175–80.

27. Van Steenburgh, E.W., 'Durationless moments in Hume's *Treatise,*' Gi12, 181–5.

28. Connon, R.W., 'The textual and philosophical significance of Hume's MS alterations to *Treatise III,*' Gi12, 186–204.

29. Britton, K., 'Hume on some non-natural distinctions,' Gi12, 205–9.

30. Sapadin, E., 'Hume's law, *Hume*'s way,' Gi12, 210–17.

31. Sutherland, S.R., 'Hume and the concert of pleasure,' Gi12, 218–24.

32. Bloom, E.A.; Bloom, L.D.; Klingel, J.E., 'Portrait of a Georgian lady: the letters of Hester Lynch (Thrale) Piozzi, 1784–1821,' *B. of the John Rylands University of Manchester Library* 60 (1978), 303–8.

33. Downie, J.A., 'An unknown Defoe broadsheet on the regulation of the press?,' *The Library* 5th ser. 33 (1978), 51–8.

34. Horne, T.A. *The social thought of Bernard Mandeville: virtue and commerce in early eighteenth-century England.* London; Macmillan; 1978. Pp xii, 123.

35. Kerkham, C.R., 'Richard Vaughan Yates, 1785–1856, traveller in Wales,' *National Library of Wales J.* 20 (1978), 265–72.

36. Lang, M., 'Maria Edgeworth's *The Parent's Assistant* (1796): a document of social education,' *History of Education* 7 (1978), 21–33.

37. Mougel, F.-C., 'Une société de culture en Grande-Bretagne au XVIIIe siècle: la Société des Dilettanti,' *Revue historique* 259 (1978), 389–414.

38. Kerslake, J. *Early Georgian portraits* [in the National Portrait Gallery]. London; HMSO; 1977. Pp xvii, 391.

39. Price, G., 'Gaelic in Scotland at the end of the eighteenth century,' *B. of the Board of Celtic Studies* 27 (1978), 561–8.

40. Stewart, J.D., 'New light on Michael Rysbrack: Augustan England's "classical baroque" sculptor,' *Burlington Magazine* 120 (1978), 215–22.

41. Woodforde, J. *Georgian houses for all.* London; Routledge; 1978. Pp xiv, 177.

42. Andrews, S., 'Boswell, Rousseau and Voltaire,' *History Today* 28 (1978), 507–15.

43. Ardall, P.S., 'Another look at Hume's account of moral evaluation,' *J. of the History of Philosophy* 15 (1977), 405–21.

44. *Sir Joseph Banks at the Dale.* Cambridge University Library; 1977. Pp 8.

45. Beard, G. *The work of Robert Adam.* Edinburgh; J. Bartholomew; 1978. Pp xi, 244.

46. Reed, J.W.; Pottle, F.A. (ed.). *Boswell, laird of Auchinleck, 1778–1782.* New York/London; McGraw Hill; 1977. Pp xxxvi, 570.

47. Botwinick, A., 'A case for Hume's nonutilitarianism,' *J. of the History of Philosophy* 15 (1977), 423–35.

48. Brown, I.G., ' "The resemblance of a great genius": commemorative portraits of Robert Adam,' *Burlington Magazine* 120 (1978), 444–51.

49. Cornforth, J. *English interiors, 1790–1848: the quest for comfort.* London; Barrie & Jenkins; 1978. Pp 144.

50. Cowie, L.W., 'The Prince Regent's cook,' *History Today* 28 (1978), 522–9.

51. Doig, A., 'James Adam, James Essex and an altar-piece for King's College Chapel, Cambridge,' *Architectural History* 2 (1978), 79–82.

52. Ferber, M., 'Blake's idea of brotherhood,' *P. of the Modern Languages Association* 93 (1978), 438–47.

53. Gandy, C.I., 'A bibliographical survey of writings on Edmund Burke, 1945–1975,' *British Studies Monitor* 8/1 (1978), 3–21.

54. Goldsmith, M.M., 'Mandeville and the spirit of capitalism,' *J. of British Studies* 17/1 (1977), 63–81.

55. Höpfl, H.M., 'From savage to Scotsman: conjectural history in the Scottish enlightenment,' ibid. 17/2 (1978), 19–40.

56. Howells, E.G., 'Hume, Shaftesbury and the Peirce-James controversy,' *J. of the History of Philosophy* 15 (1977), 449–62.

57. Hyde, M. *The Thrales of Streatham Park*. Cambridge, Mass./ London; Harvard UP; 1977. Pp xvii, 373.

58. Leob, L.E., 'Hume's moral sentiments and the structure of the treatise,' *J. of the History of Philosophy* 15 (1977), 395–403.

59. MacDonagh, O., 'Highbury and Chawton: social convergence in *Emma*,' *Historical Studies* 18 (1978), 37–51.

60. Mijuskovic, B., 'Hume on space (and time),' *J. of the History of Philosophy* 15 (1977), 387–94.

61. Pittion, J.P., 'Hume's reading of Bayle: an inquiry into the source and role of the Memoranda,' ibid. 373–86.

62. Popkin, R.H., 'Joseph Priestley's criticism of David Hume's philosophy,' ibid. 437–47.

63. Selleck, A.D. *Cookworthy 1705–80, and his circle*. Plymouth; Baron Jay Ltd; 1978. Pp 279.

64. Summerson, J. *Georgian London* (revd ed.). Harmondsworth; Penguin; 1978. Pp 349.

65. Tait, A.A., 'The sale of Robert Adam's drawings,' *Burlington Magazine* 120 (1978), 451–5.

66. Whiter, L. *Spode: a history of the family, factory and wares from 1733 to 1833*. London; Barrie & Jenkins; 1978. Pp xiii, 246.

67. Humphreys, R.A. *Robert Southey and his 'History of Brazil'*. London; Grant & Cutler; 1978. Pp 24.

68. Winch, D. *Adam Smith's politics: an essay in historiographic revision*. Cambridge UP; 1978. Pp xi, 204.

69. Tilney, C., ' "A compleat trial of principle": Southey, Wellington, and *The Quarterly Review*,' *National Library of Wales J.* 20 (1978), 377–86.

70. Dreyer, F.A., 'The genesis of Burke's *Reflections*,' *J. of Modern History* 50 (1978), 462–79.

71. Fowler, J.; Cornforth, J. *English decoration in the 18th century* (2nd ed.). London; Barrie & Jenkins; 1978. Pp 288.

72. Gaunt, W. *The world of William Hogarth*. London; Cape; 1978. Pp ix, 134.
73. Goldberg, N.L. *John Crome the elder*. Oxford; Phaidon; 1978. 2 vols. Pp xxv, 321; xvi, 166.
74. Ladd, F.J. *Architects at Corsham Court: a study in Revival style architecture and landscaping, 1749–1849*. Bradford-on-Avon; Moonraker Press; 1978. Pp xv, 184.
75. Lane, C. *Sporting aquatints and their engravers, vol. 1: 1775–1820*. Leigh-on-Sea; F. Lewis; 1978. Pp 118.
76. Lawes, J., 'Voluntary schools and basic education in Northampton 1800–1871,' *Northamptonshire Past and Present* 6 (1979), 85–91.
77. Loades, A., 'Coleridge as theologian: some comments on his reading of Kant,' *J. of Theological Studies* new ser. 29 (1978), 410–26.
78. Macdonald, W.R., 'Aberdeen periodical publishing 1786–91,' *The Bibliotheck* 9 (1978), 1–12.
79. Marcuse, M.J., 'The *Gentlemen's Magazine* and the Lauder/Milton controversy,' *B. of Research in the Humanities* 81 (1978), 179–209.
80. Bendall, J. *The origins of the Scottish enlightenment*. London; Macmillan; 1978. Pp vii, 257.
81. Joppien, R., 'John Webber's South Sea drawings for the Admiralty: a newly discovered catalogue among the papers of Sir Joseph Banks,' *British Library J*. 4 (1978), 49–77.
82. Stevenson, S.; Bennett, H. *Van Dyck in check trousers: fancy dress in art and life, 1700–1900*. Edinburgh; Scottish National Portrait Gallery; 1978. Pp 117.
83. Willis, P. *Charles Bridgeman and the English landscape garden*. London; Zwemmer; 1977. Pp xxi, 233.
84. Burton, A. and P. *The green bag travellers: Britain's first tourists*. London; André Deutsch; 1978. Pp 152.
85. Scrivener, M.H., 'Godwin's philosophy: a revaluation,' *J. of the History of Ideas* 39 (1978), 615–26.
86. Levy, D., 'Adam Smith's "natural law" and contractual society,' ibid. 665–74.
87. Farr, J., 'Hume, hermeneutics, and history: a "sympathetic" account,' *History and Theory* 17 (1978), 285–310.
88. Gilley, S., 'English attitudes to the Irish in England, 1780–1900,' Bc1, 81–110.
89. Livingston, D.W., 'Hume's conservatism,' Bc8, 213–33.
90. Burke, J.J., 'Hume's *History of England*: waking the English from a dogmatic slumber,' Bc8, 235–50.

(j) *Science*

1. Berman, M. *Social change and scientific organization: the Royal*

Institution, 1799–1844. London; Heinemann Educational; 1978. Pp xxv, 224.

2. Razzell, P.E. *The conquest of smallpox: the impact of inoculation on smallpox mortality in eighteenth century Britain.* Firle; Caliban Books; 1977. Pp x, 190.

3. Razzell, P.E. *Edward Jenner's cowpox vaccine: the history of a medical myth.* Firle; Caliban Books; 1977. Pp 130.

4. Rolt, L.T.C.; Allen, J.S. *The steam engine of Thomas Newcomen* (revd. ed.). Hartington; Moorland Publishing Co.; 1977. Pp 160.

5. Steffens, H.J. *The development of Newtonian optics in England.* New York; Science History Publications; 1977. Pp viii, 190.

6. West, J.L. *The Taylors of Lancashire: bonesetters and doctors, 1750–1890.* Manchester; the author; 1977. Pp 134.

7. King-Hele, D. *Doctor of revolution: the life and genius of Erasmus Darwin.* London; Faber; 1977. Pp 361.

8. Baugh, D.A., 'The sea-trial of John Harrison's chronometer,' *Mariner's Mirror* 64 (1978), 235–40.

9. Davies, A.C., 'The life and death of a scientific instrument: the marine chronometer 1770–1920,' *Annals of Science* 35 (1978), 509–25.

10. Porter, R., 'George Hoggart Toulmin's theory of man and the earth in the light of the development of British geology,' ibid. 339–52.

11. Anderson, R.G.W.; Simpson, A.D.C. (ed.). *The early years of the Edinburgh Medical School: a symposium.* Edinburgh; Royal Scottish Museum; 1976. Pp viii, 124.

12. Cowan, Z., 'John Lethbridge, diver,' *History Today* 28 (1978), 825–9.

13. McLoughlin, G. *A short history of the first Liverpool infirmary, 1749–1824.* London; Phillimore; 1978. Pp ix, 116.

14. Webster, C., 'The crisis of the hospitals during the industrial revolution,' *Human Implications of Scientific Advance* (P. of the XVth International Congress of the History of Science, ed. E.G. Forbes; Edinburgh UP; 1978), 214–23.

H. GREAT BRITAIN 1815–1914

See also Gb21, c10, d11, f2, 4, 8, 11, 28, 29, 42, 48, 51, i5, 7, 9, 76, j1, 6, 9; If30, 31, 33, 37

(a) *General*

1. Richardson, J., 'Queen Adelaide: a portrait,' *History Today* 28 (1978), 188–93.

2. Parssinen, T.M., 'Mesmeric performers,' *Victorian Studies* 21 (1977), 87–104.
3. Handcock, W.D. (ed.). *English Historical Documents, vol. 12: 1874–1914.* London; Eyre & Spottiswode; 1977. Pp xxiii, 725.
4. Young, G.M. *Portrait of an age: Victorian England*; annotated by G. Kitson Clark. London; Oxford UP; 1977. Pp 423.
5. Hooper, P. *William Whiting (1825–1878): master of Winchester College Quiristers and author of the hymn 'For those in peril on the sea'.* Southampton; Paul Cave Publications; 1978. Pp 176.
6. Henstock, A. (ed.). *Early Victorian country town: a portrait of Ashbourne in the mid 19th century.* Ashbourne Local History Group; 1978. Pp 76.
7. Morgan, G., 'John Cam Hobhouse,' *History Today* 28 (1978), 650–8.
8. Berridge, V., 'Victorian opium eating: responses to opiate use in nineteenth-century England,' *Victorian Studies* 21 (1978), 437–61.
9. Schedvin, M.B. & C.B., 'The nomadic tribes of urban Britain: a prelude to Botany Bay,' *Historical Studies* 18 (1978), 254–76.
10. Palgrave-Moore, P. *The mayors and lord mayors of Norwich, 1836–1974.* Norwich; Elvery Dowers Publications; 1978. Pp x, 98.
11. Smiley, L. *Life at Castle Fraser 150 years ago.* Edinburgh; National Trust for Scotland; 1978. Pp 38.
12. *Barton on Humber in the 1850's, part 1: leisure and pleasure.* Barton Branch of the WEA; 1977. Pp 56.
13. Powell, V. *Margaret, countess of Jersey: a biography.* London; Heinemann; 1978. Pp xii, 196.

(b) *Politics*

1. Ochojna, A.D., 'The influence of local and national politics on the development of urban passenger transport in Britain 1850–1900,' *J. of Transport History* new ser. 4 (1978), 125–46.
2. Moore, R. *The emergence of the Labour Party, 1880–1924.* London; Hodder & Stoughton; 1978. Pp viii, 216.
3. Hamer, D.A. *The politics of electoral pressure: a study in the history of Victorian reform agitation.* Hassocks; Harvester Press; 1977. Pp 386.
4. Gatrell, V.A.C., 'A Manchester parable,' *Studies in Local History*, ed. J.A. Benyon et al. (Cape Town; Oxford UP; 1976), 28–36.
5. Meier, P. *William Morris: the Marxist dreamer* (translated by F. Gubb). Hassocks; Harvester Press; 1978. 2 vols. Pp xiv, 597; lx, lxx.
6. Marshall, J.D.; McClintock, M.E. (ed.). *The history of the Lancashire County Council, 1889 to 1974.* London; Martin Robertson; 1977. Pp xiv, 456.

7. Morris, A.J.A. *C.P. Trevelyan, 1870–1958: portrait of a radical.* Belfast; Blackstaff Press; 1977. Pp viii, 211.

8. Stevens, J. *England's last revolution: Pentrich 1817.* Buxton; Moorland Publishing Company; 1977. Pp 167.

9. Prest, J. *Politics in the age of Cobden.* London; Macmillan; 1977. Pp viii, 165.

10. Wiltshire, D. *The social and political thought of Herbert Spencer.* Oxford UP; 1978. Pp xi, 269.

11. Mitchell, J.C.; Cornford, J., 'The political demography of Cambridge, 1832–1868,' *Albion* 9 (1977/8), 242–72.

12. Hughes, J.V. *The wealthiest commoner: C.R.M. Talbot (1803–1890).* [Aberavon; the author; 1977]. Pp 36.

13. Moylan, P.A. *The form and reform of county government.* Leicester UP; 1978. Pp 96.

14. Reid, F. *Keir Hardie: the making of a socialist.* London; Croom Helm; 1978. Pp 211.

15. Williams, G.A. *The Merthyr rising.* London; Croom Helm; 1978. Pp 237.

16. Pugh, M., 'New light on Edwardian voters: the model elections of 1906–12,' *B. of the Institute of Historical Research* 51 (1978), 103–7.

17. Hopkinson, D., 'Vintage Liberals,' *History Today* 28 (1978), 364–71.

18. Mason, J.W., 'The duke of Argyll and the land question in late nineteenth-century Britain,' *Victorian Studies* 21 (1978), 149–70.

19. Prothero, I., 'London trade unionism in the 1830s and 1840s,' *Soc. for the Study of Labour History B.* 36 (1978), 10–13.

20. Samuel, R., 'The London labour movement,' ibid. 13–15.

21. Lovell, J., 'The new unions,' ibid. 15–17.

22. Druker, J., 'Women's history and trade union records,' ibid. 28–35.

23. Gilbert, B.B., 'David Lloyd George: the reform of British landholding and the budget of 1914,' *Historical J.* 21 (1978), 117–41.

24. Moore, D.C., 'Some thoughts on thoroughness and carefulness suggested by comparing the reports of the Aylesbury meeting of 24 February 1830 in *The Times* and the *Bucks Gazette*,' *J. of British Studies* 17 (1977/8), 141–2. With: Davis, R.W., 'Rebuttal,' ibid. 143–4.

25. Lloyd, T., 'The politics of William Morris's *News from Nowhere*,' *Albion* 9 (1977/8), 273–87.

26. Baer, M.B., 'Social structure, voting behaviour, and political change in Victorian London,' ibid. 227–41.

27. Heesom, A.J., 'Problems of patronage: Lord Londonderry's appointment as lord lieutenant of County Durham,' *Durham University J.* (1978), 169–77.

28. Westergard-Thorpe, W., 'Towards a syndicalist International: the 1913 London Congress,' *International R. of Social History* 23 (1978), 33—78.

29. Rubinstein, D., 'The Independent Labour Party and the Yorkshire miners: the Barnsley by-election of 1897,' ibid. 102—34.

30. Davison, G., 'Explanation of urban radicalism: old theories and new histories,' *Historical Studies* 18 (1978), 68—87.

31. Caine, B., 'John Stuart Mill and the English women's movement,' ibid. 52—67.

32. Beales, D., 'Victorian politics observed [review article],' *Historical J.* 21 (1978), 697—707.

33. Moss, D.J., 'A study in failure: Thomas Attwood, M.P. for Birmingham, 1832—1839,' ibid. 545—70.

34. Harvey, A.D. *Britain in the early nineteenth century*. London; Batsford; 1978. Pp vii, 395.

35. Jenkins, R. *Asquith* (revd. ed.). London; Collins; 1978. Pp 572.

36. Malament, B.C., 'W.E. Gladstone: an other Victorian?,' *British Studies Monitor* 8/1 (1978), 22—38.

37. Barnes, J.C.F., 'The trade union and radical activities of the Carlisle handloom weavers,' *T. of the Cumberland & Westmorland Antiquarian & Arch. Soc.* 78 (1978), 149—61.

38. Murphy, P.J., 'The origins of the 1852 lock-out in the British engineering industry reconsidered,' *International R. of Social History* 23 (1978), 242—66.

39. Kesner, R.M., 'The Transvaal, the Orange River colony, and the South African Loan and War Contribution Act of 1903,' *Albion* 10/1 (1978), 28—53.

40. Harvey, A.D., 'The third party in British politics, 1818—21,' *B. of the Institute of Historical Research* 51 (1978), 146—59.

41. Pugh, M. *Electoral reform in war and peace, 1906—18*. London; Routledge; 1978. Pp xi, 228.

42. Hibbert, C. *Disraeli and his world*. London; Thames & Hudson; 1978. Pp 128.

43. Grigg, J. *Lloyd George: the people's champion 1902—1911*. London; Eyre Methuen; 1978. Pp 391.

44. Vincent, J. *Disraeli, Derby and the Conservative Party: journals and memoirs of Edward Henry, Lord Stanley, 1849—69*. Hassocks; Harvester Press; 1978. Pp xviii, 404.

45. Matthew, H.C.G. (ed.). *The Gladstone diaries, vol. 5: 1855—1860; vol. 6: 1861—1868*. Oxford; Clarendon; 1978. Pp lxxii, 545; vii, 706.

46. Reid, A., 'Politics and economics in the formation of the British working class: a response to H.F. Moorhouse,' *Social History* 3 (1978), 347—61.

47. Layton-Henry, Z., 'Democracy and reform in the Conservative Party,' *J. of Contemporary History* 13 (1978), 653—70.

48. Hanham, H.J. *Elections and party management: politics in the*

time of Disraeli and Gladstone (2nd ed. with new introduction). Hassocks; Harvester Press; 1978. Pp xxi, 468.

49. Marsh, P. *The discipline of popular government: Lord Salisbury's domestic statecraft 1881–1902.* Hassocks; Harvester Press; 1978. Pp viii, 373.

50. Vincent, J., 'Gladstone and Ireland,' *P. of the British Academy* 63 (1978 for 1977), 193–238.

51. Jones, A.; Bentley, M., 'Salisbury and Baldwin,' Bc13, 25–40.

52. Burton, M. *100 years of Liberalism: general elections in mid and north Oxfordshire.* Oxford; Mid-Oxon Liberal Association; 1977. Pp 19.

53. Cirket, A.F., 'The 1830 riots in Bedfordshire — background and events,' Bc10, 75–112.

(c) *Constitution, administration and law*

1. Stanley, C.R., 'A centenary tribute to Frederick Goodyer, 1836–1876,' *T. of the Leicestershire Arch. and Historical Soc.* 51 (1977 for 1975–6), 15–28.

2. Schreuder, D., 'Locality and metropolis in the British Empire: a note on some connections between the British North America Act (1887) and Gladstone's first Irish Home Rule Bill (1886),' *Studies in Local History*, ed. J.A. Benyon et al. (Cape Town; Oxford UP; 1976), 48–58.

3. Bellairs, C.E. *Conservative social and industrial reform: a record of conservative legislation between 1800 and 1974* (revd. ed.). London; Conservative Political Centre; 1977. Pp 128.

4. Murray, B.K., 'Lloyd George and the land: the issue of site value rating,' *Studies in Local History*, ed. J.A. Benyon et al. (Cape Town; Oxford UP; 1976), 37–47.

5. Collins, B.; Anderson, M., 'The administration of the 1851 census in the county of East Lothian,' *Local Population Studies* 20 (1978), 32–7.

6. Bush, G. *Bristol and its municipal government, 1820–1851.* Bristol Record Society, 1976. Pp viii, 254.

7. Thomas, R.M. *The British philosophy of administration: a comparison of British and American ideas 1900–1939.* London; Longman; 1978. Pp xix, 280.

8. Stead, P.J. (ed.). *Pioneers in policing.* Maidenhead, McGraw-Hill; 1977. Pp 307.

9. Porter, J.H., 'Northampton Boot and Shoe Arbitration Board before 1914,' *Northamptonshire Past and Present* 6 (1979), 93–9.

10. Smith, M.E. (ed.). *The parish registers of St Martin, Coney Street, York, 1813–1837.* York Family History Soc.; 1978. Pp ii, 40.

11. Ratcliffe, B.M., 'Great Britain and tariff reform in France,' Bc2, 98–135.

12. Marrison, A.J., 'The development of tariff reform policy during Joseph Chamberlain's first campaign, May 1903 — February 1904,' Bc2, 214—41.

(d) *External affairs*

1. Trainor, L., 'Policy-making and the Colonial Office: Robert Meade, the Berlin Conference, and New Guinea, 1884—5,' *J. of Imperial and Commonwealth History* 6 (1978), 119—43.
2. Nanda, B.R. *Gokhale: the Indian moderates and the British raj.* Delhi/London; Oxford UP; 1977. Pp xii, 520.
3. Fry, M.G. *Lloyd George and foreign policy; vol. 1: the education of a statesman, 1890—1916.* Montreal/London; McGill-Queen's UP; 1977. Pp xv, 314.
4. Steiner, Z.S. *Britain and the origins of the first World War.* London; Macmillan; 1977. Pp vi, 305.
5. Tyrrell, A., 'Making the millenium: the mid-nineteenth century peace movement,' *Historical J.* 21 (1978), 75—95.
6. McLean, D., 'English radicals, Russia and the fate of Persia, 1907—1913,' *English Historical R.* 93 (1978), 338—52.
7. Bullen, R., 'Party politics and foreign policy: whigs, tories and Iberian affairs, 1830—6,' *B. of the Institute of Historical Research* 51 (1978), 37—59.
8. Lester, R.I. *Confederate finance and purchasing in Great Britain.* Charlottesville; University of Virginia Press; 1975. Pp xii, 267.
9. Bley, H. *Bebel und die Strategie der Kriegsverhütung 1904—1913: eine Studie über Bebels Geheimkontakte mit der britischen Regierung und Edition der Dokumente.* Göttingen; Vandenhoek & Ruprecht; 1975. Pp 254.
10. Hayes, P.M. *The twentieth century, 1880—1939.* London; A. & C. Black; 1978. Pp viii, 343.
11. Eldridge, C.C. *Victorian imperialism.* London; Hodder & Stoughton; 1978. Pp viii, 248.
12. Fairbank, J.K.; Bruner, K.F.; Matheson, E.M. (ed.). *The IG in Peking: letters of Robert Hart, Chinese Maritime Customs. 1868—1907.* 2 vols. Cambridge, Mass.; Belknap Press; 1975. Pp xxix, 1625.
13. Sandford, K.A.P. *Great Britain and the Schleswig-Holstein question, 1848—64: a study in diplomacy, politics and public opinion.* Buffalo; University of Toronto Press; 1975. Pp x, 204.
14. Trinder, B., 'The distant scene: Banbury and the United States in the mid-nineteenth century,' *Cake & Cockhorse* 7 (1978), 163—74.
15. Bumsted, J.M., 'Settlement by chance: Lord Selkirk and Prince Edward Island,' *Canadian History R.* 59/2 (1978), 170—88.
16. Jenkins, B., 'William Gregory, champion of the Confederacy,' *History Today* 28 (1978), 322—30.

17. McNab, D., 'Herman Merivale and the native question, 1837—1861,' *Albion* 9 (1978), 359—84.
18. Schreuder, D., 'Gladstone as "troublemaker": Liberal foreign policy and the German annexation of Alsace-Lorraine, 1870—1871,' *J. of British Studies* 17/2 (1978), 106—35.
19. Connolly, C.N., 'Manufacturing "spontaneity": the Australian offers of troops for the Boer War,' *Historical Studies* 18 (1978), 106—17.
20. McLean, D., 'A professor extraordinary: E.G. Browne and his Persian campaign, 1908—1913,' *Historical J.* 21 (1978), 399—408.
21. Hibbert, C. *The great mutiny, India 1857.* London; Allen Lane; 1978. Pp 472.
22. Stiffoni, G., 'L'emigrazione liberale spagnola in Inghilterra e in Francia (1832—1834): un problema storiografico aperto,' *Nuova Rivista Storica* 62 (1978), 133—52.
23. Newbould, I.D.C., 'Lord Durham, the Whigs and Canada, 1838: the background to Durham's return,' *Albion* 8 (1976), 351—74.
24. Bradshaw, D.F., 'A decade of British opposition to the Suez Canal project, 1854—1864,' *Transport History* 9 (1978), 15—23.
25. Robertson, J.C., 'British policy in East Africa, March 1891 to May 1935,' *English Historical R.* 93 (1978), 835—44.
26. Graham, G.S., 'Napoleon's naval gaolers,' *J. of Imperial and Commonwealth History* 7 (1978), 3—17.
27. Shields, R.A., 'The imperial government and the Canadian-Spanish negotiations, 1878—83,' *B. of the Institute of Historical Research* 51 (1978), 160—73.
28. Howard, C.H.D., 'The Vienna Diary of Berta de Bunsen, 28 June — 17 August 1914,' ibid. 209—25.
29. Bradshaw, D.F., 'Stephenson de Lesseps, and the Suez Canal: an Englishman's blind spot,' *J. of Transport History* 4 (1978), 239—43.
30. Fletcher, R., 'An English advocate in Germany: Eduard Bernstein's analysis of Anglo-German relations 1900—1914,' *Canadian J. of History* 13 (1978), 209—35.
31. Gruner, W.D., 'Frieden, Krieg und politisch-soziales System: Uberlegungen zu den britisch-deutschen Beziehungen im 19. und 20. Jahrhundert,' *Zeitschrift für bayerische Landesgeschichte* 41 (1978), 921—58.
32. Kesner, R.M., 'Britain and the rehabilitation of the Cypriot economy,' *J. of European Economic History* 7 (1978), 169—90.

(e) *Religion*

1. Weaver, M.J., 'Wilfrid Ward, George Tyrrell and the meanings of modernism,' *Downside R.* 96 (1978), 21—34.
2. Prochaska, F.K., 'Little vessels: children in the nineteenth-century

English missionary movement,' *J. of Imperial and Commonwealth History* 6 (1978), 103–18.

3. Richards, N.J., 'British nonconformity and the Liberal Party 1868–1906,' *J. of Religious History* 9 (1977), 387–401.

4. Hammond, P.C. *The parson and the Victorian parish.* London; Hodder & Stoughton; 1977. Pp 224.

5. Toon, P.; Smout, M. *John Charles Ryle, evangelical bishop.* Cambridge; J. Clarke; 1976. Pp 123.

6. (Anon.) *Hundert Jahre Deutsche Evangelische Kirche, Bradford-Huddersfield-Leeds: Fakten, Berichte, Erinnerungen, Grüsse.* [The Church; 1977]. Pp 68.

7. Harrison, F.M.W., 'The Nottinghamshire Baptists and social conditions,' *Baptist Q.* 27 (1978), 212–24.

8. Williamson, J. *Josephine Butler, the forgotten saint.* Leighton Buzzard; Faith Press; 1977. Pp 122.

9. Nimmo, D., 'Towards and away from Newman's theory of doctrinal development: pointers from Mark Pattison in 1838 and 1846,' *J. of Theological Studies* 29 (1978), 160–2.

10. McLeod, H., 'Recent studies in Victorian religious history,' *Victorian Studies* 21 (1978), 245–55.

11. Gilley, S., 'Wilfrid Ward and his Life of Newman,' *J. of Ecclesiastical History* 29 (1978), 177–94.

12. Bentley, J. *Ritualism and politics in Victorian Britain: the attempt to legislate for belief.* Oxford UP; 1978. Pp xiv, 162.

13. Edwards, D.L. *Leaders of the Church of England, 1828–1978.* (Revd. ed.). London; Hodder & Stoughton; 1978. Pp 383.

14. Edwards, M.S. *S.E. Keeble: the rejected prophet.* Chester; Wesley Historical Soc.; 1977. Pp 71.

15. Machin, G.I.T. *Politics and the churches in Great Britain, 1832 to 1868.* Oxford; Clarendon; 1977. Pp x, 438.

16. Holmes, J.D. *More Roman than Rome: English Catholicism in the nineteenth century.* London; Burns & Oates; 1978. Pp 278.

17. Colloms, B. *Victorian country parsons.* Lincoln; Neb./London; University of Nebraska Press; 1977. Pp 288.

18. Daniel, W.H., 'The response of the Church of England to the Civil War and Reconstruction in America,' *Historical Magazine of the Protestant Episcopal Church* 47 (1978), 51–72.

19. Harrison, F.M.W., 'The Nottinghamshire Baptists: the political scene,' *Baptist Q.* 27 (1978), 267–79.

20. Ollerhead, P.E., 'The Baptists in Crewe, 1840–1940,' ibid. 261–6.

21. Williams, D.S.M., 'The "Mongolian Mission" of the London Missionary Society: an episode in the history of religion in the Russian Empire,' *Slavonic and East European R.* 56 (1978), 329–45.

22. Roberts, J., 'The Van mission,' *T. of the Untarian Historical Society* 16 (1978), 188–93.

23. Hill, A.M., 'The successors of the Remnant: a bicentenary account

of St Mark's Unitarian Church, Edinburgh. Part II: from 1822 to 1976,' ibid. 149—75.

24. Bonsall, H.E.; Robertson, E.H. *The dream of an ideal city: Westbourne Park, 1877—1977.* London; Westbourne Park Baptist Church; 1978. Pp vii, 247.

25. Ker, I.T.; Gornall, T.; Dessain, C.S. *The letters and diaries of John Henry Newman, vols. 1 and 31.* Oxford; Clarendon; 1978, 1977. Pp xviii, 346; xviii, 328, + supplement of letters found too late for vols. 11—30 (pp 111).

26. Drummond, A.L.; Bullock, J. *The Church in late Victorian Scotland, 1874—1900.* Edinburgh; St Andrews Press; 1978. Pp ix, 332.

27. Lummis, W.M. *Padre George Smith of Rorke's Drift.* Norwich; Wensum Books; 1978. Pp 96.

28. Stephenson, A.M.G. *Anglicanism and the Lambeth Conferences.* London; SPCK; 1978. Pp xvi, 341.

29. Stevens Cox, J. (ed.). *Extracts from the chaplain's journal, Ilchester gaol, 1823—1827.* St Peter Port; Toucan Press; 1978. Ilchester and District Occasional Papers 9, pp. 150—8.

30. Brown, C.G., 'Frederick Denison Maurice in the United States, 1860—1900,' *J. of Religious History* 10 (1978), 50—69.

31. Neveu, B., 'Mgr Duchesne et son Mémoire sur les Ordinations Anglicanes (1895 ou 1896),' *J. of Theological Studies* 29 (1978), 443—82.

32. Carwardine, R., 'The Welsh evangelical community and "Finney's Revival",' *J. of Ecclesiastical History* 29 (1978), 463—81.

33. Ransford, O. *David Livingstone: the dark interior.* London; Murray; 1978. Pp xi, 332.

34. Gunson, N. *Messengers of grace: evangelical missionaries in the South Seas, 1799—1860.* Oxford UP; 1978. Pp x, 437.

35. Cairns, D., 'A radical Sutherland minister,' *Aberdeen University R.* 159 (1978), 256—60.

36. Rashid, S., 'Richard Whately and the struggle for rational Christianity in the mid-nineteenth century,' *Historical Magazine of the Protestant Episcopal Church* 47 (1978), 293—311.

37. Fisher, B., 'Ecclesiology and the deep chancel: from Cambridge to New York,' ibid. 313—31.

38. Le Quesne, A.L. *After Kilvert.* London; Oxford UP; 1978. Pp x, 233.

39. Binney, A.; McKenny, J. (ed.). *A City Road diary: the record of three years in Victorian London, by Helen McKenny.* Bognor Regis; World Methodist Historical Soc.; 1978. Pp viii, 111.

40. Porter, A., 'Late nineteenth-century Anglican missionary expansion: a consideration of some non-Anglican sources of inspiration,' Bc7, 349—65.

41. Piggin, S., 'Assessing nineteenth-century missionary motivation: some consideration of theory and method,' Bc7, 327—37.

42. Robson, G., 'The failures of success: working class evangelists in early Victorian Birmingham,' Bc7, 381—91.
43. Yates, W.N., ' "The only true friend": ritualist concepts of priestly vocation,' Bc7, 407—15.
44. Matthew, H.C.G., 'Gladstone, Vaticanism and the question of the east,' Bc7, 417—42.
45. Varley, J., 'A Bedfordshire clergyman of the reform era and his bishop,' Bc10, 113—40.

(f) *Economic affairs*

1. Daunton, M.J., 'Inter-union relations on the waterfront: Cardiff 1888—1914,' *International R. of Social History* 22 (1977), 350—78.
2. Kerr, G.M., 'British 0-8-0 tank locomotives,' *J. of Transport History* 8 (1977), 121—32.
3. Barker, R., 'Printed propaganda in the "battle of the gauges",' ibid. 110—20.
4. Fisher, J.R., 'The Farmers' Alliance: an agricultural protest movement of the 1880's,' *Agricultural History R.* 26 (1978), 15—25.
5. Fox, N.E., 'The spread of the threshing machine in central southern England'; Macdonald, S., 'Further progress with the early threshing machine: a rejoinder,' ibid. 26—8, 29—32.
6. Urving, R.J., 'The profitability and performance of British railways, 1870—1914,' *Economic History R.* sec. ser. 31 (1978), 46—66.
7. Levit, I.; Smout, T.C., 'Some weights and measures in Scotland, 1843,' *Scottish Historical R.* 56 (1977), 146—52.
8. Kennett, D.H., 'The pattern of coaching in early nineteenth-century Norfolk,' *Norfolk Archaeology* 36 (1977), 355—72.
9. Trett, R.; Tuck, D.W., 'Alfred Dodman and Company of King's Lynn,' ibid. 373—82.
10. Snell, J.B. *Britain's railways under steam* (2nd revd. ed.). London; Allan; 1977. Pp 224.
11. Booker, F. *The Great Western Railway: a new history.* Newton Abbot; David & Charles; 1977. Pp 206.
12. Russell, J.H. *The Banbury and Cheltenham Railway, 1887—1962.* Oxford; Oxford Publishing; 1977. Pp 140.
13. Williams, H. *Stage coaches in Wales.* Barry; S. Williams; 1977. Pp 120.
14. Kirby, M.W. *The British coalmining industry, 1870—1946: a political and economic history.* London; Macmillan; 1977. Pp viii, 278.
15. Tucker, M.T. *Vincent & Son Ltd, cabinet makers, Brick Lane, London: a short record of the firm's history, work and equipment.* London; Greater London Industrial Archaeology Soc.; 1977. Pp 8.

16. Wilson, H.S. *TPO: a history of the Travelling Post Offices of Great Britain; Part 3: Scotland and Ireland* (ed. by Peter Johnson). Leicester; Railway Philatelic Group; 1977. Pp 78.
17. Morgan, A.N. *David Morgan, 1833–1919: the life and times of a master draper in South Wales.* Risca; Starling Press; 1977. Pp 181.
18. Burchill, F.; Ross, R. *A history of the potters' union.* Hanley; Ceramic and Allied Trades Union; 1977. Pp xvi, 292.
19. Meek, R.L. *Smith, Marx and after: ten essays in the development of economic thought.* London; Chapman & Hall; 1977. Pp ix, 193.
20. Chapman, S.D., 'The international houses: the continental contribution to British commerce, 1800–1860,' *J. of European Economic History* 6 (1977), 5–48.
21. Rees, P., 'Chatsworth Street cutting, part of the original terminus of the Liverpool and Manchester Railway,' *Industrial Archaeology R.* 2 (1977–8), 38–51.
22. Preece, G.P.J., 'Railway and canal coal-drops at Sharpness docks [Glos.],' ibid. 78–84.
23. Shipley, S., 'London journeymen 1810 to 1830,' *Soc. for the study of Labour History B.* 36 (1978), 9–10.
24. Mills, D.R., 'The technique of house repopulation: experience from a Cambridgeshire village, 1841,' *Labour Historian* 13 (1978), 86–98.
25. Carter, H.; Wheatley, S., 'Some aspects of the spatial structure of two Glamorgan towns in the nineteenth century,' *Welsh History R.* 9 (1978), 32–56.
26. Munting, R., 'Ransomes in Russia: an English agricultural engineering company's trade with Russia to 1917,' *Economic History R.* 2nd ser. 31 (1978), 257–69.
27. Kenwood, A.G., 'Fixed capital formation on Merseyside, 1800–1913,' ibid. 214–37.
28. Coupe, G., 'Tottington: the growth and development of a Lancashire industrial village,' *T. of the Lancashire and Cheshire Antiquarian Soc.* 79 (1977), 95–122.
29. Colyer, R.J., 'Limitations to agrarian development in nineteenth-century Wales,' *B. of the Board of Celtic Studies* 27 (1978), 602–17.
30. Gray, A. *The London to Brighton Line, 1841–1977.* Blandford Forum; Oakwood Press; 1977. Pp 127.
31. Hackett, D. *The history of the future: the Bemrose Corporation, 1826–1976.* London; Scolar Press; 1976. Pp 144.
32. Perren, R. *The meat trade in Britain, 1840–1914.* London; Routledge; 1978. Pp x, 258.
33. Simmons, J. *The railway in England and Wales, 1830–1914; vol. 1: the system and its working.* Leicester UP; 1978. Pp 295.
34. Dewey, C., 'The end of the imperialism of free trade: the eclipse

of the Lancashire lobby and the concession of fiscal autonomy to India,' *The imperial impact: studies in the economic history of Africa and India* (ed. C. Dewey, A.G. Hopkins; London, Athlone Press, 1978), 35—67

35. Wrigley, C.C., 'Neo-mercantile policies and the new imperialism,' ibid. 20—34.

36. Von Tunzelmann, G.N. *Steam power and British industrialization.* Oxford; Clarendon; 1978. Pp xii, 344.

37. Howell, D.W. *Land and people in nineteenth-century Wales.* London; Routledge; 1977. Pp xvi, 207.

38. Davies, P.N. *Sir Alfred Jones: shipping entrepreneur par excellence.* London; Europa; 1978. Pp lxii, 162.

39. O'Brien, P.K.; Heath, D.; Keyder, C., 'Agricultural efficiency in Britain and France, 1815—1914,' *J. of European Economic History* 6 (1977), 339—91.

40. Heertje, A.; Weatherall, D., 'An unpublished letter of David Ricardo: to Thomas Smith of Easton Grey, 27 April 1819,' *Economic J.* 88 (1978), 569—71.

41. Lockhart, D.G., 'The planned villages of Aberdeenshire: the evidence from newspaper advertisements,' *Scottish Geographical Magazine* 94 (1978), 95—102.

42. Perkins, E.J., 'Foreign interest rates in American financial markets: a revised series of dollar-sterling exchange rates, 1835—1900,' *J. of Economic History* 38 (1978), 392—417.

43. Ferns, J.L., 'The Walker Company of Rotherham: practical proof of its greatness,' *Industrial Archaeology* 12 (1978), 206—20.

44. Mounfield, P.R., 'Early technological innovation in the British footwear industry,' *Industrial Archaeology R.* 3 (1978), 129—42.

45. Hassan, J.A., 'Relationships between coal, gas and oil production: a nineteenth-century Scottish case-study,' ibid. 277—89.

46. Clark, S., 'Chorlton Mills and their neighbours,' ibid. 207—39.

47. Huttman, J.P., 'British meat imports in the free trade era,' *Agricultural History* 52 (1978), 247—62.

48. Benson, J., 'The thrift of English coal-miners, 1860—95,' *Economic History R.* 2nd ser. 31 (1978), 410—18.

49. Engel, A., 'Oxford colleges finances, 1871—1913: a comment,' ibid. 437—45. With 'A Reply' by J.P.D. Dunbabin, ibid. 446—9.

50. Tranter, N.L., 'The demographic impact of economic growth and decline: Portpatrick 1820—1891,' *Scottish Historical R.* 57 (1978), 87—105.

51. Perry, P.J., 'High farming in Victorian Britain: the financial foundations,' *Agricultural History* 52 (1978), 364—79.

52. Davidson, R., 'The Board of Trade and industrial relations 1896—1914,' *Historical J.* 21 (1978), 571—91.

53. Cain, P.J., 'The British railway rates problem 1894—1913,' *Business History* 20 (1978), 87—99.

54. Gourvish, T.R., 'The performance of British railway management

after 1860: the railways of Watkin and Forbes,' ibid. 186—200.

55. Jones, S., 'The cotton industry and joint-stock banking in Manchester 1825—1850,' ibid. 165—85.

56. Jones, G.G., 'The oil-fuel market in Britain 1900—14: a lost cause revisited,' ibid. 131—52.

57. Osborne, B.S., 'Commonlands, mineral rights and industry: changing evaluations in an industrializing society,' *J. of Historical Geography* 4 (1978), 231—49.

58. Clay, E.W. *Waide's 100 years, 1878—1978: a short history to mark the centenary of Thomas Waide & Sons Limited, printers and carton manufacturers of Kirkstall Hill, Leeds.* [Leeds; the firm; 1978]. Pp 60.

59. Fraser, M.; Jeeves, A. (ed.). *All that glittered: selected correspondence of Lionel Phillips, 1890—1924.* Cape Town; Oxford UP; 1977. Pp 428.

60. Turner, J.H. *The London Brighton and South Coast Railway, 2: establishment and growth.* London; Batsford; 1978. Pp xv, 320.

61. Ambirajan, S. *Classical political economy and British policy in India.* Cambridge UP; 1978. Pp vii, 301.

62. Preston, B. *Occupations of father and son in mid-Victorian England.* Dept of Geography; Univ. of Reading; 1977. Pp ii, 40.

63. Owen, C.C. *The development of industry in Burton upon Trent.* Chichester; Phillimore; 1978. Pp xvi, 279.

64. Jackson, A.A. *London's local railways.* Newton Abbot; David & Charles; 1978. Pp 384.

65. Orbell, J. *From Cape to Cape: the history of Lyle Shipping Company.* Edinburgh; P. Harris; 1978. Pp xii, 329.

66. Patrick, A. *Maltings in Nottinghamshire: a survey in industrial archaeology.* Notts County Council; 1977. Pp 24 + 23.

67. Williams, J.R. *Quarryman's champion: the life and activities of William John Parry of Coetmor.* Denbigh; Gwasg Gee; 1978. Pp 258.

68. Morgan, J.S. *The Corris Railway Company.* London; Gemini Publications; 1977. Pp 63.

69. Hartland, G.C.J., 'Steam power in Banbury,' *Cake & Cockhorse* 7 (1978), 175—83.

70. Williams, K.; Reynolds, D. *The Kingsbridge branch (the primrose line).* Oxford; Oxford Publishing Co.; 1977. Pp viii, 248.

71. Almond, J.K., 'Tindale Fell Spelter Works, East Cumbria, and its closure in 1895,' *T. of the Cumberland & Westmorland Antiquarian & Arch. Soc.* 78 (1978), 177—85.

72. Hiscock, R.H., 'The proprietory chapel of St. John, Gravesend,' *Archaeologia Cantiana* 93 (1978 for 1977), 1—24.

73. Caplan, M., 'The new poor law and the struggle for union chargeability,' *International R. of Social History* 23 (1978), 267—300.

74. Bowman, A.K., 'Dugald Drummond: a great Scottish locomotive engineer,' *Transport History* 9 (1978), 3—14.

75. George, A.D., 'The development of new passenger transport industries in Manchester 1877—1938,' ibid. 38—51.

76. Gwynned Jones, J., 'Church reconstruction in north Cardiganshire in the nineteenth century,' *National Library of Wales J.* 20 (1978), 352—60.

77. Broeze, F.J.A., 'British intercontinental shipping and Australia, 1813—1850,' *J. of Transport History* 4 (1978), 189—207.

78. Atkins, P.J., 'The growth of London's railway milk trade, 1845—1914,' ibid. 208—26.

79. Merrett, L.H., 'Staffordshire industries,' *Industrial Archaeology* 13 (1978), 60—6.

80. Wasson, E.A., 'The third earl Spencer and agriculture, 1818—1845,' *Agricultural History R.* 26 (1978), 89—99.

81. Cain, P.J., 'J.A. Hobson, Cobdenism, and the radical theory of economic imperialism, 1898—1914,' *Economic History R.* 2nd ser. 31 (1978), 565—84.

82. Sanderson, M., 'The professor as industrial consultant: Oliver Arnold and the British steel industry,' ibid. 585—600.

83. Thorne, R. *Liverpool Street Station.* London; Greater London Council; 1978. Pp 88.

84. Bick, D.E. *The old metal mines of mid-Wales, part 5: Aberdovey, Dinas Mawddwy and Llangynog.* Newent; The Pound House; 1978. Pp 52.

85. Hillier, R., 'The origins of engineering in Peterborough: the Queen Street Iron Works,' *Northamptonshire Past and Present* 6 (1978), 101—6.

86. Matthews, M.H., 'The geography of the British heavy chemical industry in the nineteenth century,' *Tijdschrift voor Economische en Social Geografie* 69 (1978), 333—44.

87. Francis, A.J. *The cement industry, 1796—1914: a history.* Newton Abbot; David & Charles; 1977. Pp 319.

88. Mair, C. *A star for seamen: the Stevenson family of engineers.* London; Murray; 1978. Pp x, 278.

89. Jones, R.C. *Arian: the story of money and banking in Wales.* Swansea; C. Davies; 1978. Pp 170.

90. Farnie, D.A., 'The Manchester Ship Canal, 1894—1913,' Bc2, 173—213.

91. White, P.R., 'Stott Park bobbin mill, Colton, Cumbria: an historical outline, 1835—1971,' Bc6, 335—48.

(g) *Social structure and population*

1. Williams, L.J.; Boyns, T., 'Occupation in Wales, 1851—1971,' *B. of Economic Research* 29 (1977), 71—83.

2. Rubinstein, D., 'Cycling in the 1890s,' *Victorian Studies* 21 (1977), 47—71.

3. Bailey, P., ' "A mingled mass of perfectly legitimate pleasures": the Victorian middle class and the problem of leisure,' ibid. 7—18.

4. Spring, D. (ed.). *European landed elites in the nineteenth century.* Baltimore/London; Johns Hopkins UP; 1977. Pp vii, 147.

5. Slater, T.R., 'Family, society and the ornamental villa on the fringes of English county towns,' *J. of Historical Geography* 4 (1978), 129—44.

6. Gadian, D.S., 'Class consciousness in Oldham and other north-west industrial towns,' *Historical J.* 21 (1978), 161—72.

7. Stone, J.S., 'More light on Emily Faithfull and the Victoria Press,' *The Library* 5th ser. 33 (1978), 63—7.

8. Tomes, N., ' "A torrent of abuse": crimes of violence between working-class men and women in London 1840—1875,' *J. of Social History* 11 (1977/8), 328—45.

9. Figlio, K., 'Chlorosis and chronic disease in nineteenth-century Britain: the social constitution of somatic illness in a capitalist society,' *Social History* 3 (1978), 167—97.

10. Berridge, V., 'East End opium dens and narcotic use in Britain,' *London J.* 4 (1978), 3—28.

11. Korr, C.P., 'West Ham United Football Club and the beginnings of professional football in East London 1895—1914,' *J. of Contemporary History* 13 (1978), 211—32.

12. Longmate, N. *The hungry mills* [the cotton famine]. London; Temple Smith; 1978. Pp 319.

13. Wohl, A.S. (ed.). *The Victorian family: structure and stresses.* London; Croom Helm; 1978. Pp 224.

14. Crafts, N.F.R., 'Average age at first marriage for women in mid-nineteenth-century England and Wales: a cross-section study,' *Population Studies* 32 (1978), 21—5.

15. Rubinstein, D., 'Cycling eighty years ago,' *History Today* 28 (1978), 544—7.

16. Gorham, D., 'The "Maiden tribute of modern Babylon" reexamined: child prostitution and the idea of childhood in late-Victorian England,' *Victorian Studies* 21 (1978), 353—79.

17. Maxwell, R., 'Henry Mayhew and the life of the streets,' *J. of British Studies* 17/2 (1978), 87—105.

18. Cannadine, D., 'The theory and practice of the English leisure classes,' *Historical J.* 21 (1978), 445—67.

19. Mills, D.R., 'The residential propinquity of kin in a Cambridgeshire village, 1841,' *J. of Historical Geography* 4 (1978), 265—76.

20. Oakley, W. *Winged wheel: the history of the first hundred years of the Cyclists' Touring Club.* Godalming; The Club; 1977. Pp 248.

21. Campin, J. *The rise of the plutocrats: wealth and power in Edwardian England.* London; Constable; 1978. Pp 340.

22. Munn, P. *The Charlotte Dymond murder: Cornwall, 1844.* Bodmin; Bodmin Books; 1978. Pp 188.

23. Gibson, I. *The English vice: beating, sex and shame in Victorian England and after.* London; Duckworth; 1978. Pp xii, 364.

24. Harrison, F. *The dark angel: aspects of Victorian sexuality.* London; Sheldon Press; 1977. Pp xi, 288.

25. Stott, M. *Organization woman: the story of the National Union of Townswomen's Guilds.* London; Heinemann; 1978. Pp 240.

26. Vicinus, M. (ed.). *A widening sphere: changing roles of Victorian women.* Bloomington/London; Indiana UP; 1977. Pp xix, 326.

27. Hammerton, A.J., 'Feminism and female emigration 1861—1886,' Hg26, 52—71.

28. Walkowitz, J., 'The making of an outcast group: prostitutes and working women in nineteenth-century Plymouth and Southampton,' Hg26, 72—93.

29. Kent, C., 'Image and reality: the actress and society,' Hg26, 94—116.

30. Smith, F.B., 'Sexuality in Britain 1800—1900: some suggested revisions,' Hg26, 182—98.

31. Ryan-Johansson, S., 'Sex and death in Victorian England: an examination of age- and sex-specific death rates, 1840—1910,' Hg26, 163—81.

32. Kanner, B., 'The women of England in a century of social change, 1815—1914: a select biography, part II,' Hg26, 199—270.

33. Calder, J. *The Victorian home.* London; Batsford; 1977. Pp 238.

34. Fletcher, R. (ed.). *The biography of a Victorian village: Richard Cobbold's account of Wortham, Suffolk, 1860.* London; Batsford; 1977. Pp 168.

35. *Barton on Humber in the 1850's, part 2: the town and the people.* Barton on Humber; Workers' Education Association Branch; 1978. Pp 86.

36. Marshall, J.D., 'Cleator and Cleator Moor: some aspects of their social and urban development in the mid-19th century,' *T. of the Cumberland and Westmorland Antiquarian & Arch. Soc.* 78 (1978), 163—75.

37. Gash, N., 'After Waterloo: British society and the legacy of the Napoleonic Wars,' *T. of the Royal Historical Soc.* 5th ser. 28 (1978), 145—57.

38. Shepherd, M.A., 'The origins and incidence of the term "labour aristocracy",' *Soc. for the Study of Labour History* 37 (1978), 51—67.

39. Keene, T., 'Cadbury housing at Bournville,' *Industrial Archaeology* 13 (1978), 43—7.

40. Crow, D. *The Edwardian woman.* London; Allen & Unwin; 1978. Pp 231.

41. Pullar, P. *Gilded butterflies: the rise and fall of the London season.* London; Hamish Hamilton; 1978. Pp 192.
42. Hibbert, C. (ed.). *Memoirs of the public and private life of Queen Caroline, by Joseph Nightingale.* London; Folio Soc.; 1978. Pp 363.
43. Winstanley, M.J. *Life in Kent at the turn of the century.* Folkestone; Dawson; 1978. Pp 236.
44. Delamont, S.; Duffin, L. (ed.). *The nineteenth century woman: her cultural and physical world.* London; Croom Helm; 1978. Pp 213.
45. Brent, C. (ed.). *Lewes in 1871: a household and political directory.* Brighton; University of Sussex; 1978. Pp viii, 76.
46. Gordon, C. *A richer dust: echoes from an Edwardian album.* London; Elm Tree Books; 1978. Pp 191.
47. Walvin, J. *Leisure and society, 1830–1950.* London; Longman; 1978. Pp ix, 181.
48. Lawton, R. (ed.). *The census and social structure: an interpretative guide to nineteenth century census for England and Wales.* London; Cass; 1978. Pp xiii, 330.
49. Hart-Davis, D. *Monarchs of the glen: a history of deer-stalking in the Scottish highlands.* London; Cape; 1978. Pp x, 249.
50. Walvin, J. *Beside the seaside: a social history of the popular seaside holiday.* London; Allen Lane; 1978. Pp 176.
51. Langley, J. *Always a layman.* Brighton; Sussex Soc. for the Study of Labour History; 1976. Pp 67.
52. Matson, J. *Dear Osborne: Queen Victoria's family life in the Isle of Wight.* London; Hamilton; 1978. Pp 166.
53. Devine, T.M., 'Social stability and agrarian change in the eastern lowlands of Scotland, 1810–1840,' *Social History* 3 (1978), 331–46.
54. Harrison, R. (ed.). *Independent collier: the coalminer as archetypal proletarian reconsidered.* Hassocks; Harvester Press; 1978. Pp viii, 276.
55. Digby, A. *Pauper palaces.* London; Routledge; 1978. Pp x, 266.
56. Walton, J.K. *The Blackpool landlady: a social history.* Manchester UP; 1978. Pp x, 229.
57. Englander, D. (ed.). *The diary of Fred Knee.* Manchester; Soc. for the Study of Labour History; 1977. Pp viii, 122.
58. May, J.P., 'The Chinese in Britain, 1860–1914,' Bc1, 111–24.
59. Holmes, C., 'J.A. Hobson and the Jews,' Bc1, 125–57.
60. Bell, P., 'Aspects of Anglo-Indian Bedford,' Bc10, 181–203.
61. Askwith, B. *A Victorian young lady.* Wilton; Michael Russell; 1978. Pp 155.

(h) *Social Policy*

1. Evans, E.J. (ed.). *Social policy, 1830–1914: individualism, col-*

lectivism and the origins of the welfare state. London; Routledge; 1978. Pp xvi, 302.

2. Perkin, H., 'Individualism versus collectivism in nineteenth-century Britain: a false antithesis,' *J. of British Studies* 17 (1977/8), 105—18.

3. Elliott, B., 'Sources for the study of juvenile delinquency in the nineteenth century,' *Local Historian* 13 (1978), 74—8.

4. Tomlinson, M.H., ' "Prison palaces": a re-appraisal of early Victorian prisons, 1835—77,' *B. of the Institute of Historical Research* 51 (1978), 60—71.

5. Simmons, H.G., 'Explaining social policy: the English Mental Deficiency Act of 1913,' *J. of Social History* 11 (1977/8), 387—403.

6. McCandless, P., 'Liberty and lunacy: the Victorians and wrongful confinement,' ibid. 366—86.

7. Thane, P. (ed.). *The origins of British social policy*. London; Croom Helm; 1978. Pp 209.

8. Thane, P., 'Introduction,' Hh7, 11—20.

9. Thane, P., 'Ratepayers and social policy,' Hh7, 21—35.

10. Crowther, M.A., 'The later years of the workhouse 1890—1929,' Hh7, 36—55.

11. Ryan, P.A., ' "Popularism" 1894—1930,' Hh7, 56—83.

12. Thane, P., 'Non-contributory versus insurance pensions 1878—1908,' Hh7, 84—106.

13. Hay, J.R., 'Employers' attitudes to social policy and the concept of "social control", 1900—1920,' Hh7, 107—25.

14. Brown, J., 'Social control and the modernisation of social policy 1890—1929,' Hh7, 126—46.

15. Treble, J.H., 'Unemployment and unemployment policies in Glasgow 1890—1905,' Hh7, 137—172.

16. Macnicol, J., 'Family allowances and less eligibility,' Hh7, 137—202.

17. Burnett, J. *A social history of housing, 1815—1970*. Newton Abbot; David & Charles; 1978. Pp viii, 344.

18. Hay, J.R. (ed.). *The development of the British welfare state 1880—1975* [documents] . London; Arnold; 1978. Pp x, 116.

19. Holcombe, L., 'Victorian wives and property: reform of the Married Women's Property Law 1857—1882,' Hg26, 3—28.

20. Hindle, R. (ed. Frankland, T.). *Salford's prison: an account of the New Bailey Prison in 1836*. Salford Local History Society; 1978. Pp 18.

21. Kerr, B., 'Henry Moule and cholera in Dorset,' *History Today* 28 (1978), 672—80.

22. Mason, F.M., 'Charles Masterman and national health insurance,' *Albion* 10/1 (1978), 54—75.

23. Hamilton, M., 'Opposition to the Contagious Diseases Acts, 1864—1886,' ibid. 14—27.

24. John, A.V., 'Colliery legislation and its consequences: 1842 and the women miners of Lancashire,' *B. of the John Rylands University Library of Manchester* 61 (1978), 78—114.

25. Horn, P., 'The employment of children in Victorian Oxfordshire,' *Midland History* 4 (1978), 61—74.

26. Brundage, A. *The making of the new poor law: the politics of inquiry, enactment and implementation, 1832—39.* London; Hutchinson; 1978. Pp xv, 204.

27. Burchall, M.J. (ed.). *Eastern Sussex workhouse census, 1851.* Brighton; Sussex Family History Group; 1978. Pp 48.

28. Coutts, F.L. *Bread for my neighbour: an appreciation of the social action and influence of William Booth.* London; Hodder & Stoughton; 1978. Pp 192.

29. Lewis, G.K. *Slavery, imperialism and freedom: studies in English radical thought.* New York/London; Monthly Review Press; 1978. Pp 346.

30. Malchow, H., 'Free water: the Public Drinking Fountain Movement and Victorian London,' *London J.* 4 (1978), 181—203.

(i) Education

1. Cottrill, D.J. *Victoria College, Jersey, 1852—1972.* London; Phillimore; 1977. Pp vii, 123.

2. Olle, J.G. *Ernest A. Savage: librarian extraordinary.* London; Library Association; 1977. Pp 225.

3. Reeder, D.A. (ed.). *Urban education in the nineteenth century: proceedings of the 1976 Annual Conference of the History of Education Society of Great Britain.* London; Taylor & Francis; 1977. Pp ix, 144.

4. Fraser, D., 'Education and urban politics c. 1832—1885,' Hi3, 11—28.

5. Stephens, W.B., 'Illiteracy and schooling in the provincial towns, 1640—1870: a comparative approach,' Hi3, 26—48.

6. Marsden, W.E., 'Education and the social geography of nineteenth century towns and cities,' Hi3, 49—74.

7. Reeder, D.A., 'Predicaments of city children: late Victorian and Edwardian perspectives on education and urban society,' Hi3, 75—94.

8. Smith, D., 'Social conflict and urban education in the nineteenth century: a sociological approach to comparative analysis,' Hi3, 95—114.

9. Garrett, K.I., 'Marie Hackett, Crosby Hall and Gresham College,' *Guildhall Studies in London History* 3/1 (1977), 42—54.

10. Welch, C.E., 'The London Society for the Extension of University Teaching, 1875—1902,' ibid. 55—65.

11. McWilliams-Tullberg, R., 'Women and degrees at Cambridge University,' Hg26, 117—45.

12. Pearse, R.N. *The story of the Mary Datchelor School, 1877–1977* (new ed.). London; Hodder & Stoughton; 1977. Pp 267.

13. Selby, D.E. *Towards a common system of national education: Cardinal Manning and educational reform, 1882–1892.* University of Leeds; 1977. Pp 60.

14. Battiscombe, G. *Reluctant pioneer: a life of Elizabeth Wordsworth.* London; Constable; 1978. Pp 320.

15. Yorke, P. *Education and the working class: Ruskin College, 1899–1909.* Oxford; Ruskin College; 1977. Pp 41.

16. Pritchard, F.C. *The story of Woodhouse Grove School.* Bradford; The School; 1978. Pp xiv, 411.

17. MacKillop, I.D., 'The London School of Ethics and Social Philosophy: an adult education movement of the 1890's,' *History of Education* 7 (1978), 119—27.

18. Horn, P. *Education in rural England, 1800–1914.* Dublin; Gill & Macmillan; 1978. Pp xiv, 351.

19. Gordon, P.; Lawton, D. *Curriculum change in the nineteenth and twentieth centuries.* London; Hodder & Stoughton; 1978. Pp 258.

20. Honey, J.R. de S. *Tom Brown's universe: the development of the Victorian public school.* London; Millington; 1977. Pp xv, 416.

21. Smith, E.H.F. *St Peter's, the founding of an Oxford college.* Gerrards Cross; Smythe; 1978. Pp 301.

22. Thrall, A. *The history of adult education in 19th century Doncaster.* Doncaster Metropolitan Borough Museums and Arts Service; 1977. Pp 102.

23. Locke, M. *Traditions and controls in the making of a polytechnic: Woolwich Polytechnic, 1890–1970.* London; Thames Polytechnic; 1978. Pp vii, 175.

(j) *Naval and military*

1. Severn, D., 'The bombardment of Algiers, 1816,' *History Today* 28 (1978), 31—9.

2. Argall, F.; Bird, R., 'Falmouth pilot cutters, 1800–1900,' *Mariner's Mirror* 64 (1978), 9—12.

3. Lindon, A., 'Hercules Linton, 1836–1900, designer of the *Cutty Sark*,' ibid. 3—8.

4. Trebilcock, C. *The Vickers Brothers: armaments and enterprise, 1854–1914.* London; Europa, 1977. Pp xl, 181.

5. Stuckey, P.J. *The sailing pilots of the Bristol Channel.* Newton Abbot; David & Charles; 1977. Pp 158.

6. Lehmann, J.H. *Remember you are an Englishman: biography of Sir Harry Smith.* London; Cape; 1977. Pp 384.

7. Hamilton, W.M., 'The "new navalism" and the British Navy League, 1895–1914,' *Mariner's Mirror* 64 (1978), 37—44.

8. Argall, F., 'Sailing barges of the Fal estuary,' *Mariner's Mirror* 64 (1978), 163—8.

9. Packard, J.J., 'Sir Robert Seppings and the timber problem,' ibid. 145—56.

10. Rodger, N.A.M., 'British belted cruisers,' ibid. 23—35.

11. Woolford, J.V., 'The Matabele war,' *History Today* 28 (1978), 537—43, 605—11.

12. Travers, T.H.E., 'The offensive and the problem of innovation in British military thought, 1870—1915,' *J. of Contemporary History* 13 (1978), 531—53.

13. Strachan, H., 'Soldiers, strategy and Sebastopol,' *Historical J.* 21 (1978), 303—25.

14. French, D., 'Spy fever in Britain, 1900—1915,' ibid. 355—70.

15. Beckett, I.F.W., 'The problem of military discipline in the Volunteer Force, 1859—1899,' *J. of the Soc. for Army Historical Research* 56 (1978), 66—78.

16. Abbott, P.E., 'N Battery, 5th Brigade, Royal Artillery at Isandhlwana, 22nd January, 1879,' ibid. 95—111.

17. Featherstone, D. *Weapons and equipment of the Victorian soldier.* Poole; Blandford Press; 1978. Pp 130.

18. Daunton, M., 'Jack ashore: seamen in Cardiff before 1914,' *Welsh History R.* 9 (1978), 176—203.

19. Harfield, A.G., 'British military presence in Cyprus in the 19th century,' *J. of the Soc. for Army Historical Research* 56 (1978), 160—70.

20. Winton, J. *The Victoria Cross at sea.* London; Joseph; 1978. Pp 256.

21. Chevenix Trench, C. *Charley Gordon: an eminent Victorian reassessed.* London; Allen Lane; 1978. Pp 320.

22. Thomas, D. *Cochrane: Britannia's last sea-king.* London; Deutsch; 1978. Pp 383.

23. Preston, A., 'Wolseley, the Khartoum Relief Expedition, and the defence of India,' *J. of Imperial and Commonwealth History* 6 (1978), 254—80.

24. Hayward, R.A. *The story and scandal of HMS Megaera.* Buxton; Moorland Publishing Co.; 1978. Pp 144.

(k) *Science and medicine*

1. Woods, R., 'Mortality and sanitary conditions in the "best governed city in the world" — Birmingham, 1870—1910,' *J. of Historical Geography* 4 (1978), 35—56.

2. Froggatt, P., 'Sir William Wilde, 1815—1876,' *P. of the Royal Irish Academy (Section C)* 77 (1977), 261—78.

3. (Anon.), 'Plate glass making in the early 19th century,' *Industrial Archaeology* 12 (1977), 111—20.

4. Makeham, P.M., 'A look at early road-making machinery,' ibid. 125–9.

5. McLaughlin, T., 'The British in the air, 1809–1903,' *History Today* 28 (1978), 73–80.

6. Howard, M. *Victorian grotesque: an illustrated excursion into medical curiosities, freaks and abnormalities, principally of the Victorian age.* London; Jupiter Books; 1977. Pp 154.

7. Rains, A.J.H. *Joseph Lister and antiseptics.* Hove; Priory Press; 1977. Pp 96.

8. Russell, C.A., 'Edward Frankland and the Cheapside chemists of Lancaster: an early Victorian pharmaceutical apprenticeship,' *Annals of Science* 35 (1978), 253–73.

9. Kittler, M.J., 'Charles Darwin's biological species concept and theory of geographical speciation: the transmutation notebooks,' ibid. 275–97.

10. Jones, O.V., 'Three Welsh obstetricians,' *T. of the Honourable Soc. of Cymmrodorion*, 1977, 173–80.

11. McLaren, A. *Birth control in nineteenth-century England.* London; Croom Helm; 1978. Pp 263.

12. Kargon, R.H. *Science in Victorian Manchester: enterprise and expertise.* Manchester UP; 1977. Pp xiii, 283.

13. Sauer, R., 'Infanticide and abortion in nineteenth-century Britain,' *Population Studies* 32 (1978), 81–94.

14. Arnold, H.J.P. *William Henry Fox Talbot: a pioneer of photography and man of science.* London; Hutchinson; 1977. Pp 383.

15. Super, R.H., 'The humanist at bay: the Arnold-Huxley debate,' Hl48, 231–45.

16. Mercer, V. *The life and letters of Edward John Dent, chronometer maker, and some account of his successors.* London; Antiquarian Horological Society; 1977. Pp xx, 829.

17. Levere, T.H., 'The rich economy of nature: chemistry in the 19th century,' Hl48, 189–200.

18. Wilson, D.B., 'Concepts of physical nature: John Herschel to Karl Pearson,' Hl48, 201–15.

19. Smith, R., 'The human significance of biology; Carpenter, Darwin and the vera causa,' Hl48, 216–30.

20. Hilts, V.L., '*Aliis exterendum*, or, the origins of the Statistical Society of London,' *Isis* 69 (1978), 21–43.

21. Geison, G.L. *Michael Foster and the Cambridge School of Physiology: the scientific enterprise in late Victorian society.* Princeton UP; 1978. Pp xxi, 402.

22. Cannon, S.F. *Science in culture: the early Victorian period.* Folkestone; Dawson; 1978. Pp xii, 296.

23. Pelling, M. *Cholera, fever and English medicine, 1825–1865.* Oxford UP; 1978. Pp x, 342.

24. Ross, J.A. *The Edinburgh School of Surgery after Lister.* Edinburgh; Churchill Livingstone; 1978. Pp x, 220.

25. Churchill, F.B., 'The Weismann-Spencer controversy over the inheritance of acquired characteristics,' *Human Implications of Scientific Advance* (P. of the XVth International Congress of the History of Science, ed. E.G. Foster; Edinburgh UP. 1978), 451–68.

(l) *Intellectual and cultural*

1. Wroughton, J., 'A student prince in Germany,' *History Today* 28 (1978), 3–13.
2. Harrington, H.R., 'Charles Kingsley's fallen athlete,' *Victorian Studies* 21 (1977), 73–86.
3. Mitchell, S., 'Sentiment and suffering: women's recreational reading in the 1860s,' ibid. 29–45.
4. Havers, M.; Grayson, E.; Shankland, P. *The royal baccarat scandal.* London; Kimber; 1977. Pp 285.
5. Scheele, G. and M. *The prince consort, a man of many facets.* London; Oresko Books; 1977. Pp 136.
6. Girouard, M. *Sweetness and light: the 'Queen Anne movement' 1860–1900.* Oxford; Clarendon; 1977. Pp 268.
7. Fasnacht, R. *Summertown since 1820.* Oxford; St Michael's Publications; 1977. Pp ix, 111.
8. Healey, E. *Lady unknown: the life of Angela Burdett-Coutts.* London; Sidgwick & Jackson; 1978. Pp 253.
9. Bassin, E. *The old songs of Skye: Frances Tolmie and her circle.* London; Routledge; 1977. Pp xxi, 227.
10. Warwick, L. *The Mackenzies called Compton: the story of the Compton Comedy Company, incorporated in the history of Northampton Theatre Royal and Opera House, 1884–1927.* Northampton; the author; 1977. Pp 328.
11. French, M. *A Victorian village: a record of the parish of Quethiock in Cornwall.* [Falmouth; Glasney Press; 1977]. Pp 112.
12. Mirsky, J. *Sir Aurel Stein: archaeological explorer.* Chicago/ London; Chicago UP; 1977. Pp xiii, 585.
13. Lloyd, F. *Woodley in the nineteenth century.* [Reading; Central Library; 1977]. Pp 92.
14. Wynn Jones, M. *George Cruickshank.* London; Macmillan; 1978. Pp 123.
15. Robinson, G. *Hedingham harvest: Victorian family life in rural England.* London; Constable; 1977. Pp 207.
16. Steele, E.D., 'The Leeds patriciate and the cultivation of learning, 1819–1905: a study of the Leeds Philosophical and Literary Society,' *P. of the Leeds Phil. and Lit. Soc.* 16 (1978), 183–202.
17. Zimmer, L.B., 'The "negative argument" in J.S. Mill's utilitarianism,' *J. of British Studies* 17 (1977/8), 119–37. With: Himmel-

farb, G., 'Reply to Louis B. Zimmer on Mill's "negative argument",' ibid. 138—40.

18. Oman, C., 'The first gothic revival in English church plate,' *Burlington Magazine* 120 (1978), 226—9.

19. Markus, J., 'Bishop Bloughram and the literary men,' *Victorian Studies* 21 (1978), 171—95.

20. Roberts, B.F., 'Printing at Aberdare, 1854—1974,' *The Library* 5th ser. 33 (1978), 125—42.

21. Clegg, J., 'John Ruskin's correspondence with Angelo Allessandri,' *B. of the John Rylands University Library of Manchester* 60 (1978), 404—33.

22. Chaloner, W.H., 'How immoral were the Victorians? A bibliographical reconsideration,' ibid. 362—75.

23. Baker, M. *The rise of the Victorian actor.* London; Croom Helm; 1978. Pp 249.

24. Guichard, K.M. *British etchers, 1850—1940.* London; Robin Garton; 1977. Pp 87 (+ 81 pp. of plates).

25. Dale, P.A. *The Victorian critics and the idea of history: Carlyle, Arnold, Pater.* Cambridge, Mass./London; Harvard UP; 1977. Pp 295.

26. O'Donnell, R., 'W.J. Donthorn (1799—1859): architecture with "great hardness and decision in the edges",' *Architectural History* 21 (1978), 83—92.

27. Roberts, B.F., 'Richard Ellis, M.A. (Edward Lhuyd and the Cymmrodorion),' *T. of the Hon. Soc. of Cymmrodorion* (1977), 131—72.

28. Britain, I.M., 'Bernard Shaw and the ethics of English socialism,' *Victorian Studies* 21 (1978), 381—401.

29. Murray, K.M.E. *Caught in the web of words: James A.H. Murray and the 'Oxford English Dictionary'.* New Haven/London; Yale UP; 1977. Pp xiv, 386.

30. Gordon, E. *The Royal Scottish Academy of Painting, Sculpture & Architecture, 1826—1976.* Edinburgh; Skilton; 1976. Pp xxiv, 272.

31. Christ, C., 'Victorian masculinity and the angel in the house,' Hg26, 146—62.

32. Mitchell, S., 'The forgotten women of the period: penny weekly family magazines of the 1840's and 1850's,' Hg26, 29—51.

33. Bingham, M. *Henry Irving and the Victorian theatre.* London; Allen & Unwin; 1978. Pp 312.

34. Marlow, J. *Mr and Mrs Gladstone: an intimate biography.* London; Weidenfeld & Nicolson; 1977. Pp xi, 324.

35. Rowell, G. *Queen Victoria goes to the theatre.* London; Elek; 1978. Pp 144.

36. Swanson, V.G. *Sir Lawrence Alma-Tadema: the painter of the Victorian vision of the ancient world.* London; Ash & Grant; 1977. Pp 144.

37. *Victoria and Albert at Cambridge: the royal visits of 1843 and 1847 as they were recorded by Joseph Romilly, Registary of the University.* Cambridge University Library; 1977. Pp 30.

38. Corrigan, P.; Gillespie, V. *Class struggle, social literacy, and idle time: the provision of public libraries in England.* Brighton; Noyce; 1978. Pp 37.

39. Dixon, R.; Muthesius, S. *Victorian architecture.* London; Thames & Hudson; 1978. Pp 288.

40. Bradley, I.P. *William Morris and his world.* London; Thames & Hudson; 1978. Pp 127.

41. Levey, M. *The case of Walter Pater.* London; Thames & Hudson; 1978. Pp 232.

42. Ransome, E. (ed.). *The terrific Kemble: a Victorian self-portrait from the writings of Fanny Kemble.* London; Hamilton; 1978. Pp xv, 272.

43. Foster, D.; Arnold, P. *100 years of test cricket, England v. Australia.* London; Hamlyn; 1977. Pp 92.

44. Tjoa, H.G. *George Henry Lewes: a Victorian mind.* Cambridge, Mass./London; Harvard UP; 1977. Pp xi, 172.

45. Frith, D. *England versus Australia: a pictorial history of the test matches since 1877.* Guildford; Lutterworth Press; 1977. Pp 304.

46. Purser, A. *Looking back at popular entertainment.* Wakefield; EP Publishing; 1978. Pp 96.

47. Robertson, D. *Sir Charles Eastlake and the Victorian art world.* Princeton/Guildford; Princeton UP; 1978. Pp xvii, 468.

48. Knoeflmacher, U.C.; Tennyson, G.B. (ed.). *Nature and the Victorian imagination.* Berkeley/London; University of California Press; 1977. Pp xxiii, 519.

49. Millard, C., 'The mind's eye: images of nature: a photo essay,' Hl48, 3—26.

50. Ford, G.H., 'The taming of space: felicitious space: the cottage controversy,' Hl48, 29—48.

51. Creese, W.L., 'Imagination in the suburb,' Hl48, 49—67.

52. Frank, E.E., 'The domestication of nature: five houses in the Lake District,' Hl48, 68—92.

53. Loomis, C.C., 'Explorations: the Arctic sublime,' Hl48, 95—112.

54. Robertson, D., 'Mid-Victorians amongst the Alps,' Hl48, 113—36.

55. Levine, G., 'High and low: Ruskin and the novelists,' Hl48, 137—52.

56. Patten, R.L., 'A surprising transformation: Dickens and the hearth,' Hl48, 153—70.

57. Griffin, A., 'The interior garden and John Stuart Mill,' Hl48, 171—86.

58. Kirchoff, F., 'A science against sciences: Ruskin's floral mythology,' Hl48, 246—58.

59. Johnson, B., 'The perfection of species and Hardy's Tess,' Hl48, 259—72.

60. Axton, W.F., 'Victorian landscape-painting: a change in outlook,' Hl48, 281–308.
61. Meisel, M., 'Half sick of shadows: the aesthetic dialogue in Pre-Raphaelite painting,' Hl48, 309–40.
62. Landow, G.P., 'The rainbow: a problematic image,' Hl48, 341–69.
63. Tennyson, G.B., 'The sacramental imagination,' Hl48, 370–90.
64. Knoeflmacher, U.L., 'Mutations of the Wordsworthian child of nature,' Hl48, 391–425.
65. Poston, L., 'Browning and the altered romantic landscape,' Hl48, 426–39.
66. Miller, J.H., 'Nature and the linguistic movement,' Hl48, 440–51.
67. Paterson, J., 'Lawrence's vital source: nature and character in Thomas Hardy,' Hl48, 455–69.
68. Litz, A.W., 'That strange abstraction "Nature": T.S. Eliot's Victorian inheritance,' Hl48, 470–88.
69. Knoeflmacher, U.C.; Tennyson, G.B., 'Afterflow and aftermath: nature, literature, science,' Hl48, 489–99.
70. Weintraub, S. *Four Rossettis: a Victorian biography*. London; W.H. Allen; 1978. Pp xiii, 303.
71. Hyman, A. *Sullivan and his satellites: a survey of English operettas, 1860–1914*. London; Elm Tree Books; 1978. Pp xvi, 224.
72. Alsop, S.M. *Lady Sackville: a biography*. London; Weidenfeld & Nicolson; 1978. Pp xii, 275.
73. Ambler, R.W., 'The transformation of harvest celebrations in nineteenth-century Lincolnshire,' *Midland History* 3/4 (1976), 298–306.
74. Walkley, C.; Foster, V. *Crinolines and crimping irons: Victorian clothes – how they were cleaned and cared for*. London; Owen; 1978. Pp 199.
75. Lucas, P., 'Provincial culture and "The Penny Brotherhood": the case of Joseph Richardson,' *T. of the Cumberland and Westmorland Antiquarian & Arch. Soc.* 78 (1978), 187–98.
76. McKibbin, R.I., 'Social class and social observation in Edwardian England,' *T. of the Royal Historical Soc.* 5th ser. 28 (1978), 175–99.
77. Bailey, P. *Leisure and class in Victorian England: rational recreation and the contest for control, 1830–1885*. London; Routledge; 1978. Pp x, 260.
78. Wilson, D.; Eisenberg, J. *Leonard Woolf: a political biography*. London; Hogarth Press; 1978. Pp 282.
79. Coustillas, P. (ed.). *London and the life of literature in late Victorian England: the diary of George Gissing, novelist*. Hassocks, Harvester Press; 1978. Pp vii, 617.
80. Knights, B. *The idea of the clerisy in the nineteenth century*. Cambridge UP; 1978. Pp ix, 274.
81. Huggett, F.E. *Victorian England as seen by 'Punch'*. London; Sidgwick & Jackson; 1978. Pp 192.

82. Young, P.M. *Alice Elgar: enigma of a Victorian lady*. London; Dibson; 1978. Pp 201.
83. Lively, J.; Rees, J. (ed.). *Utilitarian logic and politics: James Mill's 'Essay on Government', Macaulay's critique, and the ensuing debate*. Oxford; Clarendon; 1978. Pp 270.
84. Hill, A. *The family fortune: a saga of Sussex cricket*. Shoreham-by-Sea; Scan Books; [1978]. Pp xv, 152.
85. Dubbey, J.M. *The mathematical work of Charles Babbage*. Cambridge UP; 1978. Pp vii, 235.
86. Soffer, R.N. *Ethics and society in England: the revolution in the social sciences, 1870–1914*. Berkeley/London; University of California Press; 1978. Pp ix, 325.
87. Davies, C. *Brian Hatton: a biography of the artist* (1887–1916). Lavenham; T. Dalton; 1978. Pp xii, 172.
88. Strong, R. *And when did you last see your father?: the Victorian painter and British history*. London; Thames & Hudson; 1978. Pp 176.
89. Guiterman, H. *David Roberts R.A., 1796–1864*. London; [the author?]; 1978. Pp 34.
90. Agius, P. *British furniture, 1880–1925*. Woodbridge; Antique Collectors' Club; 1978. Pp 195.
91. Spalding, F. *Magnificent dreams: Burne-Jones and the late Victorians*. Oxford; Phaidon; 1978. Pp 80.
92. Munby, A.N.L. *Essays and papers* (ed. by N. Barker). London; Scolar Press; 1978. Pp xiii, 241.
93. Rees, T. *Theatre lighting in the age of gas*. London; Soc. for Theatre Research; 1978. Pp x, 238.
94. Dyer, J., 'Worthington George Smith,' Bc10, 141–79.

I. BRITAIN SINCE 1914

See also Ha10, b2, 6, 7, 52, c3, 7, d25, 31, e6, 23, 24, 28, f12, 14, 18, 30, 31, 75, g1, 41, 47, 50, h10, 11, 14, 17, 18, i1, 19, 23, j6, l10, 20, 24, 30, 68, 78, 90

(a) *General*

1. Illsley, W.A. (ed.). *The third statistical account of Scotland: The County of Angus*. Arbroath; Herald Press; 1977. Pp 630.
2. Beauman, K.B. *Green sleeves: the story of the WVS-WRVS*. London; Seeley; 1977. Pp ix, 193.
3. Zuckerman, S. *From apes to warlords: the autobiography (1904–1946) of Solly Zuckerman*. London; Hamilton; 1978. Pp xv, 447.

4. Parker, D. *Radio: the great years.* Newton Abbot; David & Charles; 1977. Pp 160.

5. Hankinson, A. *The mountain men: an early history of rock climbing in North Wales.* London; Heinemann Educational; 1977. Pp ix, 202.

6. Boardman, P. *The world of Philip Geddes: biologist, town planner, re-educator, peace-warrior.* London; Routledge; 1978. Pp x, 528.

7. *'A street door of our own': a short history of life on an LCC estate.* [London; Honor Oak Estate Association; 1977]. Pp 48.

8. Packet, C.N. *Association of lieutenants of counties and custodes rotulorum, a brief history (1907–1977).* [Bradford; the author]; 1977. Pp 48.

9. Blacker, K.C.; Lunn, R.S.; Westgate, R.G. *London's buses, vol. 1: the independent era, 1922–1934.* St Albans; H.J. Publications; 1977. Pp xii, 491.

10. Unwin, P. *The Stationers' Company, 1918–1977: a livery company in the modern world.* London; Benn; 1978. Pp 144.

11. Pollard, M. *North Sea surge: the story of the east coast floods of 1953.* Lavenham; T. Dalton; 1978. Pp 136.

12. Chown, C.H.I.; Fennerley, F.C. *Rotary in Ilford: 50 years of service, 1928–1978.* Ilford; Rotary Club; 1978. Pp 83.

13. Stoney, B. *Sibyl, Dame of Sark: a biography.* London; Hodder & Stoughton; 1978. Pp 272.

14. McNee, G. *The story of Celtic [Football Club]: an official history.* London; Paul; 1978. Pp 245.

15. Calvocoressi, P. *The British experience, 1945–75.* London; Bodley Head; 1978. Pp 253.

16. Cannadine, D., 'Politics, propaganda and art: the case of two "Worcestershire Lads",' *Midland History* 4 (1978), 97–122.

17. Fry, C. *Can you find me? A family history.* Oxford UP; 1978. Pp xii, 272.

18. Partridge, F. *A pacifist's war.* London; Hogarth Press; 1978. Pp 223.

19. Winstone, H.V.F. *Gertrude Bell.* London; Cape; 1978. Pp xiii, 322.

20. Marquis, A.G., 'Words as weapons: propaganda in Britain and Germany during the first world war,' *J. of Contemporary History* 13 (1978), 467–98.

21. Payton, J., ' "To free men alone belongs the privilege of being governed by their servants",' Bc13, 168–74.

22. Liversidge, D. *The Mountbattens: from Battenberg to Windsor.* London; A Barker; 1978. Pp xi, 163.

23. Gunston, B. *By Jupiter: the life of Sir Roy Fedden.* London; Royal Aeronautical Soc.; 1978. Pp ix, 157.

(b) *Politics*

1. Haste, C. *Keep the home fires burning: propaganda in the First World War.* London; Allen Lane; 1977. Pp x, 230.

2. Kingham, N. *United we stood: the official history of the Ulster Women's Unionist Council, 1911–1974.* Belfast; The Appletree Press; 1975. Pp 95.

3. Trory, E. *Imperialist war: further recollections of a Communist organiser.* Brighton; The Crabtree Press; 1977. Pp 242.

4. Guthrie, R.; McLean, I., 'Another part of the periphery: reactions to devolution in an English development area,' *Parliamentary Affairs* 31 (1978), 180–91.

5. Griffin, N.J., 'The response of British Labour to the importation of Chinese workers: 1916–1917,' *The Historian* 40 (1978), 252–70.

6. Miller, W.L. *Electoral dynamics in Britain since 1918.* London; Macmillan; 1977. Pp xiv, 242.

7. Jones, B. *The Russia complex: the British Labour Party and the Soviet Union.* Manchester UP; 1977. Pp x, 229.

8. Harrington, W.; Young, P. *The 1945 revolution.* London; Davis-Poynter; 1978. Pp 218.

9. Margach, J. *The abuse of power: the war between Downing Street and the media from Lloyd George to Callaghan.* London; Allen; 1978. Pp 199.

10. Rowbotham, R. *A new world for women: Stella Browne, socialist feminist.* London; Pluto Press; 1977. Pp 128.

11. Eatwell, R.; Wright, A., 'Labour and lessons of 1931,' *History* 63 (1978) 38–53.

12. Freedon, M. *The new liberalism: an ideology of social reform.* Oxford; Clarendon; 1978. Pp xi, 291.

13. Harvey, J. (ed.). *The war diaries of Oliver Harvey.* London; Collins; 1978. Pp 399.

14. McKibbin, R.I., 'Arthur Henderson as Labour leader,' *International R. of Social History* 23 (1978), 79–101.

15. Malament, B., 'British Labour and Roosevelt's New Deal: the response of the Left and the unions,' *J. of British Studies* 17/2 (1978), 136–67.

16. Newberry, J.V., 'Anti-war suffragettes,' *History* 62 (1977), 411–25.

17. Shrapnel, N. *The performers* [i.e. in parliament]. London; Constable; 1978. Pp 213.

18. Turner, J.A., 'The British Commonwealth Union and the general election of 1918,' *English Historical R.* 93 (1978), 528–59.

19. Webb, K. *The growth of nationalism in Scotland.* Glasgow; Molendinar Press; 1978. Pp x, 147.

20. Cook, C.; Ramsden, J. (ed.). *Trends in British politics since 1945.* London; Macmillan; 1978. Pp xv, 197.

21. Ramsden, J., 'The changing base of British conservatism,' Ib20, 28–46.

22. McLean, I., 'Labour since 1945,' Ib20, 47–66.

23. Steel, D., 'Nationalisation and public ownership,' Ib20, 109–31.

24. Cook, C., 'The challenge to the two-party system,' Ib20, 132—56.
25. Henig, S., 'The Europeanisation of British politics,' Ib20, 180—92.
26. Mackintosh, J.P. (ed.). *British Prime Ministers in the twentieth century: vol. 2: Churchill to Callaghan.* London; Weidenfeld & Nicolson; 1978. Pp 247.
27. Addison, P., 'Winston Churchill,' Ib26, 1—36.
28. Dowse, R.E., 'Clement Attlee,' Ib26, 37—72.
29. Blake, R., 'Anthony Eden,' Ib26, 73—117.
30. Sainsbury, K., 'Harold Macmillan,' Ib26, 118—44.
31. Iremonger, L., 'Edward Heath,' Ib26, 145—70.
32. Mackintosh, J.P., 'Harold Wilson,' Ib26, 171—215.
33. Redhead, B., 'James Callaghan,' Ib26, 216—39.
34. Whitley, P., 'The structure of democratic socialist ideology in Britain,' *Political Studies* 26 (1978), 209—31.
35. Beichmann, A., 'Hugger-mugger in Old Queen Street: the origins of the Conservative Research Department,' *J. of Contemporary History* 13 (1978), 671—88.
36. McEwen, J.M. 'The press and the fall of Asquith,' *Historical J.* 21 (1978), 863—83.
37. Cousins, P.F., 'Participation and pluralism in South London,' *London J.* 4 (1978), 204—20.
38. Brand, J. *The national government in Scotland.* London; Routledge; 1978. Pp ix, 330.
39. White, S., 'Ideological hegemony and political control: the sociology of anti-Bolshevism in Britain, 1918—1920,' *Scottish Soc. of Labour History J.* 9 (1975), 3—20.
40. Watt, D.C., 'Every war must end: war-time planning for post-war security, in Britain and America, in the wars of 1914—18 and 1939—45: the role of historical example and of professional historians,' *T. of the Royal Historical Soc.* 5th ser. 28 (1978), 159—73.
41. Wright, A.W., 'Fabianism and guild socialism: two views of democracy,' *International R. of Social History* 23 (1978), 224—41.
42. Spear, S., 'Pacifist radicalism in the post-war British party: the case of E.D. Morel, 1919—24,' ibid. 193—223.
43. Rawkins, P.M., 'Outsiders as insiders: the implications of minority nationalism in Scotland and Wales,' *Contemporary Politics* 10 (1978), 519—34.
44. Klieman, A.S., 'Emergency powers and liberal democracy in Britain,' *J. of Commonwealth and Comparative Politics* 16 (1978), 190—211.
45. Garner, J. *The Commonwealth Office, 1925—68.* London; Heinemann Educational; 1978. Pp xix, 474.
46. Birch, A.H. *Political integration and disintegration in the British Isles.* London; Allen & Unwin; 1977. Pp 183.

47. Barker, E. *Churchill and Eden at war.* London; Macmillan; 1978. Pp 346.
48. Hatfield, M. *The house the Left built: inside Labour policy-making 1970—75.* London; Gollancz; 1978. Pp 272.
49. Ramsden, J. *A history of the Conservative Party, vol. 3: the age of Balfour and Baldwin, 1902—1940.* London; Longman; 1978. Pp xiv, 413.
50. Cowling, M., 'The present position,' Bc13, 1—24.
51. Utley, T.E., 'The significance of Mrs Thatcher,' Bc13, 41—51.
52. Minogue, K., 'On hyperactivism in modern British politics,' Bc13, 117—30.
53. Griffiths, R., 'British conservatism and the lessons of the continental right,' Bc13, 131—40.
54. Biffen, J., 'The conservatism of Labour,' Bc13, 155—67.
55. Gale, G., 'The popular communication of a conservative message,' Bc13, 175—93.
56. Dony, J.G., 'The 1919 peace riots at Luton,' Bc10, 205—33.

(c) *Constitution, administration and law*

1. Poulton, R. *Kings and commoners, 1901—1936.* Tadworth; World's Work; 1977. Pp 152.
2. Stuart, D. *County borough: the history of Burton upon Trent, 1901—1974; part 2: 1914—1974.* [Burton Town Hall; 1977]. Pp 299.
3. Dunn, J.A., 'The importance of being earmarked: transport policy and highway finance in Great Britain and the United States,' *Comparative Studies in Society and History* 20 (1978), 29—53.
4. Thornhill, W. (ed.). *The modernization of British government.* Totowa, N.J.; Rowman & Littlefield; 1975. Pp ix, 322.
5. Ryle, M.T., 'Developments in the parliamentary system,' Ic4, 7—29.
6. Jones, G.W., 'Development of the Cabinet,' Ic4, 31—62.
7. Clarke, R., 'The machinery of government,' Ic4, 63—95.
8. Allen, P., 'The civil service,' Ic4, 97—115.
9. Garner, J.F., 'The redress of grievances,' Ic4, 117—39.
10. Thornhill, W., 'The nationalized industries,' Ic4, 141—66.
11. Cross, C.A., 'The local government system,' Ic4, 167—207.
12. Carter, K.S., 'The local government service,' Ic4, 209—36.
13. Lawrence, R.J., 'Northern Ireland,' Ic4, 237—59.
14. Plimmer, C. and D. *A matter of expediency: the jettison of Admiral Sir Dudley North.* London; Quartet Books; 1978. Pp 179.
15. Sellwood, A.V. *Police Strike — 1919.* London; W.H. Allen; 1978. Pp 214.
16. Peele, G., 'The developing constitution,' Ib20, 1—27.

17. Philip, A.B., 'Devolution or regionalism,' Ib20, 157—80.
18. Harrison, R., 'New light on the police and the hunger marchers,' *Soc. for the Study of Labour History* 37 (1978), 17—49.

(d) *External affairs*

1. Raffo, P., 'The founding of the League of Nations Union,' *Canadian J. of History* 12 (1977), 193—206.
2. Megaw, M.R., 'The scramble for the Pacific: Anglo-United States rivalry in the 1930s,' *Historical Studies* 17 (1977), 458—73.
3. Stafford, D.A.T., 'SOE and British involvement in the Belgrade coup d'état of March 1941,' *Slavic Review* 36 (1977), 399—419.
4. Offner, A.A., 'Appeasement revisited: the United States, Great Britain, and Germany, 1933—1940,' *J. of American History* 64 (1977), 373—93.
5. Douglas, R., 'Chamberlain and Eden, 1937—38,' *J. of Contemporary History* 13 (1978), 97—116.
6. Stanwood, F., 'Revolution and the "old reactionary policy": Britain in Persia, 1917,' *J. of Imperial and Commonwealth History* 6 (1978), 144—65.
7. Bowden, T. *The breakdown of public security: the case of Ireland 1916—1921 and Palestine 1936—1939.* London; Sage Publications; 1977. Pp xiv, 342.
8. Thorne, C., 'Chatham House, Whitehall, and far eastern issues; 1941—45,' *International Affairs* 54 (1978), 1—29.
9. Koliopoulos, J.S. *Greece and the British connection, 1935—1941.* Oxford; Clarendon; 1977. Pp 315.
10. Medlicott, W.M.; Dakin, D.; Lambert, M.E. (ed.). *Documents on British foreign policy, 1919—1939; 1st series, vol. 21: German reparation and Allied military control, 1923.* London; HMSO; 1978. Pp cxv, 1027.
11. Medlicott, W.M.; Dakin, D.; Lambert, M.E. (ed.). *Documents on British foreign policy, 1919—1929; 2nd series, vol. 16: The Rhineland crisis and the ending of sanctions, March 2—July 30, 1936.* London; HMSO; 1977. Pp lxi, 811.
12. Dutton, D.J., 'The Calais Conference of December 1915,' *Historical J.* 21 (1978), 143—56.
13. Smith, T., 'A comprehensive study of French and British decolonization,' *Comparative Studies in Society and History* 20 (1978), 70—102.
14. Niedhart, G., 'Appeasement: Die Britische Antwort auf die Krise des Weltreichs und des internationalen Systems vor dem zweiten Weltkrieg,' *Historische Zeitschrift* 226 (1978), 67—88.
15. Dutton, D., 'The deposition of King Constantine of Greece, June 1917: an episode in Anglo-French diplomacy,' *Canadian J. of History* 12 (1978), 325—45.
16. Olu Agbi, S., 'The Foreign Office and Yoshida's bid for rapproche-

ment with Britain in 1936–1937: a critical reconsideration of the Anglo-Japanese conversation,' *Historical J.* 21 (1978), 173–9.

17. Morris, J. *Farewell the trumpets: an imperial retreat.* London; Faber; 1978. Pp 576.

18. Sharp, T. *The wartime alliance and the zonal division of Germany.* Oxford UP; 1976. Pp ix, 220.

19. Hetherington, P. *British paternalism and Africa, 1920–1940.* London; Cass; 1978. Pp xvi, 196.

20. Louis, W.R. *Imperialism at bay: the United States and the decolonization of the British Empire.* Oxford; Clarendon; 1977. Pp xvi, 595.

21. Milburn, J.F. *British business and Ghanaian independence.* London; C. Hurst; 1978. Pp x, 156.

22. Bunselmeyer, R.E. *The cost of war: British economic war aims and the origins of reparation.* Hamden, Conn.; Archon Books; 1975. Pp 249.

23. Mondon, L.M., 'The process of decolonization,' Ic4, 261–88.

24. Holt, S.C., 'Britain and Europe,' Ic4, 289–311.

25. Fest, W. *Peace or partition: the Habsburg monarchy and British policy, 1914–1918.* London; Prior; 1978. Pp xiv, 276.

26. Newman, M., 'The origins of Munich: British policy in Danubian Europe 1933–1937,' *Historical J.* 21 (1978), 371–86.

27. Orde, A. *Great Britain and international security, 1920–1926.* London; Royal Historical Society; 1978. Pp viii, 244.

28. Resis, A., 'The Church-Stalin secret "percentages" agreement on the Balkans, Moscow, October 1944,' *American Historical R.* 83 (1978), 368–87.

29. Thornton, A.P. *Imperialism in the twentieth century.* Minneapolis; University of Minnesota Press; 1977. Pp xiv, 363.

30. Egerton, G.W., 'Britain and the "great betrayal": Anglo-American relations and the struggle for United States ratification of the treaty of Versailles, 1919–1920,' *Historical J.* 21 (1978), 885–911.

31. Goold, J.D., 'Lord Hardinge as ambassador to France, and the Anglo-French dilemma over Germany and the Near East, 1920–1922,' ibid. 913–37.

32. Kedourie, E. *England and the Middle East: the destruction of the Ottoman empire, 1914–1921* (2nd ed.). Hassocks; Harvester Press; 1978. Pp 238.

33. White, S., ' "Anti-Bolshevic control officers" and British foreign policy, 1918–1920,' *Co-Existence* 13/2 (1976), 144–56.

34. Dilks, D., 'The twilight war and the fall of France; Chamberlain and Churchill in 1940,' *T. of the Royal Historical Soc.* 5th ser. 28 (1978), 61–86.

35. Coupland, I.F.S., 'The Hyderabad (Berar) Agreement of 1933: a case study in Anglo-Indian diplomacy,' *J. of Imperial and Commonwealth History* 6 (1978), 281–99.

36. Buckley, R., 'Britain and the emperor: the Foreign Office and constitutional reform in Japan, 1945—1946,' *Modern Asian Studies* 12 (1978), 553—70.

37. Wingarten, A.; Malcolm, J., 'British foreign policy to 1985: J. Food and agricultural policy — the international context,' *International Affairs* 54 (1978), 393—404.

38. Freedman, L., 'British foreign policy to 1985: IV, Britain and the arms trade,' ibid. 377—92.

39. Wight, M., 'Is the Commonwealth a non-Hobbesian institution?,' *J. of Commonwealth and Comparative Politics* 16 (1978), 119—33.

40. Cohen, M.J. *Palestine — retreat from the mandate: the making of British policy, 1936—45.* London; Elek; 1978. Pp xiii, 239.

41. Douglas-Home, C. *Evelyn Baring: the last proconsul.* London; Collins; 1978. Pp 344.

42. Wasserstein, B. *The British in Palestine: the mandatory government and the Arab-Jewish conflict 1917—1929.* London; Royal Historical Soc.; 1978. Pp xii, 278.

43. Tarver, L., 'In wisdom's house: T.E. Lawrence in the Near East,' *J. of Contemporary History* 13 (1978), 585—608.

44. Arslanian, A.H., 'British wartime pledges, 1917—18: the Armenian case,' ibid. 517—30.

45. Fraser, T.G., 'India in Anglo-Japanese relations during the First World War,' *History* 63 (1978), 366—82.

46. Sharp, A., 'Britain and the protection of minorities at the Paris Peace Conference 1919,' Bc15, 170—88.

47. Harkness, D., 'Britain and the independence of the Dominions: the 1921 crossroads,' Bc9, 141—59.

(e) Religion

1. Winnett, A.R. *Attempt great things: the diocese of Guildford, 1927—1977.* Guildford Diocesan Board of Finance; 1977. Pp 84.

2. Hardyman, J.T.; Orchard, R.K. *Two minutes from Sloane Square: a brief history of the Conference of Missionary Societies in Great Britain and Ireland, 1912—1977.* London; The Conference; 1977. Pp 56.

3. Hill, F., 'From Canon Foster to the Lincolnshire Archives Office,' *Lincolnshire History and Archaeology* 13 (1978), 71—3.

4. Robbins, K.G., 'Free churchmen and the twenty years' crisis,' *Baptist Q.* 27 (1978), 346—57.

5. Norman, E.R., 'Christianity and politics,' Bc13, 69—81.

6. Thompson, D.M., 'Theological and sociological approaches to the motivation of the ecumenical movement,' Bc7, 467—79.

7. Wilson, B.R., 'Becoming a sectarian: motivation and commitment,' Bc7, 481—506.

(f) *Economic affairs*

1. Costigliola, F.C., 'Anglo-American financial rivalry in the 1920s,' *J. of Economic History* 37 (1977), 911–34.
2. Tomlinson, J.D., 'Unemployment and government policy between the wars: a note,' *J. of Contemporary History* 13 (1978), 65–78.
3. Pressnell, L.S., '1925: the burden of sterling,' *Economic History R.* 2nd ser. 31 (1978), 67–88.
4. Griffin, C.P., 'The Leicestershire miners and the mining dispute of 1926,' *International R. of Social History* 22 (1977), 299–312.
5. Taylor, A.J., '1926 – general strike and miners' lock-out,' *University of Leeds R.* 20 (1977), 172–91.
6. Hannah, L.; Kay, J.A. *Concentration in modern industry: theory, measurement, and the U.K. experience.* London; Macmillan; 1977. Pp xiv, 144.
7. Tucker, D.G., 'Refuse destructors and their use for generating electricity: a century of development,' *Industrial Archaeology R.* 2 (1977–8), 5–27.
8. Richards, P.S., 'Point of Ayr Colliery [Flintshire] : the geology, geography and history of a coalmine,' ibid. 28–37.
9. Mant, A. *The rise and fall of the British manager.* London; Macmillan; 1977. Pp 142.
10. Pasold, E.W. *Ladybird, ladybird: a story of private enterprise.* Manchester UP; 1977. Pp xvi, 668.
11. Beaumont, P.B., 'Experience under the fair wages resolution of 1946,' *Industrial Relations J.* 8 (1977), 34–42.
12. Evans, E.W.; Creigh, S.W. (ed.). *Industrial conflict in Britain.* London; Cass; 1977. Pp vii, 292.
13. Lowe, R., 'The erosion of state invention in Britain, 1917–24,' *Economic History R.* 2nd ser. 31 (1978), 270–86.
14. Nockolds, H. *Lucas: the first hundred years.* Vol. 2: the successors. Newton Abbot; David & Charles; 1978. Pp 432.
15. Bartlett, J.N. *Carpeting the millions: the growth of Britain's carpet industry.* Edinburgh; Donald; 1978. Pp xiii, 296.
16. Hoe, S. *The man who gave his company away: a biography of Ernest Bader, founder of the Scott Bader Commonwealth.* London; 1978. Pp xiii, 242.
17. Campbell, R.H., 'The North British Locomotive Company between the wars,' *Business History* 20 (1978), 201–34.
18. Capie, F., 'The British tariff and industrial protection in the 1930's,' *Economic History R.* 2nd ser. 31 (1978), 399–409.
19. Fearon, P., 'The vicissitudes of a British aircraft company: Handley Page Ltd. between the wars,' *Business History* 20 (1978), 63–86.
20. Hemingway, J. *Conflict and democracy: studies in trade union government.* Oxford; Clarendon; 1978. Pp 184.

21. Patinkin, D. *Keynes, Cambridge and 'the general theory': the process of criticism and discussion connected with the development of The General Theory.* London; Macmillan; 1977. Pp xii, 182.

22. Nash, J.; Learmonth, B.; Cluett, D., 'Croydon aerodrome,' *Transport History* 8 (1977), 254–72.

23. Percival, G. *The government's industrial estates in Wales, 1936–1975.* Pontypridd; Welsh Development Agency; [1978]. Pp 125.

24. Swann, B.; Turnbull, M. *Records of interest to social scientists, 1919 to 1939: employment and unemployment* [at Public Record Office]. London; HMSO; 1978. Pp v, 590.

25. Soldon, N.C. *Women in British trade unions, 1874–1976.* Dublin; Gill and Macmillan; 1978. Pp xiii, 226.

26. Whetham, E.H. *The agrarian history of England and Wales, vol. 8: 1914–39.* Cambridge UP; 1978. Pp xxiii, 353.

27. Sinclair, P., 'Economic debates,' Ib20, 67–87.

28. Taylor, R., 'Scapegoats for national decline: the trade unions since 1945,' Ib20, 88–108.

29. Lowe, R., 'The failure of consensus in Britain: the National Industrial Conference, 1919–1921,' *Historical J.* 21 (1978), 649–75.

30. Shaw, G. *Processes and patterns in the geography of retail change, with special reference to Kingston upon Hull, 1880–1950.* University of Hull; 1978. Pp ix, 109.

31. Barty-King, H. *Food for man and beast: the story of the London Corn Trade Association, the London Cattle Food Trade Association, and the Grain and Feed Trade Association, 1878–1978.* London; Hutchinson; 1978. Pp 107.

32. Holt, G.O. *The north west.* Newton Abbot; David & Charles; 1978. Pp 256.

33. Taylor, D. *Fortune, fame and folly: British hotels and catering from 1878 to 1978.* London; IPC Business Press; 1977. Pp vii, 177.

34. Hebden, J., 'Men's and women's pay in Britain, 1968–1975,' *Industrial Relations J.* 9/2 (1978), 56–70.

35. Gill, C.G., 'Employer organisation in the UK chemical industry,' ibid. 37–47.

36. Concannon, H., 'The growth of arbitration work in ACAS,' ibid. 12–18.

37. Wolpin, K.I., 'An economic analysis of crime and punishment in England and Wales, 1894–1967,' *J. of Political Economy* 86 (1978), 815–40.

38. Archer, J.K., 'De Havilland aircraft (1908–1960),' *Transport History* 9 (1978), 60–9.

39. Neeld, P., 'Wolverhampton motorcycles: the growth and decline of an industry,' ibid. 52–9.

40. Hugill, A. *Sugar and all that: a history of Tate & Lyle.* London; Gentry Books; 1978. Pp 320.

41. Bibby, J.B. and C.L. *A miller's tale: a history of J. Bibby & Sons Ltd, of Liverpool.* Liverpool; J. Bibby & Sons; 1978. Pp xi, 218.
42. *Reviews of United Kingdom statistical sources, vol. 10: ports and inland waterways, and civil aviation.* Oxford; Pergamon; 1978.
43. Hoole, K. *North eastern branch lines since 1925.* London; I. Allan; 1978. Pp 128.
44. Nock, O.S. *The last years of British Railways steam: reflections ten years after.* Newton Abbot; David & Charles; 1978. Pp 143.
45. Bayliss, D.A. *The Post Office Railway, London.* Sheffield; Turntable Publications; 1978. Pp 96.
46. Newton, D. *Men of mark: makers of East Midland Allied Press.* Peterborough; The Press; 1977. Pp xv, 239.
47. Palfreyman, D. *John Jeyes: the making of a household name.* Thetford; Jeyes Group Ltd; 1977. Pp 127.
48. Munby, D.L.; Watson, A.H. *Inland transport statistics, Great Britain, 1900–1970. Vol. 1: Railways, public road passenger transport, London's transport.* Oxford; Clarendon; 1978. Pp xii, 693.
49. Klapper, C.F. *Golden age of buses.* London; Routledge; 1978. Pp xii, 248.
50. Johnson, E.S. *The shadow of Keynes: understanding Keynes, Cambridge and Keynesian economics.* Oxford; Blackwell; 1978. Pp xiv, 253.
51. Blackaby, F.T. (ed.). *British economic policy 1960–74.* Cambridge UP; 1978. Pp xviii, 687.
52. Robertson, A.J., 'Clydeside revisited: a reconsideration of the Clyde shipbuilding industry, 1919–38,' Bc2, 258–78.
53. Flinn, M.W., 'Exports and the Scottish economy in the depression of the 1930s,' Bc2, 279–93.

(g) *Social Structure and Population*

1. Bulmer, M. *Mining and social change: Durham County in the twentieth century.* London; Croom Helm; 1978. Pp 318.
2. Caffrey, K. *'37–'39: last look round.* London; Gordon and Cremonesi; 1978. Pp 175.
3. Hamilton, P. *Three years of the duration: the memoirs of a munition worker, 1914–1918.* London; Owen; 1978. Pp 125.
4. Sproule, A. *The social calendar.* Poole; Blandford Press; 1978. Pp 144.
5. Thomas, K. *Commuting flows and the growth of London's new towns, 1951–1971.* Milton Keynes; The Open University; 1977. Pp 35.
6. Miles, R.; Phizacklea, A. *The TUC, black workers and New Commonwealth immigration.* Bristol; the University (SSRC Research Unit on Ethnic Relations, working paper no. 6); 1977. Pp 44.

7. Guppy, A. *Children's clothes, 1939–1970: the advent of fashion.* Poole; Blandford Press; 1978. Pp 346.
8. Hall, R. (ed.). *Dear Dr Stopes: sex in the 1920s.* London; Deutsch; 1978. Pp 218.
9. Clarke, H.E. *The Waterloo Cup, 1922–1977.* Hindhead; Spur Publications; 1978. Pp viii, 440.
10. Deakin, N., 'The vitality of a tradition [immigration in the 20th century],' Bc1, 158–85.

(h) *Social policy*

1. *St Katharine's College, Liverpool: notes and memoirs for the golden jubilee of Warrington Training College Incorporated.* [The College] ; 1977. Pp 82.
2. *Bell, book and boys: one hundred years of the Whitstable Boys' School.* [The School] ; 1977. Pp xiv, 76.
3. Duclaud-Williams, R.H. *The politics of housing in Britain and France.* London; Heinemann; 1978. Pp viii, 280.
4. Potter, S. *Transport and new towns.* Vol. 1: The historical perspective – the development of transportation planning for new communities, 1898–1939. Vol. 2: The transport assumptions underlying the design of Britain's new towns, 1946–1976. Milton Keynes; The Open University; 1976. Pp iv, 63; ix, 64–272.
5. Seaman, R.D.H. *St Peter's College, Saltley, 1944–1978.* Birmingham; The College; 1978. Pp 215.
6. Navarro, V. *Class struggle, the state and medicine: an historical and contemporary analysis of the medical sector in Great Britain.* London; Martin Robertson; 1978. Pp xviii, 156.
7. Morgan, M.C. *Bryanston, 1929–1978.* Blandford; Bryanston School; 1978. Pp 123.
8. Gray, J.G. *Prophet in plimsoles: an account of the life of Colonel Ronald B. Campbell.* Edinburgh; Edina Press; 1978. Pp xiii, 135.
9. Thornton, A.H.; Stephens, M.D. (ed.). *The university and its region: the extra-mural contribution.* Nottingham; the University; 1977. Pp 192.
10. Egerton, V. *A history of Hollings College, 1901–1976.* Manchester; the author; 1978. Pp viii, 116.
11. Booth, A.E., 'An administrative experiment in unemployment policy in the thirties,' *Public Administration* 56 (1978), 139–57.
12. Henderson, J.L. *Irregularly bold: a study of Bedales School.* London; Deutsch; 1978. Pp 154.
13. Worsthorne, P., 'Too much freedom,' Bc13, 141–54.
14. Aldcroft, D.H., 'control of the liquor trade in Great Britain, 1914–21,' Bc2, 242–57.

(i) *Naval and Military*

1. Jordan, G. (ed.). *Naval warfare in the twentieth century, 1900–1945: essays in honour of Arthur Marder*. London; Croom Helm; 1977. Pp 243.
2. Douglas, W.A.B., 'Conflict and innovation in the Royal Canadian Navy,' Ii1, 210–32.
3. Kemp, P., 'From Tryon to Fisher: the regeneration of a navy,' Ii1, 16–31.
4. Mackay, R.F., 'Historical reinterpretation of the Anglo-German naval rivalry,' Ii1, 32–44.
5. Kennedy, P.M., 'Fisher and Tirpitz: political admirals in the age of imperialism,' Ii1, 45–59.
6. Schofield, B., ' "Jacky" Fisher, H.M.S. *Indomitable*, and the Dogger Bank action: a personal memoir,' Ii1, 60–69.
7. Sweetman, J., 'Coronel: anatomy of a disaster,' Ii1, 70–89.
8. Higham, R., 'The peripheral weapon in wartime: a case study,' Ii1, 90–104.
9. Gusewell, J., 'Science and the admiralty during World War I: the case of the Board of Invention and Research,' Ii1, 105–17.
10. Slesson, J., 'Admiralty command policy in two world wars: reflections based on Arthur Marder's story of Jutland,' Ii1, 118–27.
11. Gretton, P., 'The U-Boat campaign in two world wars,' Ii1, 128–40.
12. Braisted, W.R., 'On the American KGD and red-orange plans 1919–39,' Ii1, 167–85.
13. Hunt, B.; Schurman, D., 'Prelude to Dieppe: thoughts on combined operations policy in the "Raiding Period", 1940–42,' Ii1, 186–209.
14. Hodges, G.W.T., 'African manpower statistics for the British forces in East Africa, 1914–1918,' *J. of African History* 19 (1978), 101–16.
15. Bialer, U., ' "Humanization" of air warfare in British foreign policy on the eve of the Second World War,' *J. of Contemporary History* 13 (1978), 79–96.
16. Parsons, E.B., 'Why the British reduced the flow of American troops to Europe in August–October 1918,' *Canadian J. of History* 12 (1977), 173–9.
17. Campbell, J.P., 'D-Day 1943: the limits of strategic deception,' ibid. 207–37.
18. Roskill, S.W. *Churchill and the admirals*. London; Collins; 1977. Pp 351.
19. Mason, U.S. *The Wrens, 1917–77*. Reading; Educational Explorers; 1977. Pp 160.
20. Lamb, D. *Mutinies, 1917–1920*. Oxford; Solidarity; 1977. Pp 32.

21. Jones, I.W. *Luftwaffe over Clwyd: the air war over Denbighshire and Flintshire, 1939—45*. Llandudno; Pegasus Press; 1977. Pp 46.

22. Richards, D. *Portal of Hungerford: the life of Marshall of the Royal Air Force Viscount Portal of Hungerford*. London; Heinemann; 1977. Pp xii, 436.

23. Jones, R.V. *Most secret war* [memoirs]. London; Hamilton; 1978. Pp xx, 556.

24. Thorne, C. *Allies of a kind: the United States, Britain and the war against Japan, 1941—1945*. London; Hamilton; 1978. Pp xxiii, 772.

25. Bidwell, S. *The Women's Royal Army Corps*. London; Cooper; 1977. Pp xv, 141.

26. Marder, A.J. *From the Dreadnought to Scapa Flow; vol. 3: Jutland and after (May 1916—December 1916)*. 2nd ed. revised and enlarged. Oxford UP; 1978. Pp 400.

27. Allison, W.; Fairley, J. *The monocled mutineer* [Private Percy Toplis]. London; Quartet Books; 1978. Pp 206.

28. Hill, R. *The great coup* [bombing in the second World War]. London; Arlington Books; 1977. Pp 208.

29. McNish, R. *Iron Division: the history of the 3rd Division*. London; I. Allan; 1978. Pp 192.

30. Perrett, B. *Tank tracks to Rangoon: the story of British Armour in Burma*. London; Hale; 1978. Pp 255.

31. Sims, J. *Arnhem spearhead: a private soldier's story*. London; Imperial War Museum; 1978. Pp xiii, 118.

32. Moulton, J.L. *Battle for Antwerp: the liberation of the city and the opening of the Scheldt, 1944*. London; I. Allan; 1978. Pp 208.

33. Piekalkiewicz, J. *Arnhem, 1944* (translated by H.A. and A.J. Barker). London; I. Allan; 1977. Pp 112.

34. Adams, R.J.Q. *Arms and the wizard: Lloyd George and the Ministry of Munitions, 1915—1916*. London; Cassell; 1978. Pp xv, 252.

35. Barker, R. *The hurricanes* [aeroplanes]. London; Pelham; 1978. Pp xi, 207.

36. Bowyer, C. *Sopwith camel: king of combat*. Falmouth; Glasney Press; 1978. Pp 192.

37. Glubb, J.B. *Into battle: a solider's diary of the Great War*. London; Cassell; 1978. Pp 223.

38. Jackson, W.G.F. *'Overlord': Normandy 1944*. London; Davis-Poynter; 1978. Pp 250.

39. Leasor, J. *Boarding party* [south-east Asian war]. London; Heinemann; 1978. Pp xvi, 204.

40. McAughtry, S. *The sinking of the Kenbane Head*. Belfast; Blackstaff Press; 1977. Pp 139.

41. Revell, A. *The vivid air: Gerald and Michael Constable Maxwell,*

fighter pilots in both world wars. London; Kimber; 1978. Pp 255.

42. Turnbull, P. *Dunkirk: anatomy of disaster.* London; Batsford; 1978.

43. Warner, P. *The Zeebrugge raid.* London; Kimber; 1978. Pp 238.

44. Winter, D. *Death's men: soldiers of the Great War.* London; Allen Lane; 1978. Pp 283.

45. Englander, D.; Osborne, J., 'Jack, Tommy and Henry Dubb: the armed forces and the working class,' *Historical J.* 21 (1978), 593—619.

46. Franks, N.L.R. *Fighter leader: the story of Wing Commander Ian Gleed, DSO, DFC, Croix de Guerre.* London; Kimber; 1978. Pp 207.

47. Carver, M.B.C. *Harding of Petherton: Field Marshal.* London; Weidenfeld & Nicolson; 1978. Pp ix, 246.

48. Lucas, J.; Barker, J. *The killing ground: the battle of the Falaise Gap, August 1944.* London; Batsford; 1978. Pp 176.

49. Hoyt, E.P. *The life and death of HMS Hood.* London; A. Barker; 1977. Pp vii, 144.

50. Haines, G. *Cruiser at war.* London; I. Allan; 1978. Pp 144.

51. Lewin, R. *Ultra goes to war: the secret story.* London; Hutchinson; 1978. Pp 398.

52. Thetford, O. *British naval aircraft since 1912.* (4th ed.). London; Putnam; 1978. Pp 480.

53. Fawkes, R. *Fighting for a laugh: entertaining the British and American armed forces, 1939—1946.* London; Macdonald & Janes's; 1978. Pp 192.

54. Callahan, R. *Burma, 1942—1945.* London; Davis-Poynter; 1978. Pp 190.

55. Pack, S.W.C. *Invasion North Africa, 1942.* London; I. Allan; 1978. Pp 112.

56. Paul, C. *Sywell: the story of an English aerodrome, 1928—1978.* Sywell; the aerodrome; 1978. Pp ix, 94.

57. Young, R.A. *The flying bomb.* London; I. Allan; 1978. Pp 160.

58. Baker, J. (Lord). *Enterprise versus bureaucracy: the development of structural air-raid precautions during the 2nd World War.* Oxford; Pergamon; 1978. Pp 110.

59. Terraine, J. *To win a war: 1918, the year of victory.* London; Sidgwick & Jackson; 1978. Pp 284.

60. Verney, P. *Anzio 1944: an unexpected fury.* London; Batsford; 1978. Pp 265.

61. Macdonald, L. *They call it Passchendaele: the story of the Third Battle of Ypres and of the men who fought in it.* London; Joseph; 1978. Pp xv, 253.

62. Hancock, T.N. *Bomber country: a history of the Royal Air Force in Lincolnshire.* Lincolnshire Library Service; 1978. Pp 142.

63. James, E.A. *British regiments, 1914—1918.* London; Samson Books; 1978. Pp 140.

Ii64

64. James, E.A. *British regiments, 1914–1918.* London; Samson Books; 1978. Pp 140.
65. Goulding, J.; Moyes, P. *RAF Bomber Command and its aircraft, 1941–1945.* London; I. Allan; 1978. Pp 128.

(j) *Intellectual and cultural*

1. Ibberson, M. *For joy that we are here: rural music schools, 1929–1950.* London; Bedford Square Press; 1977. Pp 97.
2. Trenn, T.J. *The self-splitting atom: the history of the Rutherford-Soddy collaboration.* London; Taylor & Francis; 1977. Pp xii, 175.
3. Nuttall, G.F., 'The genius of R.T. Jenkins,' *T. of the Honourable Soc. of Cymmrodorion*, 1977, 181–94.
4. Hodges, S. *Gollancz: the story of a publishing house, 1928–1978.* London; Gollancz; 1978. Pp 256.
5. Hallett, M. *John Logie Baird and television.* Hove; Priory Press; 1978. Pp 95.
6. Masterman, J.C. *On the chariot wheel: an autobiography.* Oxford UP; 1975. Pp x, 384.
7. Elsom, J. *The history of the National Theatre.* London; Cape; 1978. Pp x, 342.
8. Fisher, D., 'Rockefeller philanthropy and the British Empire: the creation of the London School of Hygiene and Tropical Medicine,' *History of Education* 7 (1978), 129–43.
9. Handley, G. *The College of All Saints, 1964–1978: an informal history of one hundred years, 1878–1978.* London; The College; 1978. Pp 47.
10. Holt, J.C. *The University of Reading: the first fifty years.* Reading UP; 1977. Pp xii, 372.
11. Howarth, T.E.B. *Cambridge between two wars.* London; Collins; 1978. Pp 258.
12. Law, J. (ed.). *The Lion and Unicorn Press: a short history and a list of publications, 1953–1978.* London; Lion and Unicorn Press; 1978. Pp 24.
13. Greenall, R.L., 'Rural life and the camera in the twenties,' *Northamptonshire Past and Present* 6 (1979), 107–9.
14. Westendorp, T.A., ' "De vorlog geschreven": verkenning van het terrein van de twintigste-eeuwse oorlogsliteratur in Engeland en Amerika,' *Tijdschrift voor Geschiedenis* 91 (1978), 490–507.
15. Armes, R. *A critical history of the British cinema.* London; Secker & Warburg; 1978. Pp 374.
16. Mitchell, D.; Evans, J. *Benjamin Britten, 1913–1976: pictures from a life: a pictorial biography.* London; Faber; 1978. Pp 216.
17. Spender, S. *The thirties and after: poetry, politics, people (1933–75).* London; Fontana; 1978. Pp 286.

116

18. Roberts, J. *Everton: the official centenary history*. London; Mayflower; 1978. Pp 240.
19. Hurd, M. *The ordeal of Ivor Gurney*. Oxford UP; 1978. Pp x, 230.
20. Bamford, T.W. *The University of Hull: the first fifty years*. Oxford UP; 1978. Pp x, 290.
21. Peacock, F.C. (ed.). *Jealott's Hill: fifty years of agricultural research, 1928–1978*. Bracknell; Imperial Chemical Industries; 1978. Pp viii, 160.
22. Norton, B., 'Fisher and the neo-Darwinian synthesis,' *Human Implications of Scientific Advance* (P. of the XVth International Congress of the History of Science, ed. E.G. Forbes; Edinburgh, 1978), 481–94.
23. Letwin, S.R., 'On conservative individualism,' Bc13, 52–68.
24. Casey, J., 'Tradition & authority,' Bc13, 82–100.
25. Scruton, R., 'The politics of culture,' Bc13, 101–16.
26. Werskey, G. *The visible college* [20th century scientists]. London; Allen Lane; 1978. Pp 376.

J. MEDIEVAL WALES

(a) *General*

1. Davies, R.R. *Lordship and society in the March of Wales, 1282–1400*. Oxford; Clarendon; xvi, 512.
2. Davies, W. *An early Welsh microcosm: studies in the Llandaff Charters*. London; Royal Historical Society; 1978. Pp xi, 208.
3. Richter, M., 'The political and institutional background to national consciousness in medieval Wales,' Bc9, 37–55.

(b) *Politics*

1. Miller, M., 'The foundation-legend of Gwynedd in the Latin texts,' *B. of the Board of Celtic Studies* 27 (1978), 515–32.
2. Davies, W., 'Land and power in early medieval Wales,' *Past and Present* 81 (1978), 3–23.

(c) *Constitution, Administration and Law*

1. Jenkins, D., 'The significance of the Law of Hywel,' *T. of the Honourable Soc. of Cymmrodorion*, 1977, 54–76.

(d) *External Affairs*

1. Carr, A.D., 'A Welsh knight in the Hundred Years War: Sir

Gregory Sais,' *T. of the Honourable Soc. of Cymmrodorion*, 1977, 40—53.

(e) *Religion*

1. Jones, J.T., 'Saint David,' *National Library of Wales J.* 20 (1978), 209—39.

(f) *Economic Affairs*

1. Morgan, R., 'The foundation of the borough of Welshpool,' *The Montgomeryshire Collections* 65 (1978 for 1977), 7—24.
2. Taylor, A.J., 'The earliest burgesses of Flint and Rhuddlan,' *Flintshire Historical Soc. J.* 27 (1978 for 1975/6), 152—60.
3. Carr, A.D., 'Medieval fisheries in Anglesey,' *Maritime Wales* 3 (1978), 5—9.

(g) *Social Structure and Population*

1. Jones, F., 'Cadets of Golden Grove III: Vaughan of Derllys and Vaughan of Plas Gwyn,' *T. of the Honourable Soc. of Cymmrodorion*, 1977, 77—102.
2. Griffiths, R.A. *Boroughs of Medieval Wales.* Cardiff; University of Wales Press; 1978. Pp 338.
3. Knight, J.K., 'Usk Castle and its affinities,' Bc6, 139—54.

(h) *Naval and Military*

1. Griffiths, R.A., 'The three castles at Aberystwyth,' *Archaeologia Cambrensis* 126 (1977 for 1976), 74—87.
2. Warner, P. *Famous Welsh battles: where battles were fought, why they were fought, how they were won and lost.* London; Fontana; 1977. Pp 160.
3. Taylor, A.J., 'Castle-building in thirteenth-century Wales and Savoy,' *P. of the British Academy* 63 (1978 for 1977), 215—92.

(i) *Intellectual and Cultural*

1. Huws, D., 'A Welsh manuscript of Bede's *De natura rerum*,' *B. of the Board of Celtic Studies* 27 (1978), 491—504.
2. Thorpe, L. (ed.). *The journey through Wales; and, The description of Wales, by Gerald of Wales.* Harmondsworth; Penguin; 1978. Pp 333.

(j) *Topography*

1. Bird, A.J. *History on the ground: an inventory of unrecorded*

material relating to the mid-Anglo-Welsh borderland, with intro-
ductory chapters. Cardiff; University of Wales Press; 1977. Pp
xiv, 135.

2. Davies, D. *Welsh place-names and their meanings.* [Brecon; the
author; 1977] . Pp 60.

3. Caple, R.; Jarvis, P.H.; Webster, P.V., 'The deserted village of
Runston, Gwent: a field survey,' *B. of the Board of Celtic
Studies* 27 (1978), 638–52.

4. Jones, H.C. *Place names in Glamorgan.* Risca; Starling Press;
1976. Pp 56.

5. Pratt, D., 'Fourteenth-century Bromfield and Yale – a gazetteer
of lay and ecclesiastical territorial units,' *Denbighshire Historical
Soc. T.* 27 (1978), 89–149.

6. White, R.B., 'Bodbenwyn,' *Anglesey Antiquarian Soc. and Field
Club T.* (1977/8), 19–33.

K. SCOTLAND BEFORE THE UNION

(a) *General*

1. Brown, J.M. (ed.). *Scottish society in the fifteenth century.*
London; Arnold; 1977. Pp xi, 273.

2. Macdougall, N.A.T., 'The sources: a reappraisal of the legend,'
Ka1, 10–32.

3. Bannerman, J., 'The Lordship of the Isles,' Ka1, 209–40.

4. Lockhart, S.M. *Seven centuries: a history of the Lockharts of Lee
and Carnwath.* Carnwath; the author; 1977. Pp x, 317.

5. Royal Commission on the Ancient and Historical Monuments of
Scotland. *Lanarkshire: an inventory of the prehistoric and
Roman monuments.* Edinburgh; HMSO; 1978. Pp xxxiv, 173.

6. Bogdan, N.Q.; Wordsworth, J.W. *The medieval excavations at the
High Street, Perth, 1975–76: an interim report.* Perth High
Street Arch. Excavation Committee, 1978. Pp 32.

7. Donaldson, G. *Scottish kings* (revd. ed.). London; Batsford; 1977.
Pp 224.

8. Grant, A., 'The development of the Scottish peerage,' *Scottish
Historical R.* 57 (1978), 1–27.

9. Landsborough, D.M. *Our Galloway ancestors revisited: a genealogical and historical investigation particularly in the Galloway
region of Scotland . . .* Thornton Heath; the author; 1978. Pp
148.

10. Mackay, R.L. *The Clan Mackay: its origin, history and dispersal*
(3rd ed.). [Wolverhampton; the author; 1978] . Pp 39.

11. Mackie, J.D. *A history of Scotland* (2nd ed.). London; Allen Lane;
1978. Pp 414.

12. MacLennan, R.G. *The history of the MacLennans.* Ullapool; the author; 1978. Pp 264.
13. McNaughton, D. *The clan McNaughton.* Edinburgh; Albyn Press; 1977. Pp 87.

(b) *Politics*

1. Goldwater, E.D., 'The Scottish franchise: lobbying during the Cromwellian Protectorate,' *Historical J.* 21 (1978), 27—42.
2. Miller, M., 'Eanfrith's Pictish son,' *Northern History* 14 (1978), 47—66.

(c) *Constitution, administration and law*

1. Lyall, R.J., 'The medieval Scottish coronation service: some seventeenth-century evidence,' *Innes R.* 28 (1977), 3—21.
2. Brown, J.M., 'The exercise of power,' Ka1, 33—65.
3. Robertson, J.J., 'The development of the law,' Ka1, 136—52.

(d) *External affairs*

1. Evans, N.E., 'The meeting of the Scottish and Russian ambassadors in London in 1601,' *Slavonic and East European R.* 55 (1977), 519—28.
2. Crawford, B.E., 'Scotland's foreign relations: Scandinavia,' Ka1, 85—100.
3. Macdougall, N.A.T., 'Scotland's foreign relations: England and France,' Ka1, 101—11.
4. Stewart, A.M. (ed.). *Scots in the Baltic: proceedings of a seminar held in the University of Aberdeen, Saturday, 29th October, 1977.* University of Aberdeen; [1978?]. Pp 44 + 8.
5. Mennie, D.M., 'Some Baltic Scots in literature,' Kd4, 3—8.
6. Manson, T.M.Y., 'Bothwell abroad,' Kd4, 9—18.
7. Dukes, P., 'Scots in Russia,' Kd4, 19—30.
8. Smouth, T.C., 'Scottish trade with Scandinavia and the Baltic: 16th—18th centuries,' Kd4, 31—33.
9. Gray, M., 'Scotland and the herring trade with the Baltic,' Kd4, 34—8.
10. Stewart, A.M., 'Scots in the southern Baltic countries,' Kd4, 41—4.

(e) *Religion*

1. Cowan, I.B. *Regional aspects of the Scottish Reformation.* London; Historical Association (Pamphlet G92); 1978. Pp 40.
2. Kirk, J. (ed.). *The records of the synod of Lothian and Tweed-*

dale, 1589–1596, 1640–1649. Edinburgh; Stair Soc.; 1977. Pp xxx, 325.

3. McRoberts, D., 'The Greek bishop of Dromore [Irish bishop of Greek extraction resident in Scotland] ,' *Innes R.* 28 (1977), 22–38.

4. Murray, A.L.; Donaldson, G., 'Sutherland in 1575 and 1586: problems of the reformed ministry,' *Scottish History R.* 56 (1977), 182–4.

5. Cowan, I.B., 'Church and society,' Ka1, 112–35.

6. Eeles, F.C.; Clouston, R.W.M., 'The church and other bells of Wigtownshire,' *P. of the Soc. of Antiquaries of Scotland* 107 (1978 for 1975/6), 261–74.

7. Hay, G., 'The late medieval development of the High Kirk of St Giles, Edinburgh,' ibid. 242–61.

8. Lamb, R.G., 'The Burri stacks of Culswick, Shetland, and other paired stack-settlements,' ibid. 144–54.

9. Towill, E.S. *The saints of Scotland.* Edinburgh; St Andrew Press; 1978. Pp ix, 148.

10. Lynch, M., 'The "Faithful Brethren" of Edinburgh: the acceptable face of protestantism,' *B. of the Institute of Historical Research* 51 (1978), 194–9.

11. Mackay, P.H.R. *Sanctuary and the privileges of St John.* Edinburgh; West Lothian History Soc.; 1978. Pp 24.

12. Baker, D., ' "A nursery of saints": St Margaret of Scotland reconsidered,' Bc12, 119–41.

13. Cruden, S., 'The cathedral and relics of St Magnus, Kirkwall,' Bc6, 85–97.

(f) *Economic affairs*

1. Woodward, D., 'Anglo-Scottish trade and English commercial policy during the 1660s,' *Scottish Historical R.* 56 (1977), 153–74.

2. Zupko, R.E., 'The weights and measures of Scotland before the Union,' ibid. 119–45.

3. Lythe, S.G.E., 'Economic life,' Ka1, 66–84.

4. Graham-Campbell, J.A., 'The Viking-age silver and gold hoards of Scandinavian character from Scotland,' *P. of the Soc. of Antiquaries of Scotland* 107 (1978 for 1975/6), 114–35.

(g) *Social Structure and Population*

1. Schofield, J., 'Excavations south of Edinburgh High Street, 1973–4,' *P. of the Soc. of Antiquaries of Scotland* 107 (1978 for 1975/6), 155–241.

2. Barrow, G.W.S., 'The aftermath of war: Scotland and England in

the late thirteenth and early fourteenth centuries,' *T. of the Royal Historical Soc.* 5th ser. 28 (1978), 103—25.

3. Cameron, D.K. *The ballad and the plough: a portrait of the life of the old Scottish farmtouns.* London; Gollancz; 1978. Pp 253.

(h) *Naval and Military*

1. Macgregor, A., 'Two antler crossbow nuts and some notes on the early development of the crossbow,' *P. of the Soc. of Antiquaries of Scotland* 107 (1978 for 1975/6), 317—21.
2. Alcock, L., 'A multi-disciplinary chronology for Alt Clut, Castle Rock, Dumbarton,' *P. of the Soc. of Antiquaries of Scotland* 107 (1978 for 1975/6), 101—13.
3. Macivor, I., 'Craignethan Castle, Lanarkshire: an experiment in artillery fortification,' Bc6, 238—61.

(i) *Intellectual and cultural*

1. Durkan, J.; Russell, J., 'John Grierson's book-list,' *Innes R.* 28 (1977), 39—49.
2. Stell, G., 'Architecture: the changing needs of society,' Ka1, 153—83.
3. MacQueen, J., 'The literature of fifteenth-century Scotland,' Ka1, 184—208.
4. Lyall, R.J., 'Dunbar and the Franciscans,' *Medium Aevum* 46 (1977), 253—8.
5. Findlay, A.M., ' "Cunninghamia" — Timothy Pont's contribution to Scottish cartography re-examined,' *Scottish Geographical Magazine* 94 (1978), 36—47.
6. Durkacz, V., 'The source of the language problem in Scottish education, 1688—1709,' *Scottish Historical R.* 57 (1978), 28—39.
7. Durkan, J., 'Henry Scrimgeour, renaissance bookman,' *Edinburgh Bibliographical Soc. T.* 5 (1978), 1—31.
8. Adam, I. *Witch hunt: the great Scottish witchcraft trials of 1697.* London; Macmillan; 1978. Pp 256.
9. Cambridge, E., 'The early building-history of St Andrews cathedral, Fife, and its context in northern transitional architecture,' *Antiquaries J.* 57 (1978), 277—88.
10. Durkan, J.; Pringle, R.V., 'St Andrews additions to Durkan & Ross: some unrecorded Scottish pre-Reformation ownership inscriptions in St Andrews University Library,' *The Bibliotheck* 9 (1978), 13—20.
11. Thompson, F. *A Scottish bestiary: the lore and literature of Scottish beasts.* Glasgow Molendinar Press; 1978. Pp 92.
12. Larner, C.; Lee, C.H.; McLachlan, H.V. *A source-book of Scottish witchcraft.* Glasgow; Dept of Sociology (of the University); 1977. Pp xv, 335.

13. Fenwick, H. *Scotland's abbeys and cathedrals.* London; Hale; 1978. Pp 288.

L. IRELAND TO ca. 1640

(a) *General*

1. Binchy, D.A., 'Irish history and Irish law, II,' *Studia Hibernica* 16 (1977–8 for 1976), 7–45.
2. Clarke, A., 'Colonial identity in early seventeenth-century Ireland,' Bc9, 57–71.
3. Moody, T.W., 'Irish history and Irish mythology,' *Hermathena* 124 (1978), 7–24.
4. Ó Corráin, D., 'Nationality and kingship in pre-Norman Ireland,' Bc9, 1–35.
5. Cregan, D.F., 'Early modern Ireland [review article],' *Irish Historical Studies* 20 (1978 for 1977), 272–85.
6. Bottigheimer, K.S., 'Kingdom and colony: Ireland in the westward enterprise, 1536–1660,' Bc14, 45–65.
7. Canny, N., 'Rowland White's "Discors touching Ireland", c. 1569,' *Irish Historical Studies* 20 (1978 for 1977), 439–63.

(b) *Politics*

1. Dalton, G.F., 'The alternating dynasties, 734–1002,' *Studia Hibernica* 16 (1976 [1977–8]). 46–53.
2. Fallon, Niall. *The Armada in Ireland.* London; Stanford Maritime; 1977. Pp x, 236.
3. Lydon, J.F., 'The Braganstown massacre, 1329,' *J. of the County Louth Arch. and Historical Soc.* 19 (1978 for 1977), 5–16.
4. Martin, F.X. *No hero in the house: Diarmait Mac Murchada and the coming of the Normans to Ireland.* Dublin; National University of Ireland; 1977. Pp 26.
5. Sheehy, M. *When the Normans came to Ireland.* Cork; Mercier Press; 1975. Pp 105.
6. Ellis, S.G., 'Tudor policy and the Kildare ascendancy in the lordship of Ireland, 1496–1534,' *Irish Historical Studies* 20 (1978 for 1977), 235–71.

(c) *Constitution, Administration and Law*

1. Treadwell, V., 'The establishment of the form of the Irish customs, 1603–13,' *English Historical R.* 93 (1978), 580–602.
2. Ellis, S.G., 'The struggle for control of the Irish mint, 1460–c. 1506,' *P. of the Royal Irish Academy* 78 C (1978), 17–36.

3. Ellis, S.G., 'Privy seals of chief governors in Ireland, 1392–1560,' *B. of the Institute of Historical Research* 51 (1978), 187–94.
4. Treadwell, V., 'The Irish customs administration in the sixteenth century,' *Irish Historical Studies* 20 (1978 for 1977), 384–417.

(d) *External Affairs*

1. Dillon, M., 'The Irish settlements in Wales,' *Celtica* 12 (1977), 1–11.
2. Coombes, J.; Ware, N.J., 'The letter-book of General de Zubiaur: a calendar of the "Irish" letters,' *J. of the Cork Historical and Arch. Soc.* 83 (1978), 50–8.

(e) *Religion*

1. Mooney, C. *The friars of Broad Lane: the story of a Franciscan friary in Cork, 1229–1977.* Cork; Tower Books; 1977. Pp 101.
2. Bradshaw, B., 'Sword, Word and strategy in the Reformation in Ireland,' *Historical J.* 21 (1978), 475–502.
3. Conlan, P. *Franciscan Ireland: the story of seven hundred and fifty years of the friars minor in Ireland with notes on all the major sites associated with the friars and a brief description of the other members of the Franciscan family in Ireland.* Dublin; Mercier Press; 1978. Pp 116.
4. Hanson, R.P.C., 'The date of St. Patrick,' *B. of the John Rylands University Library of Manchester* 61 (1978), 60–77.
5. Morrisey, T., 'The Irish student diaspora in the sixteenth century and the early years of the Irish College at Salamanca,' *Recusant History* 14 (1978), 242–60.
6. Miller, D.W., 'Presbyterianism and "modernization" in Ulster,' *Past and Present* 80 (1978), 66–90.
7. Hood, A.B.E. (ed.). *St. Patrick: his writings and Muirchu's 'Life'.* London; Phillimore; 1978. Pp 101.

(f) *Economic affairs*

1. Dykes, D.W., 'The Anglo-Irish coinage of Edward III,' *British Numismatic J.* 46 (1976), 44–50.
2. Mac Niocaill, G., 'Land-transfer in sixteenth-century Thomond: the case of Domhnall Óg Ó Cearnaigh,' *North Munster Antiquarian J.* 17 (1977 for 1975), 43–5.
3. Mac Niocaill, G., 'Cairt le Walter de Lacy [a charter of Walter de Lacy],' *Galvia* 11 (1977), 54–6.
4. Aalen, F.A.H. *Man and the landscape in Ireland.* London; Academic Press; 1978. Pp xi, 343.
5. Nicholls, K.W. *Land, law and society in sixteenth century Ireland.* Dublin; National University; [1976?]. Pp 26.

6. Woodward, D., 'Sixteenth-century shipping: the charter-party of the *Grace* of Newton, 1572,' *Irish Economic and Social History* 5 (1978), 64—9.

(g) *Social structure and population*

1. Barnwell, S., 'Plunkett of Loughcrew,' *Irish Genealogist* 5 (1977), 422—7.
2. Barnwell, S., 'The ancestry of St. Oliver Plunket: a genealogical puzzle,' ibid. 428—30.
3. Gallwey, H., 'The Cusack family of counties Meath and Dublin (continued,' ibid. 464—70.
4. Gallwey, H., 'Tobin of Kilnagranagh,' ibid. 491—5.
5. Nicholls, K., 'The Kavanaghs,' ibid. 435—47.
6. Ó Corráin, D., 'The families of Corcumroe,' *North Munster Antiquarian J.* 17 (1977 for 1975), 21—30.
7. Slevin, G., 'Funeral entries from County Clare in the seventeenth century,' ibid. 63—7.
8. Canny, N., 'Dominant minorities: English settlers in Ireland and Virginia, 1550—1650,' Bc15, 51—69.
9. Canny, N., 'The permissive frontier: social control in English settlements in Ireland and Virginia, 1550—1650,' Bc14, 17—44.
10. Maclysaght, E. *The surnames of Ireland* (3rd revd. ed.). Dublin; Irish Academic Press; 1978. Pp xxi, 377.
11. Robinson, P., 'British settlement in County Tyrone, 1610—1666,' *Irish Economic and Social History* 5 (1978), 5—26.

(h) *Naval and Military*

1. Harbison, P., 'Native Irish arms and armour in medieval Gaelic literature,' *Irish Sword* 12 (1977 for 1976), 173—99, 270—84.

(i) *Intellectual and cultural*

1. Bradshaw, B., 'Fr. Wolfe's description of Limerick city, 1574,' *North Munster Antiquarian J.* 17 (1977 for 1975), 47—53.
2. Dolley, M., 'A further note on the fourteenth-century armorial of Ireland,' ibid. 31—3.
3. Hunt, J., 'The influence of alabaster carvings on medieval sculpture in Ennis friary,' ibid. 35—41.
4. Dumville, D.N., 'Ulster heroes in the early Irish annals: a caveat,' *Éigse* 17/1 (1977), 47—54.
5. Ó Cathasaigh, T. *The heroic biography of Cormac mac Airt.* Dublin Institute of Advanced Studies; 1977. Pp 138.
6. Ó Cuív, B., 'The earl of Thomond and the poets, A.D. 1572,' *Celtica* 12 (1977), 124—45.
7. Westropp, M.S.D. *Irish glass: a history of glass-making in Ireland*

from the sixteenth century (revd. ed.). Dublin; Allen Figgis; 1978. Pp 248.

8. Harbison, P.; Potterton, H.; Sheehy, J. *Irish art and architecture from prehistoric to the present.* London; Thames & Hudson; 1978. Pp 272.

9. O'Meara, J.J. (ed.). *Navigatio Sancti Brendani abbatis: the voyage of Saint Brendan — journey to the promised land.* Dublin; Dolmen Press; 1978. Pp xxiii, 70.

10. Schauman, B.T., 'The Irish script of the MS Milan, Bibliotheca Ambrosiana, S. 45 sup (ante ca. 625),' *Scriptorium* 32 (1978), 3—18.

11. Scott, B.G., 'Iron "slave-collars" from Lagore crannog, Co. Meath,' *P. of the Royal Irish Academy* 78C:8 (1978), 213—30.

12. Sweetman, P.D., 'Archaeological excavations at Trim Castle, Co. Meath, 1971—74,' *P. of the Royal Irish Academy* 78 C:6 (1978), 127—98.

13. Walsh, L. *Richard Heaton of Ballyskenagh, 1601—1666.* Roscrea; Parkmore Press; 1978. Pp 111.

14. Bradshaw, B., 'Native reaction to the westward enterprise: a case-study in Gaelic ideology,' Bc14, 66—80.

15. Browne, T.L., 'Irish attitudes toward education and learning,' *Studies in Medieval Culture* 11 (1977), 27—32.

M. IRELAND SINCE ca. 1640

See also Le1, i8

(a) *General*

1. Maclysaght, E. *Changing times: Ireland since 1898 as seen by Edward Maclysaght.* Gerrards Cross; Smythe; 1978. Pp 248.

2. Magnusson, M. *Landlord or tenant? A view of Irish history.* London; Bodley Head; 1978. Pp 155.

3. Dolan, L. *The third earl of Leitrim.* [Dundalk] ; the author; 1978. Pp 134.

4. Mansergh, N. *The prelude to partition: concepts and aims in Ireland and India.* Cambridge UP; 1978. Pp 62.

5. Miller, D.W. *Queen's rebels: Ulster loyalists in historical perspective.* Dublin; Gill & Macmillan; 1978. Pp xiii, 194.

6. Tierney, M. *Modern Ireland since 1850* (revd. ed.). Dublin; Gill & Macmillan; 1978. Pp 241.

(b) *Politics*

1. Fitzpatrick, D. *Politics and Irish life, 1913—1921.* Dublin; Gill & Macmillan; 1977. Pp xxi, 394.

2. Fitzpatrick, D., 'The geography of Irish nationalism, 1910–1921,' *Past and Present* 78 (1978), 113–44.

3. Mair, P. *The break-up of the United Kingdom: the Irish experience of regional change, 1918–49.* Glasgow; Univ. of Strathclyde Centre for the Study of Public Policy; 1978. Pp 21.

4. O'Mahony, T.P. *The politics of dishonour: Ireland, 1916–1977.* Dublin; Talbot Press; 1977. Pp viii, 151.

5. Malcolmson, A.P.W. *John Foster: the politics of the Anglo-Irish ascendancy.* Oxford UP; 1978. Pp xxviii, 504.

6. O'Connell, M.R. (ed.). *The correspondence of Daniel O'Connell, vol. 4: 1829–1832.* Dublin; Stationery Office; 1977. Pp ix, 494.

7. Carty, X. *In bloody protest: the tragedy of Patrick Pearse.* Dublin; Able Press; 1978. Pp 154.

8. Boyce, D.G.; Hazelhurst, C., 'The unknown chief secretary: H.E. Duke and Ireland, 1916–18,' *Irish Historical Studies* 20 (1977), 286–311.

9. Faulkner, B. *Memoirs of a statesman.* London; Weidenfeld & Nicolson; 1978. Pp xiii, 306.

10. Mandle, W.F., 'The I.R.B. and the beginnings of the Gaelic Athletic Association,' *Irish Historical Studies* 20 (1977), 418–38.

11. Moody, T.W. *The Ulster question, 1603–1973* (3rd ed.). Dublin; Mercier Press; 1978. Pp viii, 134.

12. Powell, J.E., 'Kilmainham — the treaty that never was,' *Historical J.* 21 (1978), 949–59.

13. Wilkinson, B. *The zeal of the convert* [Erskine Childers]. Gerrards Cross; Smythe; 1978. Pp viii, 256.

14. Ó Broin, L., 'Revolutionary nationalism in Ireland: the I.R.B., 1858–1924,' Bc9, 97–119.

15. Beames, M.R., 'Rural conflict in pre-famine Ireland: peasant assassinations in Tipperary 1837–1847,' *Past and Present* 81 (1978), 74–91.

(c) *Constitution, Administration and Law*

1. Fanning, R. *The Irish Department of Finance, 1922–58.* Dublin; Institute of Public Administration; 1978. Pp xxi, 707.

2. McColgan, J., 'Implementing the 1921 treaty: Lionel Curtis and constitutional procedure,' *Irish Historical Studies* 20 (1977), 312–33.

3. Oliver, J.A. *Working at Stormont: memoirs.* Dublin; Institute of Public Administration; 1978. Pp 251.

(d) *External Affairs*

1. Keatinge, P. *A place among the nations: issues of Irish foreign policy.* Dublin; Institute of Public Administration; 1978. Pp viii, 287.

Md2

2. Dwyer, T.R. *Irish neutrality and the USA, 1939–47.* Dublin; Gill
& Macmillan; 1978. Pp xi, 241.

(e) *Religion*

1. Conlan, P. *St Anthony's College of the Irish Franciscans, Louvain.*
Dublin; Assisi Press; 1977. Pp 60.
2. Walker, L.H. (ed.). *One man's famine: one man's tribute to
Brother Paul James O'Connor on his centenary, 17th April 1978.*
[Galway; Patrician Books; 1977?]. Pp 104.
3. Larkin, E. *The Roman Catholic Church and the creation of the
modern Irish state, 1878–1886.* Philadelphia; American Philosophical Soc.; 1975. Pp xxiv, 412.
4. Bowen, D. *The protestant crusade in Ireland, 1800–70: a study
of protestant-catholic relations between the Act of Union and
Disestablishment.* Dublin; Gill & Macmillan; 1978. Pp xv, 412.
5. Carroll, K.L., 'Quaker weavers at Newport, Ireland, 1720–1740,'
J. of the Friends' Historical Soc. 54 (1976), 15–27.
6. O'Donoghue, P., 'The Holy See and Ireland, 1780–1802,' *Archi-
vium Hibernicum* 34 (1976/7), 99–108.
7. Faulkner, A. (ed.). *Liber Dubliniensis: chapter documents of the
Irish Franciscans, 1719–1875.* Killiney; Franciscan Friars;
1978. Pp xvi, 400.
8. Newsinger, J., ' "I bring not peace but a sword": the religious
motif in the Irish War of Independence,' *J. of Contemporary
History* 13 (1978), 609–28.
9. Hanson, R.P.G., 'William Connor Magee,' *Hermathena* 124
(1978), 42–55.
10. MacLennan, J.M. *From shore to shore: the life and times of the
Rev. John MacLennan of Belfast, P.E.I.* Edinburgh; Knox
Press; 1978. Pp vii, 96.
11. d'Alton, I., 'A contrast in crises: southern Irish Protestantism,
1820–43,' Bc15, 70–83.
12. Holmes, R.F.G., 'Dr Henry Cooke: the Athanasius of Irish
presbyterianism,' Bc7, 367–80.

(f) *Economic affairs*

1. Pollard, M., 'White paper-making in Ireland in the 1690s,' *P. of
the Royal Irish Academy (Section C)* 77 (1977), 223–34.
2. Crawford, W.H. (ed.). *Letters from an Ulster land agent, 1774–
85: the letter-books of John Moore of Clough, County Down.*
Belfast; Public Record Office of Northern Ireland; 1976. Pp
xxxiii, 82.
3. Bowie, G., 'Early stationary steam engines in Ireland,' *Industrial
Archaeology R.* 2 (1978), 168–74.
4. Kennedy, L., 'Retail markets in rural Ireland at the end of the

128

nineteenth century,' *Irish Economic and Social History* 5 (1978), 46—63.

(g) *Social structure and population*

1. Dupâquier, J., 'Les aventures démographiques comparées de la France et de l'Irlande (XVIIIe—XXe siècles),' *Annales* 33 (1978), 143—55.
2. Goodall, D., 'The freemen of Wexford, 1776,' *Irish Genealogist* 5 (1977), 448—63.
3. Kelly, K., 'Extracts from the census of 1821: barony of Iverk, parish of Pollrone,' ibid. 552—6.
4. MacCarvill, E., 'Johnsons — lineal descendants of Uí Néill,' *North Munster Antiquarian J.* 17 (1977 for 1975), 55—62.
5. McKenna, E.E., 'Age, region and marriage in post-famine Ireland: an empirical examination,' *Economic History R.* 2nd ser. 31 (1978), 238—56.
6. O Danachair, C., 'Emigration from county Clare,' *North Munster Antiquarian J.* 17 (1977 for 1975), 69—76.
7. O'Ferrall, F., 'The population of a rural pre-famine parish: Templebredin, counties Limerick and Tipperary, in 1834,' ibid. 91—101.
8. Seoighe, M., 'Fragments from lost census returns: entries relating to the Kilfinane district,' ibid. 83—90.
9. Walton, J., 'The family of Aylward — VII,' *Irish Genealogist* 5 (1977), 506—21.
10. Clarkson, L.A., 'Household and family structure in Armagh city, 1770,' *Local Population Studies* 20 (1978), 14—31.
11. Cartland, G. and J.B. *The Irish Cartlands and Cartland genealogy.* [Bromsgrove; the authors; 1978]. Pp 174.
12. Rudnitzky, H. *The Careys.* Belfast; Blackstaff Press; 1978. Pp 70.
13. Webb, C.R., 'Some Irish poor in Lambeth, 1834—46,' *Irish Ancestor* 10 (1978), 108—15.
14. Moore, B.F.E.; Kenny, M., 'Monumental inscriptions in the church and graveyard of Agher, Co. Meath,' ibid. 129—39.
15. Hepburn, A.C., 'Catholics in the north of Ireland, 1850—1921: the urbanization of a minority,' Bc15, 84—101.
16. Clarkson, L.A., 'An anatomy of an Irish town: the economy of Armagh, 1770,' *Irish Economic and Social History* 5 (1978), 27—45.

(h) *Naval and military*

1. Wall, R., 'Irish officers in the Spanish service,' *Irish Genealogist* 5 (1977), 431—4.
2. Ó Snodaigh, P., 'Nótaí ar Óglaigh, ar Chaithearnaigh, ar Mhílístigh is ar Oráistigh Chontae na Gaillimhe, 1: Na hÓglaigh [Notes on

the Volunteers, Yeomen, Militiamen and Orangemen of co. Galway, 1: The Volunteers] ,' *Galvia* 11 (1977), 1—31.

3. Black, E., 'John Tennent, 1777—1813, United Irishman and chevalier de la legion d'honneur,' *The Irish Sword* 13 (1977), 158—9.

4. Kerrigan, P.M., 'The capture of the *Hoche* in 1798,' ibid. 123—7.

5. Lambert, E., 'General Francis Burdett O'Connor,' ibid. 128—33.

6. Muenger, E.A., 'A national reserve for Ireland: the story of an aborted force, 1910—14,' ibid.

7. Van Brock, F.W., 'Defeat at Les Platons, 1792,' ibid. 89—105.

8. de Breffny, B., 'Letters from Connaught to a Wild Goose,' *Irish Ancestor* 10 (1978), 81—98.

(i) *Intellectual and cultural*

1. Evans, D. *An introduction to modern Ulster architecture.* Belfast; Ulster Architectural Heritage Soc.; 1977. Pp vii, 93.

2. Dixon, H.; Kenmuir, K.; Kennett, J. *Historic buildings, groups of buildings, buildings of architectural importance in Donaghadee and Portpatrick.* Belfast; Ulster Architectural Heritage Soc.; 1977. Pp 49.

3. Hewon, M., 'The diaries of John Singleton of Quinville, co. Clare,' *North Munster Antiquarian J.* 17 (1977 for 1975), 103—9.

4. McAuliffe, E.; Walton, J., 'Monumental inscriptions from Chapelizod,' *Irish Genealogist* 5 (1977), 496—505.

5. Mac Lochlainn, A., 'The Irish language in Clare and north Tipperary, 1820: Bishop Mant's enquiry,' *North Munster Antiquarian J.* 17 (1977 for 1975), 77—82.

6. Ó Brion, L., 'Cúlra réabhlóideach W.B. Yeats [W.B. Yeats' revolutionary background] ,' *Galvia* 11 (1977), 32—53.

7. Morris, H., 'Extracts from Ramsey's Waterford chronicle, 1777,' *Irish Genealogist* 5 (1977), 471—90.

8. Hogan, R.; Kilroy, J. *The modern Irish drama: a documentary history; vol. 3: the Abbey Theatre — the years of Synge, 1905—1909.* Dublin; Dolmen Press; 1978. Pp 385.

9. Parkes, S.M. *Irish education in the British parliamentary papers in the nineteenth century and after (1801—1920).* Cork UP; 1978. Pp 68.

10. Campbell, G.; Crowther, S. *Historic buildings, groups of buildings, areas of architectural importance in the town of Carrickfergus.* Belfast; Ulster Architectural Heritage Soc. 1978. Pp 39.

11. Hamlyn, R., 'An Irish Shakespeare gallery,' *Burlington Magazine* 120 (1978), 515—29.

12. Iske, B. *The green cockatrice.* Dublin; Meath Arch. and Historical Soc.; 1978. Pp 205.

13. Acton, C. *Irish music and musicians.* Dublin; Eason & Son; 1978. Pp [28].

14. Ó Canainn, T. *Traditional music in Ireland.* London; Routledge; 1978. Pp x, 145.
15. Tuohy, M. *Belfast Celtic* [football club]. Belfast; Blackstaff Press; 1978. Pp 82.
16. Murphy, W.M. *Prodigal father: the life of John Butler Yeats (1832–1922).* Ithaca/London; Cornell UP; 1978. Pp 680.
17. Finneran, R.J. *The olympian and the leprechaun: W.B. Yeats and James Stephens.* Dublin; Dolmen Press; 1978. Pp 36.
18. Akenson, D.H.; Crawford, W.H. *Local poets and social history: James Orr, bard of Ballycarry.* Belfast; Public Record Office of Northern Ireland; 1977. Pp viii, 130.

(j) *Local History*

1. (Anon.) *Glimpses of old Newtownards.* [Ards Historical Soc.; 1977]. Pp 57.
2. Mullin, T.H. *Coleraine in by-gone centuries.* Coleraine; the author; 1976. Pp 189.
3. Mullin, T.H. *Coleraine in Georgian times.* Coleraine; the author; 1977. Pp 207.
4. Rutherford, G. *Parish of Islandmagee.* Belfast; Ulster Historical Foundation; 1977. Pp xv, 101.
5. Mac Lochlainn, T. *The story of Killure, Fohenagh and Kilgerill parish over a period of almost 200 years.* [Ballinasloe; the author; 1975]. Pp 54.
6. Mac Suibhne, P. *Kildare in 1798.* Naas; Leinster Leader Ltd; 1978. Pp 259.
7. O'Sullivan, H., 'The Cromwellian and Restoration settlements in the civil parish of Dundalk,' *J. of the County Louth Arch. and Historical Soc.* 19 (1978 for 1977), 24–58.
8. Flood, D.T., 'Dublin Bay in the 18th century,' *Dublin Historical Record* 31 (1978), 129–41.

AUTHOR INDEX

Abbott, P.E., Hj16
Aalen, F.H.A., Lf4
Abercrombie, N.J., Ge9
Acaster, E.J.T., Gf41
Ackerman, R.W., Ee22
Acton, C., Mi13
Adam, I., Ki8
Adams, I.H., Ba15
Adams, L., Ej15
Adams, M.M., Ei5
Adams, R., Ei59
Adams, R.J.Q., Ii34
Adams, S.L., Fb47
Addison, P., Ib27
Addison, W., Ab35
Addyman, P.V., Df7; Eh7
Agius, P., Hl90
Airs, M., Fk29
Akenson, D.H., Mi18
Albury, W.R., Fk15
Alcock, L., Kh2
Aldcroft, D.H., Ih14
Alexander, G., Fa11
Alexander, J.J.G., De1; Ei41
Alexander, M.J., Bb118
Allan, A.R., Ab26
Allen, J.S., Gj4
Allen, P., Ic8
Allison, W., Ii27
Allott, S., Bb86
Almasy, R., Fe27
Almond, J.K., Hf71
Alsop, S.M., Hl72
Altick, R.D., Bb102
Alvey, R.C., Eh6; Fa23
Ambirajan, S., Hf61
Ambler, R.W., Hl73
Anderson, B.L., Gf58
Anderson, M., Hc5
Anderson, M.W., Fe51
Anderson, R.G.W., Gj11
Anderson, W., Ba53

Andrews, C.T., Bb42
Andrews, K.R., Bc14; Fd6
Andrews, S., Gi42
Anglim, J., Fj8
Angus-Butterworth, L.M., Ej25
Anselment, R.A., Fe46
Appleby, A.B., Fh12
Appleby, J.P., Ff20; Gf42
Apted, M.R., Bc6; Fg20
Archer, J.K., If38
Archibald, M.M., Ef6
Ardal, P.S., Gi16, 43
Argall, F., Hj2, 8
Armes, R., Ij15
Armstrong, N.E.S., Ab9
Armstrong, P., Ek12
Arnold, H.J.P., Hk14
Arnold, J., Fk50
Arnold, P., Hl43
Aronstam, R.A., De4
Arslanian, A.H., Id44
Arundel, D., Bb68
Ashcroft, M.Y., Gh26
Ashley, K.M., Ei18
Ashley, M., Fb8
Askwith, B., Hg61
Aston, M., Ca33
Aston, M.A., Eg5
Aston, T.H., Ei34
Atkin, M., Dd4
Atkins, P.J., Hf78
Auksi, P., Fe40
Austen, B., Ba48
Austin, F., Ga9
Avent, R., Df8
Avery, M.E., Gb7
Axton, M., Fc4
Axton, W.F., Hl60
Aylmer, G.E., Fe58, h7

Babington, A., Ba40
Backhouse, J., Fj4

133

Bird, A.J., Jj1
Bird, B., Eb22
Birrell, J., Ef18
Bishop, H., Ej47
Bishop, T.A.M., De12
Bismanis, M.R., Ej3, 37
Bittle, W.G., Fg3
Black, E., Mh3
Blackaby, F.T., If51
Blacker, K., Ia9
Blackman, M.E., Ff14
Blackwood, B.G., Fa36
Blake, N.F., De6
Blake, R., Ib29
Blanchard, I., Ef1
Blatcher, M., Fc25
Blaxland, Bb10
Blethen, H.J., Fe10, 37
Bley, H., Hd9
Baber, J., Ga3
Bloom, E.A., Gi32
Bloom, L.D., Gi32
Blunt, C.E., Dd13
Boardman, P., Ia6
Bogaers, J.E., Cb6
Bogdan, N.Q., Ka6
Boler, J., Ei6
Bonsall, H.E., He24
Bonwick, C., Gb8
Booker, F., Hf11
Boon, G.C., Ca6, 22, 34, 35, 56, 63
Booth, A.E., Ih11
Borne, P., Ej35
Boswell, J., Gi46
Bottigheimer, K.S., La6
Botwinick, A., Gi47
Bourne, J., Bb5
Bowden, T., Id7
Bowen, D., Me4
Bowie, G., Mf3
Bowman, A.K., Hf74
Bowyer, C., Ii36
Bowyer, J., Ba61
Boyce, D.G., Ac18; Mb8
Boyce, G., Ba59
Boydell, M., Li7
Boyer, R., Ee25

Boyes, J., Bb3
Boylan, H., Ab41
Boyns, T., Hg1
Braakhuis, H.A.G., Ei56
Bradford, E., Gh28
Bradley, H.W., Ab29
Bradley, I., Hl40
Bradshaw, B., Le2, i1, 14
Bradshaw, D.F., Hd24, 29
Braisted, W.R., Ii12
Brand, J., Ib38
Brand, J.D., Ef20
Brand, P.A., Ec35, 47
Brander, M., Bb110
Brandon, P., Bb30
Brandt, R., Gi20
Branigan, K., Cb17
Braswell, B.K., De11
Bratchel, M.E., Ff26
Breckin, M.J., Gf54
Breeze, D., Cb12
Brent, C., Hg45
Brett, C.E.B., Bb12
Bricke, J., Gi25
Bridbury, A.R., Ef17
Briggs, E.R., Fe38
Bristow, E.J., Ba30
Britain, I.M., Hl28
Britnell, R.H., Ef2
Britton, K., Gi29
Broeze, F.J.A., Hf77
Bromley, R., Fh13
Brook, F., Bb26
Brooke, L.E.J., Bb58
Brookes, C., Ba31
Brooks, C.W., Fc33
Brooks, N.P., Df6
Brown, A.E., Dd2
Brown, C.G., He30
Brown, D., Ca25; Da2
Brown, I.G., Gi48
Brown, J.M., Ka1, c2
Brown, K., Fk44
Brown, P.D., Gb1
Brown, J., Hh14
Browne, D.M., Ca14
Browne, T.L., Li15

Champion, T.C., Df17
Chandler, D., Gh21
Chaplais, P., De8
Chapman, J., Gf43
Chapman, M., Gd9
Chapman, S.D., Gf35; Hf20
Charlesworth, D., Ca76
Charlton, D.B., Ca66
Charlton, J., Fb55
Cherry, B., Ej28
Cherry, J., Ek4
Chevenix Trench, C., Hj21
Chibnall, M., Ea1
Childs, W.R., Ef12
Chinchen, B., Fe32, h10
Chown, C.H.I., Ia12
Christ, C., Hl31
Christianson, P., Fb4, e55
Christie, I.R., Gb6, 9
Churchill, F.B., Hk25
Cirket, A.F., Hb53
Clanchy, M.T., Ec34
Clapson, R., Hg36
Clark, C., Eg10
Clark, J.C.D., Gb10, 11
Clark, J.P.H., Ee1
Clark, P., Fb9, e26, g16
Clark, S., Hf46
Clark, Stuart, Fk9
Clarke, A., La2
Clarke, H., Ek5
Clarke, H.E., Ig9
Clarke, M.L., Ed7; Fa4, d3
Clarke, R., Ic7
Clarkson, L.A., Mg10, 16
Clay, E.W., Hf58
Clegg, J., Hl21
Clemoes, P., Da5
Cliffe, J.T., Fg15
Clogan, P.M., Ei23
Clouston, R.W.M., Ke6
Cluett, D., If22
Cobb, H.S., Ff21
Cockburn, J.S., Fc34
Cohen, Michael J., Id40
Cohen, Murray, Fk16
Coleman, D.C., Ff7, g3

Colledge, E., Ei73
Collinge, J.M., Ab37
Collins, B., Hc5
Collins, E.J.T., Ba43
Colloms, B., He17
Colvin, H.M., Ab25, 32
Colyer, R.J., Hf29
Cornforth, J., Gi71
Concannon, H., If36
Condon, M.M., Ec44
Conlan, P., Le3, Me1
Connolly, C.N., Hd19
Connolly, P.A., Ef6
Connon, R.W., Gi28
Connor, W.J., Fc2
Constable, G., Ee35
Cook, C., Ib20, 24
Cook, M., Ac20, 26
Coombes, J., Ld2
Coombs, D., Ba57
Cooper, F.R., Ff2
Cooper, R.G., Ee4
Cope, E.S., Fc5
Cope, J.P., De13
Cope, S.R., Gf3, 22
Copeland, T.W., Gb4
Corbet, J., Ca41
Corina, M., Bb97
Cornford, J., Hb11
Cornforth, J., Gi49
Corrigan, P., Hl38
Costigliola, F.C., If2
Cotton, A.N.B., Fb34
Cottrill, D.J., Hi1
Coupe, G.F.L.A., Hf28
Coupland, I.F.S., Id35
Courtenay, W.J., Ei58
Cousins, P.F., Ib37
Coustillas, P., Hl79
Coutts, F.L., Hh28
Cowan, I.B., Ke1, 5
Cowan, Z., Gj12
Cowie, L.W., Ej10; Gi3, 50
Cowling, M., Ib50
Cowling, T.G., Fk17
Crafts, N.R.F., Gf46; Hg14
Craigen, C.D., Gf45

SUBJECT INDEX

Classicism, Hl36
Class struggle, Gg3
Cleator (Cumb.), Hg36
Clergy, Ec43; He4, 17, 38;
 assemblies of, Ee6; marriage
 of, Fe49; taxation of, Fe47;
 and see Church
Clifford, Lady Anne, Fb55;
 Richard (bishop of Worcester
 and London), Ee7
Clift, William, Ga9
Clifton, Gf38
Clocks, Ba39; Hk16
Cloth, Fa14, f21; Gf34
Clothing, Ba7, b11; Hl74
Clough (Co. Down), Mf2
Clubs, boys', Ih8; Rotary, Ia12;
 Working men's, Hl77
Clun (Salop), Jj1
Clwyd (Denbigh), Ii21
Clydeside, If52
Coaches, Bb18; Hf13
Coal, Gf6, 46, 49; Hf14, 45, 56,
 57, g54, h24; If4, 5, 8
Coalitions, Ba16
Cobbold, Richard, Hg34
Cobden, Richard, Hb4, 9, f81
Cochrane, Thomas, 10th earl of
 Dundonald, Hj22
Codes, Ii51
Coetmor (Card.), Hf67
Coinage, Ab29; Ca17, 29, 30, 35,
 47, 52, 54, 56, 62, 63, 69, 71;
 Cb8, 15; Dd8–13; Ef6–10, 20,
 21, j4, 44; Fa26, 28, f1–3, 8;
 Lf1
Coke, Sir Edward, Fb42, c23, 24,
 k4
Colchester (Essex), Bb72; Ca4, b1
Coleman, Edward, Fe50
Coleraine, Mj2, 3
Coleridge, Samuel Taylor, Gi77
Coley (Reading, Berks.), Bb34
Collectivism, Hh2
Collier, Jeremy, Fj20
Collingwood, R.G., Ac15
Colne (Lancs.), Ab10

Colonia, Cb1, 6
Colonialism, Hd17; Id19
Colonial Office, Gb18; Hd1
Colonisation, Hd15; Id23; La2
Colyton (Devon), Fh9
Combined Operations, Ii13
Comenius, John, Fk30
Common Pleas, court of, Ec41;
 Fc33
Commonwealth Office, Ib45
commotes, Jj5
Congregationalists, Fe60
Connaught, Mh8
Conservatism, Ba55
Constable Maxwell, Gerald, Ii41;
 Michael, Ii41
Constantine (emperor), Ca62;
 (king of Greece), Id15
Contraception, Fh9; Hk11
Cook, James, Gf44, h7, 25; Sir
 Thomas, Eb1, 24
Cooke (family), Fg12; Henry,
 Me12; James, Gd3
Cookworthy, William, Gi63
Cooper, Anthony Ashley, 3rd Earl
 of Shaftesbury, Gi56
Copeland (Westm.), Ec29
Coral, Gf21
Corbridge (Northumb.), Ca19, 70
Corcumroe (county Clare), Lg6
Cork (city), Le1
Cormac mac Airt, Li5
Corn, If31; drying furnace, Ca52;
 laws, Hb9
Cornwall, Ec39, g11; Hg22
Coronation, Kc1
Coronel, battle of, Ii7
Coroners, Ec3, 4, 37
Corpus Christi plays, Ei18, 20
Corro, Antonio del, Fk13
Corsham Court, Gi74
Corunna, battle of, Gh21
Cosmology, Ej24
Cotesworth, William, Gc6
Cotton, Hf34, 55; Hg12
Cotton, John, Fe21
Council, Privy, Fa10

165

171

Infanticide, Hk13
Inflation, Ef3
Innovation, technological, Hf44
Inns, Ca8; of Court, Fk13
Inscriptions, Bd7; Ca17, 23, 55,
    56, 68, b5, 11; Mg14, i4, j4
Ireland, Aa18, 37, 44, b41; Bc14;
    Fe11, i15; Gb10; Hb50, f16;
    Id7; home rule for, Hb35, c2;
    Northern, Ib2, c13, and see
    Ulster
Insurance, Hf48; health, Hh22
Intaglio, Ca73; Ej20
Intellectuals, Hl80
Invention & Research, Board of,
    Ii9
Inventories, Fg9
Irish: abroad, Gi88; Le5; Repub-
    lican Army, Mb1; Republican
    Brotherhood, Mb10, 14
Iron and Steel, Ca12; Fa15, f10,
    16, 23, 25; Gf19; Hf43, 82
Ironwork, Ca52, 54, 72
Irving, Henry, Hl33
Isandhlwana (South Africa),
    Hj16
Islandmagee (co. Antrim), Mj4
Isles, lordship of the, Ka3
Italy, Hd25; Id5
Itinerarium Cambriae, Ji2
Iverk, barony of, Mg3

Jackson, Thomas, Fk58
Jacobites, Gb3; Ka4
Jacobs, Samuel, Hg38
Jamaica, Gf7
James (kings of England), I, Fa4;
    II, Fa2, b56
James (kings of Scots), I, Ki3;
    II, Ka2; III, Ka2
Japan, Fa39; Id16, 24, 36, 45
Jealott's Hill, Ij21
Jedburgh Abbey, Ki9
Jehovah's Witnesses, Ie7
Jenkins, R.T., Ij3
Jenkinson, Hilary, Ac10
Jenner, Edward, Gj3

Jermyn, Sir Henry, Fb7
Jersey, Bb40; Df17; Fb10; Hi1
Jesuits, Fe7
Jewel, John (bishop of Salisbury), Fe5
Jewellery, Df8
Jews, Ba63; Ge6, f21; Id42
Jeyes, John, If47
John (king), Eb17, c12, 13
Johnson (family), Mg4; Francis,
    Fe2
Jones, Sir Alfred, Hf38; Philip,
    Fb53, c3; R.V., Ii23
Josselin, Ralph, Fb52
Judges, Ec14, 15, 18, 19, 36
Junius, Gb5
Juries, Fc14
Justice, Kc2
Jutland, battle of, Ii10, 26
Juxon, William (bishop of London
    and archbishop of Canterbury),
    Fe8

Kant, Immanuel, Gi77
Kavanagh (family), Lg5
Kaye, John (bishop of Lincoln),
    He45
Kebell, Mary, Fa7
Keeble, S.E., He14
Kelvin, lord, see Thomson
Kemble, Fanny, Hl42
Kempe, Margery, Ee38
Kenbane Head, S.S., Ii40
Kendal (Westm.), Fe53
Kenilworth (Warw.), Ej33
Kennel Hall Knowe (Northumber-
    land), Ca64
Kennett, J., Mi2
Kent, Ab27; Ba33, b100; Fa15,
    b9, 52, c16, e26; Hb13, g43
Ker, Neil R., Ei40
Kett, Robert, Fa16
Kettering (Northants.), Fk41
Keynes, John Maynard, If2, 21, 50
Keynsham, abbey of, Ej22
Kidderminster (Worcs.), If15
Kildare (county), Aa18; Mj6;
    earls of, Lb6